B-89
Ne

W9-CAD-341

WITHDRAWN

WITHDRAWN

NOT LIKE OUR PARENTS

NOT LIKE OUR PARENTS

HOW THE BABY BOOM GENERATION IS CHANGING AMERICA

D. QUINN MILLS

WILLIAM MORROW AND COMPANY, INC.
New York

Library of Congress Cataloging-in-Publication Data

Mills, Daniel Quinn.
    Not like our parents.
    1. United States—Social conditions—1980–
2. Baby boom generation—United States. 3. Inter-
generational relations—United States. I. Title.
HN59.2.M55   1987   305.2   87-13908
ISBN 0-688-06835-9

Printed in the United States of America

First Edition

1 2 3 4 5 6 7 8 9 10

BOOK DESIGN BY RICHARD ORIOLO

PREFACE

I have written this book in order to present to the public the revolutionary importance of generational differences in America today.

I first realized the special qualities of the baby boom generation when, as a young faculty member at the Massachusetts Institute of Technology, I watched a demonstration against the Vietnam War under the watchful eye of many campus and a few Cambridge city police. I was impressed by the courage of conviction which they showed that day. I was also intrigued by the substantial intellectual talent and imagination which had enabled them to jam the radio communications of the Cambridge police force and so send the great majority of the municipal riot-control unit into milling confusion several miles away.

In the almost two decades since I have met, worked, and socialized with baby boomers in a wide variety of situations. I have served with them as an officer in my church; I have been their partner in assorted business ventures; I have worked with them in the federal government; I have encountered them in political activities; literally thousands of them have been my students, both in undergraduate studies at MIT and in graduate business courses at MIT and Harvard University; and I have been a consultant to companies in which many of them are employed.

It was in the course of teaching at Harvard Business School that I became interested in the baby boom generation in a systematic way. At Harvard there is a long tradition of research and careful analytic thinking about the satisfaction and motivation of people in the working environment. Teaching in this tradition, I came to recognize that older executives whom I encountered were somewhat bewildered by the younger people in their companies, and that there were great difficulties of communication and cooperation across the generations. When I began to investigate this in a formal way with surveys and questionnaires, the reality of the generational differences fairly shouted at me from the results. I shared some of my early conclusions about the differences in the generations with insightful acquaintances, who soon reported to me that their own observations confirmed what I had suggested.

This book is about the baby boom generation, but it will be of great interest to older people as well. It is very important to stay in touch with young people. It helps to keep an older person young, accepting, vibrant, and hopeful.

An older man in my church once told me, "I know change must come, but I abhor every bit of it."

To my mind that was a foolish statement. The man who made it was not close enough to the enthusiasm and hopefulness of young people to see the opportunities change brings.

There is a Japanese business aphorism that if you know the values and attitudes of a person, then you can predict his or her behavior in business situations. Hence it is more important to know the person in depth than to assess his or her particular skills or interests. Older people will find in this book what baby boomers think about their lives, what their basic values are, and why they act as they do. The information will be a revelation to many.

I am not a baby boomer myself, having been denied that opportunity by the passage of a few years. But because I am so close in age to that generation, I have been able to feel much of what it feels, experience much of what it has experienced, and share many of its attitudes. On the other hand, the difference of a few years has permitted me to see the characteristics of the younger generation clearly, and to distinguish the various groups into which it can be divided. It is hard to be part of a scene and yet be dispassionate about it. The few years that divide me from the subjects of this book are a guarantor of objectivity.

ACKNOWLEDGMENTS

This book could not have been written without the assistance of many people. I am particularly indebted to Lydia desGroseilliers of LDG Associates for the survey data on which the book is based and for insights into her generation that enliven the book enormously. Adrian Zackheim, my editor, offered sage advice and continuing encouragement. William Leigh and Larry Leson of the Leigh Bureau helped with valuable suggestions. Clare DiGiovanni provided critical commentary on the book as it took shape and helped me to improve it. Bruce Friesen helped with outlines, critiques of the argument, and statistical analyses.

My sister Debbie helped continually with the book, often when she didn't know it. I am very grateful for her assistance. My daughter Lisa showed interest in the book while I worked on it over vacations and holidays, and made suggestions, which I received with great pleasure.

The Research Division of the Harvard Business School provided financial support for some of the interviewing and data analysis. I am grateful both to the school for its support and to the corporations whose gifts to the school make that support possible.

All errors and omissions that the book contains are, however, my responsibility alone.

CONTENTS

PART ONE

HOW PEOPLE FEEL ABOUT THEMSELVES

1

What a Difference a Generation Makes

A PERIOD OF CHANGE AND MISUNDERSTANDING

As 1990 approaches, we enter a period of social change in America which is characterized by powerful contradictions. For those who are not the instigators of this change, but are affected by it, these contradictions can be experienced as paradoxical or downright hypocritical.

The contention in this book is that these changes can be attributed largely to the clash of values between the generation born before 1945, and the huge baby boom generation born from 1946 to 1966. The latter group is now coming of age—and coming to power. The baby boomers are reshaping America in their own image. To their parents, the result is unexpected and often frightening.

By their own admission, the baby boomers are most readily distinguished from previous generations by their personal values. The choices in their lives are based on convictions that often seem radical to older people.

A survey of high-level managers was conducted in 1985 at the

Harvard Business School. * Responses to a seventy-three-item question-naire were exhaustively analyzed by computer. There was no important distinction between the program participants who were American citizens and those who were not, but there was a startling divergence at about age forty between those who were older and those who were younger. These results were so dramatic that they became the inspiration for this book.

Other surveys, including one done of themselves by master's degree candidates at the Harvard Business School, showed certain patterns that were strikingly consistent with those found in the survey mentioned above. The MBA candidates, who averaged twenty-six years in age, expressed attitudes similar to those of the younger managers in the executive group.

Further investigation revealed that careful qualitative surveys of the readership of business and general-interest periodicals showed significant differences among age groups, as do many public-opinion surveys.

This book is exclusively about Americans, but there are similar generational differences in other countries. Hearing the American term "baby boomer" for the first time, Europeans and Japanese in their twenties and thirties have recounted that they long felt that their generation was different from their parents' generation, and that they were glad to have a term, even one borrowed from America, to apply to themselves.

When the convictions and aspirations of the baby boomers are understood, much that seems paradoxical in their behavior disappears. However, few Americans have delved deeply enough into the feelings of baby boomers to understand them. Hence, there continues to be a very substantial misunderstanding between the generations in the United States.[1] (Because this misunderstanding has its roots in different values, people get angry. Many in the previous generation view most baby boomers as hypocritical, and boomers see their critics as dishonest.)

What the baby boomers describe as openness and honesty in personal relationships, the older generation perceives as licentiousness and tactlessness. Is it possible to be morally loose (by the old standards) and

---

* The total sample in the survey was 136 managers. One half were U.S. citizens; one half came from abroad. Most of the respondents were male; the average age was forty-four years.

morally responsible at the same time? As the baby boomers themselves attest, what is valued is not the old standard of faithfulness, but the new standard of truthfulness. Nonetheless, people fixed in the old standards see open relationships as evidence of low morality in general and have difficulty understanding the new standards.

Critics also have difficulty accepting the idealism which baby boomers often combine with an aggressive materialism. In their college years, boomers denounced the materialism of their parents, yet filled their dormitory rooms with stereos, televisions, and other accoutrements of the good life.

Their parents asked, "Isn't it rank hypocrisy to reject materialism and yet embrace it simultaneously?" It may be to a degree, but a baby boomer does not necessarily see a conflict. Boomers often find it congenial to espouse worldly renunciation while conducting a financially lucrative professional practice in architecture, medicine, or law.[2] Self-reliant, well educated, suspicious of authority, scientifically oriented enough to reject many doctrines of established religion, the baby boomer nonetheless has a spiritual aspect that requires attention. However, baby boomers reject the notion that spirituality must be connected to material sacrifice. Indeed, it is possible to identify a form of spiritual materialism, which boomers have fashioned out of their unique life experiences and which seems highly paradoxical to people steeped in America's older traditions.

As we found out in the late sixties, the boomers are deeply suspicious of political authority. They are open-minded about a wide range of political notions (including the policies espoused by America's enemies abroad). Yet they are also deeply patriotic. Right or wrong, they think for themselves and are rarely hesitant to voice their opinions.

The previous generation finds this independence and outspokenness somewhat hard to take. "Are these people loyal to our country or not?" they ask. "Americans never spoke well of the Axis powers during World War Two; how can young people express sympathy for the Vietcong, or Castro's Cuba, or the Sandinistas—and yet maintain that they are loyal to this country?"

To the baby boomers there is no conflict—they are very much American; no one abroad would mistake them for anything else. In their minds they do not have to demonstrate loyalty by an uncritical allegiance to whatever policy Washington adopts.

While the baby boomers are suspicious of institutional authority and rebellious against any demand for abstract institutional loyalty, they are often deeply loyal to the group of people with whom they live, work, or socialize, and sometimes even to broader entities, such as corporations, unions, or religious denominations. What is required is that the broader entity *earn* the baby boomer's loyalty. The type of almost unquestioning allegiance that previous generations were willing to give to a corporation is given today most often by boomers only to the small team with which he or she is most closely involved at the workplace.

Another area of apparent contradiction involves the widely varying life-styles among baby boomers as contrasted to a striking similiarity in certain attitudes and values.[3] For the baby boom generation there is much diversity, but there is also an underlying unity of convictions.

Marketing-survey data suggests that a distinction be drawn between first- and second-wave baby boomers, specifically those in their thirties and those in their twenties. The two groups are at different stages in life and consume different products because of divergent priorities. Yet the most up-to-date research indicates that they share basic values and attitudes and are more alike than different. As those who are in their twenties today move into their thirties, they will follow a trail already blazed by older boomers.

Yet even where there is a unity of values, there is no sameness. Instead, priorities in life and styles of expression differ greatly among individuals.

Some boomers have left the urban rat race to settle in Alaska or the remote recesses of the mountain states. Others have chosen to be securities brokers or investment bankers in the canyons of Manhattan. Some are devoted to their families; others have remained unattached. Some are sports-minded and wilderness-oriented; others are committed to the arts or to such indoor pursuits as collecting or conversation. Some boomers are executives, some workers; some are rich, some poor. To a large degree, differences in life-style reflect differing priorities.

Five categories of baby boomers, reflecting different priorities and variations in self-image, are identified in the chapters that follow. The categories have been created by baby boomers themselves, and describe their generation analytically.

The categories are:

- the pleasure-seekers—who are striving to enjoy life;
- the competitors—who are business- and profession-obsessed;
- the trapped—who are in difficult situations at home or at work, and who cannot bring themselves to get out;
- the contented—who are generally satisfied with their lives; and
- the "Get Highs"—who are excessively involved in alcohol and drugs, or even, many baby boomers insist, in matters of the spirit.

In recent years the media focus has been on the competitors, who are superachievers, the trapped who are dissatisfied, or the "Get Highs" among the boomers. What few of us realize is that the hidden categories are most common in the baby boom generation across the country.[4]

It is especially noteworthy that boomers hold as a fundamental tenet that a person can transform his or her own life. Even those people who have not undergone a personal transformation, as seen by a dispassionate observer, often believe that they have.

Baby boomers are such ardent individualists that it seems surprising that they are able to work together at all. But in small groups, this generation has always demonstrated the capacity to organize, delegate responsibilities, and perform as a team. This is true in sports, business, and other contexts. There is little suppression of each individual's unique attributes; instead, the group displays great tolerance for differences.

Many people have argued that Americans cannot successfully answer the challenge of other cultures, particularly the Japanese, because American individualism prohibits effective teamwork. However, because of their ability to combine individualism with teamwork, the baby boomers are potentially able to respond effectively to the challenge of nations that benefit from teamwork but suppress the individual.

Where previous generations have largely fitted themselves to the demands of work, baby boomers insist that the job be adjusted to fit them. In the previous generation, people were prepared to have one personality for the office and another for personal lives. They accepted treatment on the job that they would not accept outside the workplace.

Boomers, by contrast, insist on being themselves at work and at home. They are not prepared to accept, at the hands of a company or its managers, treatment they do not accept elsewhere. Nor are they prepared to abandon their expectations with respect to the quality of personal relationships simply because they are at work. They have taken their values into the office and are insisting that the office adjust to fit them. No previous generation has done so. The result is that corporations have great difficulty imposing traditional job practices on younger people, and find they are required to deal with a whole personality, not just a mask worn for the office.

Baby boomers are the first generation to demand that work be enjoyable. They also permit personal relationships to play a substantial role in shaping their attitudes and expectations, and so determine to a large degree how they look at their jobs. Implicit in this position is the conviction that while work is significant, other aspects of life are more important.

Whatever their skill attainments, baby boomers want professional jobs. If they are not in the traditional professions, they want to professionalize the jobs they have. Virtually all baby boomers think of themselves as professionals, and describe themselves as professional truck drivers, carpenters, bartenders, and file clerks, to cite only a few examples. One reason for this professionalizing of nonprofessional employment is that baby boomers are far more educated than is realized. A survey conducted for this book indicated that about 70 percent have had some college education. This is a far higher level of education than was attained by the older generation, and is greater than is suggested by official government statistics (which usually ask years of school completed). Being well educated, baby boomers want personal discretion and responsibility in their work. They aspire to the independence and respect that traditional professionals receive. However, these are attitudes that corporations ordinarily display *only* toward members of traditionally professional and managerial occupations. The result is that most corporations treat employees as nonprofessionals, which the employees perceive as depersonalizing and disrespectful behavior.

The derisive term "yuppie" is not used often in this book. Yet the term does contain an insight. Baby boomers are young compared with their parents' generation, and most live in urban areas. So, to identify them as young and urban—the first two words in the acronym—

contributes little. The significance of the term lies in its last element, the word professional. The coiners of the term intended to refer only to people whose occupations are law, management, medicine, accounting, and education. Ironically, however, the term "professional" applies to the entire boomer generation.

Boomers have great respect for professionalism, but are also intensively competitive. Many in the previous generation believe these two attributes are in fundamental opposition. Among the most dramatic statements of the traditionalist viewpoint are those of former Chief Justice Warren Burger of the U.S. Supreme Court. He has referred repeatedly to the recent practice of advertising by attorneys as approaching mere "shysterism." In his view, providing high-quality professional services is inconsistent with a marketplace-like competition among attorneys for clients.

While there are probably excesses in soliciting clients by attorneys, there is also a far wider range of competitive behavior that is acceptable to the baby boomers than to the Chief Justice. Always conscious of their large numbers, always jockeying for position and advantage, many baby boomers come early to intense competitiveness. Whether competing for scarce acceptances by top colleges, for starting positions on sports teams, for first place in individual sports, or even for the attention of the best teachers, the boomer long ago learned to live with contests. Rivalry was imposed on the generation by its numbers. It is only natural that when many of its most talented members have entered the traditional professions, including law, they should have continued to compete vigorously with one another.

To the previous generation, professionalism meant the regulation of each profession by those in it, and the right to exclude others. To baby boomers, professionalism implies opportunity for entry and competition for the top positions. Once again, it is the combination of what traditionalists view as seeming opposites which marks an important change that baby boomers are bringing to America.

In sports the boomers are internationally outstanding. With little support from our government, they compete, often successfully, with government-sponsored and subsidized athletes from the eastern bloc. Baby boomers fill health clubs and sporting facilities. Rather than being a generation of spectators, they are runners, hikers, swimmers, or basketball, football, soccer, racquetball, Wallyball, and tennis players.

Yet they take drugs. The previously mentioned poll of MBA degree students revealed that two thirds had taken drugs, including 40 percent who had taken cocaine. Only 15 percent answered that they were still using drugs during the time of the survey, but many have considered this answer was intentional dissembling. "The respondents were not telling the truth," they said. "The actual percentage is far higher."

Students in the better-known business schools are among the most intellectually gifted young people we have today. Because of the apparent oversupply of doctors and lawyers that has developed in recent years, business schools have been receiving applications from young people who possess top academic credentials. So we must conclude that what is occurring among MBA candidates is representative of what is occurring in America's very best young people.

"How," ask critics, "can a person be serious about physical fitness and yet use drugs? It seems to us that the one must prohibit the other."

To this question, posed by a top executive, I heard a younger manager reply as follows: "There's no inconsistency at all. I do both, sports and drugs, for the same reason—to feel good. I do sports to feel good about my body. I do drugs occasionally to feel good for an evening. I don't think that moderate use of drugs is going to harm me."

This book is about young adults as they are today, and it forecasts their effect on the future; it is also about people who are getting older and more concerned about their own lives: Should they have children or not? Is it all right not to try to have it all? Can a person get out of the rat race and still be interesting to others? When a relationship is not working out, can it be because of a mismatch in priorities? What should someone do when he or she feels trapped in an organization that refuses to recognize one's individuality?

I have tried to assess the transformations that the baby boom generation is fashioning in major U.S. institutions as we face the millenium.

The years until the end of the century will be crucible in which the convictions of baby boomers will be tested and the choices each makes in his or her life will reshape America. Where the boomers will find themselves and our society in the year 2000 is revealed in the final chapter of this book.

Why the Concept of a Generation Is Controversial

What causes a generation to be different from its parents are major historical discontinuities, such as wars, depressions, or major technological advances. When these events do not occur, the generations do not differ a great deal. However, major discontinuities occurred between the baby boom generation and its parents. The baby boomers missed historical events that were strong influences on their parents, especially the Great Depression and the Second World War.

Today psychology largely ignores generational differences among individuals. Psychologists generally assert that the personality and behavior of a person depends on upbringing and experiences unique to that individual. In recent years some theorists have added stage of life as another determinant of personality. Could it be that differences between the generations are due simply to differences in the stage of life between older and younger people?

While it is difficult to prove conclusively that someone's generation is an important aspect of his or her personality, it is not difficult to point to some key indicators that generations are important. In fact, it has been most instructive to see whether or not, as baby boomers pass through their thirties, they turn out to be just like their parents.

A decade ago the older baby boomers turned thirty and began having families. If the logic of the stage-of-life theory were to hold, then their attitudes and values should have been changing in the direction of those who were older. But surveys taken when the oldest baby boomers were forty-one, have shown that their attitudes differed from those of older people and were very similar to those of younger people. The suggestion is very strong that generation matters more than stage of life. (See Appendix B.)

This is not to say that as baby boomers get older their concerns and priorities do not change. Changes do occur. People take on new responsibilities and find new priorities. But these changes are grafted onto a largely unchanging or slowly evolving set of values and attitudes.

There is little scientific basis for the choice of a particular year to be the start of the baby boom generation, or of any particular year to mark its conclusion. But lines need to be drawn somewhere for clarity of thought and expression. The surveys done for this book suggest that the years 1946 to 1966, those most commonly used, are appropriate.

Also, because the baby boom generation is so large and complex, it is possible to find an example or two of almost anything. Hence, some support can be marshaled for virtually any proposition. This is why there is such a wide divergence of commentary about the generation. To avoid being misled by a few examples, I have talked to many people and conducted a special survey of baby boomers (described in Appendix A) to determine where the significant commonalities are.

Methods of Presentation

The methods of presentation I have adopted for this book conform to the nature of the baby boom generation. Deeply individualistic, boomers relate best to personal experiences. Therefore, many of the chapters relate experiences that boomers have conveyed to me in interviews.

The numerous stories included in this book about their lives represent the essence of a generation. It is not necessary to know the actual identities of the people involved. What matters is their experiences and concerns today. Their inner conflicts and outward behavior are characteristic of a great many Americans.

I will be much concerned with three types of personalities that are strongly influential among boomers, but who barely existed, if at all, in previous generations. The reader will soon meet two of them. One is a young financial manager, Bif. He is hardworking, very well paid, aggressive, competitive, and individualistic. Another is a self-reliant, extremely capable, somewhat hardened but very feminine young businesswoman, Susan. She is on her own to a degree virtually unheard-of before, and aspires, with reason, to a level of income and power in society rarely available to women in the past.

Finally, the Vietnam veteran is a major character, and a type who did not exist at all previously. The survivor of a complex and controversial conflict, he remains an enigmatic figure. I have interviewed many vets in preparing this book, and will let them speak for themselves.

For years the media have suggested that most baby boomers are shallow people, the essence of the "me generation." But I have not found this to be true. There is much depth of human concern and understanding among them. To plumb that depth one must ask the right questions, and then listen carefully. In my interviews I discovered that even people who appeared on the surface to have little to say often offered profound observations when listened to with attention.

Many of the ideas that are advanced in this book were developed in conversations with baby boomers and a few members of the older generation. The ideas flowed naturally in dialogue form, and I have chosen to present some of them in the same fashion.

In particular, I have relied in several chapters on a series of conversations which took place among several individuals and which I have reconstructed. The people in the dialogues are peoples with whom I am personally acquainted. The conversations occurred largely as they are recounted below. The relationships between these people, both years ago and more recently, actually existed. But I have disguised their names and the settings so that specific persons are not recognizable. Also, some license has been taken with respect to dates and times; but the essence of each situation is factual.

Should I Wear My Earring Again?

A man and a woman in their mid-thirties sat at a table on the veranda of a large restaurant at harborside, watching the sun splash gold and red as it plunged into the bay. The last rays of light glimmered from the blossoming sails of boats now being lost to sight against the dark water.

Bif was of moderate height, with a fair complexion and handsome features. A financial manager, he handled pension-fund investments for corporate clients and worked for a rapidly growing company. This was a recent position; he had had a string of other jobs in the past, including secondary-school teaching and stock brokerage. He now made a substantial salary, and his casual clothes were expensive and carefully selected.

Susan was shorter than he, slim and dark-haired. Gold earrings and a choker were brilliantly displayed against her tanned skin. She was dressed in a conservatively tailored skirt, blouse, and jacket. Susan owned an advertising agency, which she had founded three years earlier and which now employed several people. She was a professional woman, accustomed to be listened to about business matters. Her self-assurance reflected both considerable beauty and a confidence in relationships with others. But her usual equanimity was disturbed this evening.

"Do you remember that summer we spent in New Mexico?" Susan asked.

"Yes," Bif responded, his expression quizzical.

"I like to think back to those days," Susan continued. "When I met you, I was being a hippie. I had long straight hair and love beads. I wore white lipstick and huge gold earrings in my ears. I had thick black eyeliner on my eyes that came up to a point. I used to just tie a scarf around my chest instead of wearing a blouse or a shirt. I was probably dressed like that when we met.

"I remember when I was a senior in high school, I would go out to the school bus and all the girls would gather at the back of the bus. We'd all kind of squeeze together so the boys couldn't see and we'd slip out of our bras. You couldn't wear a bra in those days, but you wouldn't dare go out of the house without one. Your parents would have killed you."

Bif smiled and nodded affirmatively.

"Do you remember how you looked?" Susan asked him. "You always had that green knapsack on your back and wore those rumpled shorts that were patched in the back and stringy where they had been cut off. I remember you had a faded blue T-shirt and sandals. Your hair hung long and straight, and you gathered it into a knot at the back held by a triple-twisted rubber band. You had that big gold ring dangling from your ear."

Though many years had passed, they had never gotten completely out of touch. "Each person I've known," Susan had once told a friend, "is still a friend. I may have decided not to marry a guy, but that doesn't mean I still don't find him interesting, or that I wouldn't like to see him. But I find that I outgrow them after a while. I learn from each person I spend time with; then I get bored and want to move on. But it's still nice to see a person again and so I keep in touch."

Susan paused, looking at Bif. Then she asked, "Do you still go hiking in the mountains?"

"No," he answered, "it's been a long time since I've been in the West."

Susan hesitated before replying, her usually playful aspect subsiding into disappointment. She lifted her glass slowly and sipped the contents. Setting the glass down, she looked directly into her companion's eyes.

"It's a good thing I didn't marry you," she said.

Bif was startled. He waited for the flash of humor that so often followed one of Susan's comments; but her eyes kept the same steady gaze. The line of her lips softened not at all. He saw that she was not joking with him, or simply being provocative, as she so often was. He saw that she meant what she had said, and that the challenge implicit in her words was intentional and deeply felt.

He waited before answering to get time to judge her mood. Now he had to say something, but he was unsure why she was so serious. Where were her thoughts going?

He replied uncertainly, preparing to defend himself against whatever accusation would follow. "That's a strange thing to say," he began, "that you're glad you didn't marry me. But why?"

"Your values have changed," she answered.

"What do you mean?" Bif asked. "My values haven't changed."

"You were different then," Susan answered, less challenging now than regretful. "We were both free spirits; we weren't going to let anyone dictate our lives or tell us what to be like. You introduced me to all of it. You made me see how important it was to get away; not to let work dominate my life; not to do what other people want me to do unless I thought it was right for me. You said we had to choose between being directed by others outside us, or by what we really wanted inside us; that our parents were dedicated to obligations they had had placed on them by others and that they'd do the same to us if we let them.

"You taught me to see that the significance of the nineteen-sixties was the sense of comfort and casualness which we could feel in doing things our parents didn't do at all. We received a broader base of experience than our parents did on which to build. Those years opened up our minds, made us more liberal socially, so that we could say more, do more, explore new freedoms.

"I'm still doing it," Susan continued. "I still go out into the mountains; I still get to know new people; I still see different men. But look at you now. You don't wear your ring anymore. You dress just like a banker; you don't let your wife work; you'd have children too, if your wife could have them; you drive a big car. When I asked you if you've been out to the West lately, you said you'd like to but you just don't have the time.

"You don't have time to get outdoors. You dress like a square. You talk about dollars and investments and making money all the time. I think your values have changed a lot."

Bif grew more and more agitated. "I haven't changed at all," he insisted, his voice rising with each word, and somewhat surprised at his increasing anger. "I still like to do those things. They're still important to me. I'm just busy."

Susan didn't answer. She let his words die into the soft glow of twilight. His anger hung like an evening mist over them, then began to evaporate as a quarter moon emerged in the darkening sky.

She answered softly, "I get so upset when I look at you. I was in awe of you because of your courage to go into the desert and to live among the Indians. That's why I'm so disappointed now. Were the things you stood for then your real values? Or were they merely pretenses to be something you aren't?"

Bif shifted nervously. His mind reached back many years to a small tent in the mountains under the desert sky brilliantly decorated by stars; to a dying fire and the sweet bite of a joint. He felt again the presence of the young woman then beside him, her head resting on his arm. Memory rekindled his warmth.

Bif had encountered Susan this evening only by chance. He looked at his watch and saw that he had only a few more moments with her before leaving to join his wife. Already, however, he had decided to call her in the next few days to continue the conversation. Susan remained a beautiful woman who was interested in him, and he was flattered by her attention. But he was also troubled by her observations about him.

"Have I changed so much?" Bif asked her quietly just before rising to leave. "Is what you say true? Before I came here tonight, I didn't think I had changed. I don't want to change. I still have my gold earring. Should I wear it again?"

2

THE PLEASURE–
SEEKERS

To Bif's surprise, Susan brought to their next meeting a man she was currently dating. Of moderate height, he had a high forehead and piercing eyes. He dressed casually, but carried himself with an air of self-confidence. His thick hair was graying at the temples, and streaks of silver ran across the crown of his head. He had a slender, athletic body, and his complexion was lightly tanned. He wore a thin moustache and smiled readily. Susan had known him for several years and was quite comfortable with him, something Bif recognized instantly. Bif also made an accurate assessment of his age. He was fifty-three.

"Bif," Susan began, "this is Gary. I told him about our last conversation and he was very interested. He was in town tonight, so I invited him to come along and join us."

Susan took no notice whether Bif was pleased or not to have another man join them. When she had lived with Bif, both had felt free to bring acquaintances along at any time. Meeting new people was to her an important part of the variety life afforded, and no matter what Bif thought, she wanted Gary there this evening.

They picked a table in a quiet corner of the lounge in a large oceanside restaurant. A few customers were already gathered at the bar; and as the evening passed, a crowd from the restaurant spilled over into the lounge so that the tables became filled. They knew several of the other people and looked up periodically to nod hello to someone who had called out to them. Mostly, however, they found themselves conversing.

Susan summarized for Gary the discussion she and Bif had had a week earlier. "We left it that we would meet again to try to decide if our values had changed or not."

"You mean, if my values had changed," Bif said, smiling.

"Yes, I mean if his values had changed."

"You think," said Gary to Susan, "that you are still holding to the same values you had when you and Bif . . ." Gary hesitated.

"When we lived together?" Susan asked, finishing Gary's sentence. "Yes." Turning to Bif, she said, "He knows about that."

Bif shrugged. It was no secret.

"Well," Gary suggested to Susan. "I can't pretend to know much about your generation, but I think it would be fun for me to learn something, if you'll let me listen."

Bif shrugged in acquiescence. Susan had waited to see Bif's reaction, since she didn't want to force Gary into the discussion if Bif objected. Bringing Gary along had seemed a good idea at the time. But when she saw Bif at the bar waiting for her earlier in the evening, she had had certain doubts. Maybe she was bringing Gary into a conversation that was really just between Bif and herself. She had been suddenly afraid that Bif might really be angered by her including Gary. But since Bif now seemed agreeable to the notion of Gary taking part, Susan's concerns were allayed, and she nodded at Gary in agreement also.

"Susan, why don't you tell us what values you think are important," Gary suggested. "Then later Bif can do the same and we can compare the two and see how much Bif has changed, if he has changed at all."

Susan frowned. She had expected Bif to be on the spot, not herself, but both men were watching her with such interest that she was pleased. Also, she didn't want to decline the challenge and so appear to be a weak person. So she nodded again.

"Taking time to be with my friends is very important to me," Susan began. "Years ago I bought a house when I was working here. It's a great place in the summer and lots of people come down to be at the ocean.

Some of them sail, some of them go to the beach, and others just look for other people.

"Anyway, in the summer I started renting out rooms. First it was a girl or two. But then I moved out because I wanted to live with someone, so I wasn't there. After a couple of summers the girls moved out. One wanted to give the room to a guy she had met; so I finally agreed. Then later there were three guys and a girl. Finally, I moved back in, and it was three men and two women."

"How many rooms did you have?" Gary asked.

"There were four bedrooms," she said. "The same people came back for years. After a while I needed money, so we refinanced the house, and four of us—three men and me—owned the house. They wrote up a contract and I signed it, too. If any of us got married or brought in a special companion, he or she had to pay his or her fair share. We agreed to ten dollars per hour as a fair share for the people who did the work cleaning the house. If a person cleaned up, she or he would come out ahead on the money.

"But we had one problem. One of the guys planted a garden no one else wanted. Then at the end of the summer he charged us fifteen hundred dollars for taking care of it."

"Where do your friends at the beach live in the winter?" Gary asked.

"They go all over. Some live in Vail, some in Vermont, some in Tahoe, one in Vegas," Susan answered. "But we always plan to get together a couple of times a year to ski or party or whatever.

"That's what life's for, isn't it?" Susan asked. "It's to enjoy.

"See, the problem is," she continued, "that you've got to avoid entanglements. You've got to keep loose so you don't mess everything up. I've played around a bit, I admit that. But I never slept with the guys who rented my house.

"Anyway, they always had plenty of other things going for them." Then she added, "It's like when my friend Jerry went to be a mercenary . . ."

"A mercenary?" Gary interrupted, wanting to be sure he'd heard correctly.

"Yes, a person who fights for another government. Isn't that right—a mercenary?"

Gary nodded. "Yes."

"That was years ago," she said. "He was at Fort Bragg being trained to operate equipment on the really big cargo planes. Very few people could do it then. And he was living with a woman who was beginning to get serious about him. She was talking about getting married.

"So he saw a notice on the bulletin board. It was an advertisement for mercenaries to work for the Cambodian government. They were doing things and the U.S. didn't want to be involved. So they put Americans on the Cambodian payroll.

"Jerry was at his wits' end about how to get rid of this woman, so he decided to volunteer to be a mercenary to get away from her.

"He spent six months in Cambodia. They had great accommodations on a beach. He got thirty thousand and all expenses paid. When he came back he was very thin and had very long hair. The girl was married, so that was settled. He put some of his money in Swiss banks to avoid U.S. taxes and carried the rest in cash to Vail, where he lived with a Vietnam buddy for a while. He kept this little box hidden where he had cash, and he paid cash for everything until he ran out and had to get a job."

"Doesn't he have a career?" Gary asked. "He's got a college degree, doesn't he?"

"Yes," Susan answered. "He has some pretty good skills he can use when he needs money. But he only works when he needs money."

She paused. "I don't want to give you the wrong impression. He doesn't spend everything he gets. He's a pretty smart investor and always has money tied up in houses or gold or something.

"But he doesn't really have a career. It's his philosophy. He calls it careerlessness. He says that if you have a career it holds you in too tightly and you miss the best opportunities in your life. His hero is a guy out in San Francisco who has made a whole philosophy of careerlessness. The guy wrote an article about it and Jerry copied it, so from time to time he looks at it just to reinforce his own commitment.[1]

"See, it's not aimlessness, it's not underachievement; it's well planned and it takes a lot of work. You have to plan when to work, because you need money to do things. And you have to plan for what you're going to do next. It's like the means are the end. It's what you're doing that matters, not where you get to.

"What it is, what the guy in San Francisco said, and I think it's a great point, is that a person who has this philosophy is more free to live in the world of dreams than a person who is tied to a career. To these people, work has nothing to do with their identity."

"Are you like them?" Gary asked Susan.

"Only to a degree," she answered. "I admire them, but I'm not really like they are. I like to play and I work hard, but when I work, I do it for other reasons than they do. For me work's not only so that I can use the money to get the experiences I want. It's also to establish my identity and my worth as a person."

"What you're saying is that Bif ought to be more like these friends of yours?" Gary asked.

"He used to be," Susan responded. "He used to do all kinds of things and be a very interesting person. I used to have fun with him and learn a lot from him." She paused and thought for a moment. "Yes, I think he ought to be more like the people I've been telling you about. I think he used to be like them and he ought to be again."

"What your friends do," said Bif, "is kind of graze through life. Like some people who eat just a little bit of each thing and call it 'grazing' instead of 'eating' in order to distinguish what they're doing from having a meal."

"Is there anything wrong with looking for pleasure?" Susan asked Bif, her head up, her eyes wide and turned slightly at an angle to him. Her whole attitude seemed to challenge him to criticize if he dared.

Bif smiled. "Not at all," he answered.

"Do you know other people like the ones you described?" Gary asked.

"Lots," Susan answered.

Bif nodded in agreement.

"Then we ought to put a label on them, shouldn't we?" Gary asked. "So we can identify what kind of person they are."

"I know how I think about my friends," Susan said. "I have a label for them."

"What?" Gary asked.

"I call them the pleasure-seekers," she said.

"I'm a pleasure-seeker, too," Bif put in.

"No, you're not," Susan answered with some heat.

"Well, I'm always looking for pleasure," Bif retorted.

"I don't think you would even qualify to be an apprentice pleasure-seeker," Susan told him. "If you were really a pleasure-seeker, you'd wake up one day and go to the Caribbean, spontaneously. That's why the pleasure-seekers are here—to enjoy life spontaneously."

WHAT THE PLEASURE-SEEKERS SAY ABOUT THEMSELVES

The pleasure-seeker category, and the others that follow in later chapters, were developed from conversations like the preceding one with baby boomers and are based on my experience with them.

To check the general applicability of these categories, I commissioned an in-depth survey in which baby boomers were asked if they recognized the categories and to which they belonged. I did not develop the categories from the survey, but I employed here the alternative approach of using survey data to check the validity of the categories, and to obtain additional information about them. Many of the comments on the categories by baby boomers, presented in the following chapters, are taken from the survey.

"Five years ago, what did you think you'd be doing today?" our interviewer asked a twenty-six-year-old construction worker in New York.

"Well," he answered thoughtfully, "I thought I'd be selling drugs."

Our interviewer described a pleasure-seeker to him, then asked, "Do you know anybody like that?"

"Out of ten people I know," the man answered, "all ten would be like that. I'm a pleasure-seeker. I work to have things I want. I party a lot."

"What do you expect to be doing in five years?" he was asked.

"Nothing," he replied. "By then I hope to be rich and famous and just enjoy life."

A twenty-three-year-old electrical lineman from Wisconsin was another pleasure-seeker. "Years ago I didn't really know what I wanted to do. I knew I wanted to make a lot of money, but I didn't know how I was going to go about getting it."

Our interviewer asked him, "Aside from your family and loved ones, what is the most important thing in your life?"

"Holy cripes!" he exclaimed. "What a question! Other than loved ones? Well . . . how long are you going to give me to think about this?

I'd have to say, Me! Having fun, enjoying life. That's pretty important to me.

"I'm a pleasure-seeker," he said, upon hearing the categories. "I make money to do what I want to do."

When asked the same question about what was the most important thing in his life, a twenty-five-year-old auto-shop foreman in Texas answered over the roar of a party at his home, "Getting dirty! In several ways." Later, still amid sounds of laughter and screams, when he was asked what was the most exciting moment in his life, he answered excitedly, "It hasn't happened yet! I'm still on the phone!" At that, our interviewer let him go.

A Colorado construction foreman responded to the question about what was important in life, "I would say, having some time off to go fishing . . . just piddling around on my ranch. I own a small one." Into which category did he fit? "I like to work and I like to enjoy myself," he answered. "I also like to have a lot of money. The pleasure-seekers are pretty close."

A thirty-two-year-old factory worker from Indiana mused about how to categorize himself. "I'm just an average type of guy. I don't get caught up in my problems. I take life as it comes. I have my goals but I take my problems in stride. Society's rules don't rule me. I'm a nonconformist. Not because I don't want to conform and always be different . . . I just think you have to bend the rules a little bit."

Sometimes people were reluctant to apply the categories to themselves. Some seemed to draw back at the pleasure-seeker label. One man taught school, slept till noon whenever possible, worked at a resort, and traveled constantly. Still, he didn't want to think of himself as a pleasure-seeker.

We also encountered a group of people who longed to be pleasure-seekers, but didn't quite make it. A thirty-nine-year-old chemist from Pennsylvania categorized himself this way. "I'm contented, I guess." He sighed audibly. "At least, I'm contented part of the time. I'd like to earn enough now to get to a higher pay level in order to eventually live off my investments. People liike me are wrapped up in making an enormous amount of money fast. They look like overachievers, but essentially they're not.

"I like to be daredevilish," he continued. "I do a lot of thrill-seeking through experiments when I'm in the lab. I take an opportunity when

I get the chance to do daredevil things with new experiments as an escape for me."

Not everyone admired pleasure-seekers. "I know a lot of people who are pleasure-seekers," said one man. "I don't have a very high opinion of them. I see those people with tremendously expensive cars, expensive silk shirts, and ducks on their socks."

Many respondents suggested to us that the pleasure-seekers were almost exclusively single. "It's a single's life-style," they said.

However, we interviewed many pleasure-seekers, and of them, 70 percent were married, a larger percentage than in the baby boomer population as a whole. The lesson is clear: The pleasure-seeker is not synonymous with the single person.

WORKING AT A PLEASURE-SEEKER'S LIFE

Though it may seem a contradiction in terms, the fact is that a person has to work at a pleasure-seeker's life. To the many people who live it, being a pleasure-seeker is a good life, but not because it's easy. It's a good life because it keeps priorities straight. It puts what matters most up front. A pleasure-seeker keeps in shape and keeps looking for stimulating experiences. From a pleasure-seeker's point of view, he or she really lives life—rather than wasting it on work.

A young woman told one of our interviewers how she works at staying fit. "My mother said to me," she began, "that she's been going to these Weight Watchers classes and all they say is 'Walking. Walking reduces stress; walking keeps your weight down.' "

She continued. "I said to her, 'Mother, why do you think I walk two hours a day? I do it to stay relaxed and thin.' "

Interpersonal relationships are important to pleasure-seekers, but not so much for love, or romance, as for friendship. Usually this means friendships with women and with men. Often friendships include sex, but many pleasure-seekers don't want to fall in love for life or to be caught up in a single relationship that dominates and defines all else.

A young man told us, "I think sex is physical and is a pleasure. Love is emotional and is a hassle."

Some pleasure-seekers are less cynical about love and less hard-headed about relationships. Some have been married, sometimes more than once.

A young woman told us, "It's women who created the sexual revolution. Women destroyed the Victorian world. We got restless under the restraints and burst them in all directions. I think men have been accomplices in this, but no more."[2]

This woman sees herself as the new woman who passes through a series of sexual relationships, never marrying, loving only briefly. She always changes in each relationship and carries on her career simultaneously. Others, who do not pursue a career, are simply gathering experiences.

To a traditionalist it appears as if for pleasure-seekers sex and love are disconnected. And while this may not be uncommon, what pleasure-seekers put first *is* unusual.

There has been a big change. The older generation pursued love, but because morals were different and people were less free about sex, it was often love without sex. For the baby boomers, sex has been much freer, and it seems to the previous generation as if they are after sex without love.

For many baby boomers, however, it's a new concept of love. It's love as acceptance—not as possessiveness; accepting a person for a while, not trying to possess or change him or her. It's love as permission to the other person to develop himself or herself, not as a restriction on opportunities. It's love as an adventure, not as a competition with others to see who can land the best mate.

Thought of in this way, love is an element of a person's life-style, not an end in itself. It's there for growth and self-development, not to result in the possession of another or the surrender of oneself.

"I remember," a young woman told us, "how I learned about love from the nuns. It was all giving up yourself totally, losing yourself in some other person. I couldn't understand it then and I don't want that kind of thing now.

"Relationships are very important to me. They help me shape my life. But I want them to add to me as a person, not eliminate me."

Another young woman told us about a key experience in her life. "I remember when I lived with a man," she began. "I learned a lot from one experience. I had lived with him for three years. I thought he was taking me more and more for granted, and I was getting bored. So one day I just picked up and left. He was in the shower and when he came out, I was gone. I went back to live in my house where my friends were. It was summer.

"For a day or two I felt great. I think every woman dreams of doing something like that, when she's been with a man for a long while and he takes her for granted. She thinks, 'I'll show him,' and one day she just walks out.

"But it didn't work out well for me. I was only gone for three days when another woman moved in with him. I guess he'd been seeing her on the side. I was very replaceable. It was extremely humbling.

"It made me realize that traditional things like a man-woman relationship weren't very stable, and that they weren't really very important. You couldn't build your life around them. I felt very rejected.

"Years later I'd been seeing another man, and then one day I got a 'Dear John' letter. He was going to marry someone else. All my friends thought I must be pining away. But I wasn't. He had a nice body, and I enjoyed sleeping with him, but I didn't really care very much. He was replaceable, too; just like I had been."

The difference in how the generations perceive the sexual revolution was made graphically apparent by a poll conducted for *Time* magazine. People were asked whether they thought the changes in attitude about sexual conduct that occurred in the 1960s and 1970s were good or bad. The baby boom respondents answered, mostly good. People from the previous generation answered, mostly bad.[3]

A thirty-three-year-old single woman asked our interviewer if she had seen a column Ann Landers wrote, which was based on a poll and said that most women want affection from men but not the sex act.[4]

The woman commented, "The women who said that must be married women." She was implying that the married ones don't like the sex act and the single ones do.

"My married friends and I rarely discuss sex," she continued. "The married people talk among themselves, but not with singles.

"I don't think the married ones do it very much. I'm not married and I think I score more often in a year than my married friends do."

Sex is a topic that emerges continually in discussions with pleasure-seekers. Being attractive to others is important to them, and they devote considerable time and effort to it. Another significant topic is travel.

Pleasure-seekers want to change their environment, meet new people.

Pleasure-seekers worry about getting older. Many of them aren't married, so they are beginning to wonder who will take care of them when they start aging. Our interviews indicated that many are planning to make sure someone will be able to take care of them when their health begins to deteriorate. They're conscious of such eventualities, so they're not just impulsive and never make plans. Some pleasure-seekers insisted that being a pleasure-seeker requires as much intelligence and persistence as being in business does.

THE PLEASURE-SEEKERS' PHILOSOPHY

A few people told us that pleasure-seekers are not very interesting to talk to. "They don't have a lot to say," our interviewers were told. "All they talk about is what they did yesterday and how much fun it was."

But this opinion understates the importance of the pleasure-seekers enormously. In fact, they are among the most influential individuals in the baby boom generation. The same people who told us that pleasure-seekers seemed to be empty-headed also spent a lot of time admiring their philosophy and what they do with their lives. The essential proposition for which the pleasure-seekers stand is that one should enjoy one's life and relationships, and should not put work or career, or loyalty to nation, church, or corporation, above concern for one's own well-being. Baby boomers in general feel that they must deal seriously with the challenge the pleasure-seekers present to their own choices about how to live.

Pleasure-seeking isn't entirely an escape. It's not just being lazy or without serious commitment. To those involved, it is a serious commitment.[5]

To a certain extent, the pleasure-seekers' philosophy comes out of the experiences some of them had in Vietnam. Because of this, it shouldn't be underestimated or denigrated in any way.

From the point of view of many veterans who are now pleasure-seekers, they were sent to a senseless war by a crazy power structure. They were lucky to get out of Vietnam alive. So they decided to live the lives they had almost lost. They didn't want to give up their lives to

Lyndon Johnson or to Richard Nixon, and now they say they don't want to give them up to a corporation. They concluded that it makes no sense to try to climb a corporate ladder. There are more important things in life.

"What's more important?" we asked them.

"Having relationships with other people, enjoying life, and having a full set of experiences," they told us.

People who were not in Vietnam probably cannot fully understand why the veterans feel as they do. But their convictions arise out of very deep personal experiences which were not the experiences of other generations.

Traditionalists ought to be very careful if they are inclined to suggest that these people are soft or lazy and that's why they have a pleasure-seeker's philosophy. It is very important to recognize how firmly these convictions were built and how deeply they are rooted.

Those who graduated from college in the late 1950s were the last group to feel secure. They signed up for military service without hesitation, thinking it would be good experience for them, and it probably was. They met different types and classes of people in the service, and they matured as a result.

Then Vietnam occurred. After that, young people didn't go into the military so willingly. They didn't trust the government.

Ironically, the Great Depression made its generation economically insecure, but World War II made it feel secure about the government. Then the baby boom generation came along. The nation experienced an economic expansion in the fifties and sixties, so the new generation felt economically secure. But Vietnam made it feel insecure about America's government. So the generations are almost exact opposites. The older generation feels insecure about the economy and secure about the government. Baby boomers feel secure about the economy and insecure about the government.

To people who are economically insecure, it seems crazy to live like a pleasure-seeker—to have no career and to spend your time trying to divert or entertain yourself. But to people who feel financially secure, it makes sense. Also, to a generation which trusts the power structure, it seems sensible to try to work one's way up the ladder. But to a generation which thinks the people in power are a bit insane, then it makes better sense to keep your distance and to do your own thing.

Even though much of the impetus for the differences between the generations came from Vietnam, there were other factors. Much the same kind of thing is happening in Europe, where some nations were not involved in the Vietnam War. It appears to be caused by something deeper and of longer duration than just the Vietnam influence.

Still, in the previous generation there were also people who didn't care much for work and were mainly interested in pleasure. But there were not as many as there are among the baby boomers, and they didn't have the same reasons. They didn't have the same philosophy.

There are even some pleasure-seekers today who are somewhat business-oriented. Pleasure-seekers have to get jobs, and there's lots of competition. So to get good jobs, they act the way the people who run the companies want them to act. However, they often don't really feel like doing it.

A fascinating example of how important pleasure-seekers are in setting the standard for a desirable life for baby boomers was contained in an article appearing in the student newspaper at the Harvard Business School. In the article the author introduced himself as a young investment banker who had spent a summer in the mergers and acquisition department at a major Wall Street firm. "My suspenders have dollar signs on them," he wrote. "I fasten my French shirts with diamond-studded cufflinks; and the personalized license plate of my Mercedes 280 SL says 'I-Banker.' "

In short, he continued, "my life is a Harvard MBA's dream come true. Or it was . . . until I met the plumber." The article proceeded in tongue-in-cheek fashion to tell of an encounter with a plumber who had been offered a job in investment banking but had turned it down. To the incredulous young man, the plumber said, "Figure it out." He explained that working an eighty-hour week on Wall Street brought an investment banker a hourly rate less than the plumber's.

"But I need a big income to afford the nice things I'm accustomed to," the young man responded.

"So do I," said the plumber. He explained that he made a lot on the weekends, and at a higher hourly rate, so that his annual income surpassed the banker's. Most important, however, he said, "I'm my own boss . . . not only that, but I can be as late as I want, and I can drink on the job. . . . I've got a summer house . . . and I enjoy what I do."

"What about prestige?" the young investment banker asked the plumber. "What do you do when you tell people you're a plumber?"

"What do you do when you have to tell people you're an investment banker?" the plumber responded. "My experience is that people would rather go out drinking with a plumber."

Finally, the plumber capped his advice to the young man: "Remember, just do what makes you happy."

The young investment banker ended the story by sitting on his couch and thinking. "I feel a strange emptiness," he wrote, "and I'm not sure why."[6]

So, among baby boomers who, as a generation, value independence and leisure time, even an investment banker cannot escape a pleasure-seeker's contention that he is working too hard and wasting his life.

These are not easy notions for traditionalists to grasp. It is difficult to get into the minds of another generation. Perhaps a bit of historical perspective will help make sense of the generational changes that have taken place.

In the seventeenth century, people gave the dominating position to religion; in the eighteenth century, it was given to nationalism; in the nineteenth century, it was given to economic development. But, for the pleasure-seekers of the twentieth century, the dominant theme is their own growth and stimulation.

3

THE COMPETITORS

"The pleasure-seekers are only one group in our generation," Susan said. "There are other groups as well. Bif isn't a pleasure-seeker at all; he's into business instead. I think the difference is that the pleasure-seekers look outside themselves for stimulation. People like Bif, on the other hand, look inside themselves. They want to know whether they can meet the challenges they put in their own path—in particular, whether or not they can achieve the goals they set for themselves. And I'm not really a pleasure-seeker either. I'm kind of an intermediate person between Bif and the pleasure-seekers. So we also need a category for me.

"But let's not go to me next," Susan added. "Instead, let's see what kind of a person Bif is."

"I don't know what kind of person I am," Bif responded, smiling. "I guess in recent years I've been spending more and more time on business. I certainly didn't anticipate several years ago that I'd be into work as much as I am now. I had never thought of devoting much interest, imagination, or effort to business.

"In a sense, I don't really want to be so much involved in work. I'm not entirely comfortable with it.

"I started off with the idea that I'd work for forty hours each week and do other things in all my other time. I thought that was the kind of arrangement people had; that I'd go to work five days a week and the rest of my life was mine.

"But I discovered that I couldn't make it do for me. I couldn't keep up. I looked around and other people were working much more. My boss indicated I wasn't carrying my share of the work. In a sense, the world just wouldn't tolerate my idea of working kind of halfheartedly. It turned out to be a recipe for disaster.

"I just couldn't keep up if I didn't put a lot more effort into my work than I had expected. I couldn't do things at work in a kind of routine way while I preserved my imagination for other things. Thinking and imagination were required. Slowly I've put more and more of myself into my job.

"That's what Susan complained to me about," he continued. "But I'm not at all an extreme person. If you want to know about a person who is much more into his career than I am, I can tell you about one of my friends."

Susan and Gary indicated by nodding that he should continue.

"His name is 'Doctor Doctor.' Well, that's not his real name. Doctor Doctor is his nickname, and he got it just a short while ago. He's a few years younger than I am.

"Doctor Doctor's father was a dentist. He had several brothers, but he was the oldest. His father wanted him to take over the practice, so he went to dental school. When he graduated, he joined his father in the practice.

"Always, while in dental school, he had envied the medical school students, but he doubted that he had the capacity for medical school. He confided both his ambition and his fears to his wife.

"While he was in dental practice, people would come to him for a special problem with their jaws. Soon he was receiving referrals from other dentists. He took the referrals and did his best to treat the problems successfully. But he kept saying to himself, 'This is really a medical problem, not a dental one. I really should be a doctor and specialize in this!'

"Suddenly his father died. The practice belonged to him alone. It was time to make a move if he was ever going to. He could sell the family business and act independently.

"Still he hesitated. Many of his friends were medical doctors. Was he good enough? He was afraid that he wasn't, but he feared to admit it to himself. He wanted desperately to be the equal of or better than his old friends.

"One night he attended a workshop at a university. A prominent physician, who was a friend of the family, was there. After the workshop this man said to him, 'You can do it! Go to medical school.'

"He went home very excited. He told his wife he wanted to go to medical school. She agreed.

"So now he's gotten his medical degree and is a specialist in diseases of the jaw. Since he has two medical degrees, he's now Doctor Doctor to all of us.

"I'm not as sharp as Doctor Doctor," Bif continued. "But I told you this story for a reason. You could think that I just work hard to try to keep up with my peers. But it's more than that. It was more than that for Doctor Doctor, and that's where I'm like him. You wonder, 'Am I good enough to do this thing?' That's what drives Doctor Doctor and it's what drives me. The challenge is important. You want to prove to yourself that you can do something. You want to prove you're as good as the others.

"One final thing," Bif added after a brief hesitation. "Lots of it is simply sheer, unlimited optimism. The belief that if you just stay at it, you'll be a success. Sure, you have times of self-doubt. 'Am I good enough to do this?' But you have to rely on optimism to overcome the doubts."

Bif stopped. He was finished.

"Ten years ago I wouldn't have believed we would be having this conversation," Gary said. "I first learned about your generation from people who wrote about you in the late nineteen-sixties and early nineteen-seventies. They said you were not competitive. That was one of their big points. They said that people in your generation were competitive only in sports. That in business you were cooperative. People wanted to work with other people, not to compete with them or try to exceed them, they said."[1]

"That may have had some truth then, I don't know," Bif said. "All of us were in college then; none of us were in business. How could someone writing at that time have known how we would be in the business world? We didn't know then ourselves.

"But for today, whoever said we weren't going to be competitive is just wrong. Business is a game—it's like a sport. The way you keep score is how much money you make."

"I'm still surprised," Gary said. "When I first encountered your generation, people seemed very resistant to being measured against one another in a contest. I thought they weren't at all competitive. Instead, I thought they were into their own things; into their own psyches. I thought people in your generation spent very little time, compared to mine, thinking about how they measured up compared to other people."

"Even if you were right then," Bif said, "it's all changed by now. It's as competitive as it can possibly be."

"You're right," Susan said. "That's what we should call Bif. He's a competitor, and there are lots like him. But he's also right—he's not an extreme case. Doctor Doctor is more extreme, and so are lots of other people I know.

"I do some work with companies on Wall Street," she continued, "and that's a place you find lots of competitors. The young people make a lot of money, but they work all the time. When I ask them why companies pay them so much money, they say it's because each job is really two jobs. They travel all the time and work seventy or eighty hours a week. They think of it as having two regular jobs, and so do the companies they work for."

"I can give you an example of that," Bif said. "I have this good friend from college who works for a Wall Street investment-banking firm. He had been there fourteen months and hadn't taken a single day off. But he wanted to come to my wedding. So I scheduled it for the Sunday of Labor Day weekend, that is, for the day before Labor Day itself, the holiday. He gave his company two months' notice that he'd be gone on that day.

"So that Sunday he was at my wedding. We had the service in the morning, and by noon we were at the reception. He decided to call in to the office. So he called in and, sure enough, his team leader was there to take the call.

" 'Our whole team except you has been here for a meeting this morning on our project,' he told my friend. 'We really needed you for this meeting, and we were very disappointed that you weren't here.

We're going to get together again after lunch. Can you come in this afternoon?' "

"Good gosh," Gary said in astonishment. "Did he go in?"

"Yes, he went in," Bif answered. "He couldn't get there until that night because he was two plane trips away from New York City. He arrived at about ten that night at his office and stayed until after midnight."

"But he's not unusual," Bif continued. "There's a new set of nightclubs that have sprung up in the city that start at midnight and have a big cover charge, so mainly young Wall Street types use them. They are open all night, so that the young bankers can stay there until three or four in the morning, then go home and sleep a few hours before going in to work the next day."

"Why didn't your friend just tell them he'd be in the next day?" Gary asked.

"No competitor would do that," Bif responded. "He'd be driven crazy by the thought of all his peers there at the office working while he was at a wedding reception. They'd all be getting ahead of him."

"A lot of the consulting companies are the same way," Bif added. "People get big salaries, but they work double the normal schedule to get them."

"And they're the people you're trying to keep up with?" Susan asked him.

"Not all of them," Bif replied. "Only the ones I know personally. They work hard, but they also learn a lot. We just hired one fellow from a big Boston consulting firm. He said he worked continually all the time he was there, but that he loved it. I think he'd still like to be there. He has a good job, but I don't think there's all that much to interest him at our company. Still, I wouldn't be surprised to see him run the company one day."

"If he's patient enough," Susan interjected.

"What do you mean?" Bif asked.

"Most big companies make people wait in line for promotions, don't they?"

"That's true," Bif said. "You mean he might get impatient and leave?"

"Yes."

"So might I," Bif answered.

"I have a friend who was in the army," Susan said. "He graduated from West Point and wanted to make a career as an army officer. But in the military, promotion is based on time in grade. It's the old concept.

"They told him he would have to spend eight years as a captain. So he left. They asked him why he was getting out.

" 'Because in eight years I can do better on the outside,' he told them, 'and that's your competition, guys.' "

"You mean that if my friend and I have to wait years to get to the top, we may leave the company," Bif said. "You're right. It's not just that we're impatient. I can't afford to wait in line while other people in my age group are forming their own companies or advancing quicker. Neither can my friend.

"We're both very conscious of how many people there are who are our age. We read about it a lot in magazines and newspapers. We know there are steep pyramids in big companies. There is a lot of talent in our generation, and lots of dedication. We don't want to fall behind, or be left out. There's a very fast-moving world out there. Things change quickly. In every business, people are inventing new games. You have to really pay attention and stick it out if you're going to keep up."

"We've been talking about men," Gary said, "but there are also women competitors, aren't there?"

"I bet my second wife started out as a good example of that," Bif said. "She was very much into her profession, and she really didn't have time to be married. I think she begrudged me whatever time we spent together. She'd rather have been at the office seeing clients.

"What was worse was that she was so competitive. She competed with me constantly. She wanted her career to be as good as mine; she wanted to be in the same sort of physical condition, or to be more fit, if she could.

"A few years ago I took to working out with weights. I started reading body-building magazines and studying how to improve my physique. I'd go into the health clubs and work on the machines.

"If you do that, you'll discover that the first year or so you can really reshape your body. You don't look like Mr. America or Mr. Olympia, of course, but your muscle tone is better and you lose weight in some places and add it in others. If you work at it and watch your diet, the change can be pretty dramatic in a short time.

"She didn't have time to work out as often as I did, and she began to get very nervous. 'You don't know how much your doing this challenges me,' she told me. 'It makes me feel very uneasy, very inadequate.'

" 'You're in great shape,' I'd tell her, and she was. But still she was very uneasy.

" 'I'm afraid you're outgrowing me,' she'd say. 'I feel like I can't keep up.'

"I told her it was crazy to feel that way, but she couldn't help it. She is just that competitive."

"I'll bet you loved it," Susan put in. "I'll bet you liked to pretend you were outgrowing her. You always loved to put the pressure on." Susan laughed. "I can just hear you saying to yourself, 'She wants to outgrow me, but I'll show her. I'll get ahead of her.' You're just as competitive as she was."

"Do you know Bif's second wife?" Gary asked Susan.

"Yes," she responded.

"Did you know his first wife, too?" Gary asked.

"Sure," Susan answered. "She moved in with him after I moved out. Why do you ask?"

"I'm just surprised," Gary replied. "In my generation people usually are mad when they break up, and they stay away from each other and don't know their old mates' new spouses."

"I don't feel that way," Susan said. "I have known both of Bif's wives. I think they're both very interesting people. I still see his first wife around town from time to time. But I don't really know her well. I mean, I don't know much about their relationship. I don't know her well enough to talk about that."

Bif, who had been thinking, suddenly commented, "To be honest, Susan's probably right. I do like to see her squirm."

"Does she still work?" Gary asked Bif.

"No."

"You don't want her to?"

"That's right," Bif agreed.

"But you don't have children, do you?" Gary asked. "I mean, you haven't mentioned any children."

"No, I don't have children," Bif acknowledged.

"Then why doesn't she work?"

"You have to understand," Susan said to Gary, answering his

question, "that there are still some very traditional men around. Bif doesn't want his wife to work, even if they don't have children, and even if she would like to keep working. Isn't that right, Bif?"

Bif nodded in agreement.

"That seems unfortunate," Gary said. "It isn't necessary to compete all the time with everybody. Couldn't you have just let her do what she wanted?"

Bif frowned, and Gary saw that he had said more than he should have. He had meddled too much in Bif's private affairs. Gary decided to say no more, but Susan picked up his thought.

"You're right, Gary," Susan said, "but I don't think competitors see it that way. They're driven by a sort of personal insecurity. Their biggest fear in life is that they will no longer have something interesting to say or to show off—that they won't measure up to their friends. So they can't stop competing."

FROM HIPPIE TO COMPETITOR

In 1970 in *The Greening of America*, Charles Reich wrote that the new generation "does not believe in the antagonistic or competitive doctrine of life."[2]

In the early 1980s, less than a decade and a half later, Len Schlesinger, then of the Harvard Business School, described some young people working for a new airline as follows: "They're all capitalists. They all want to have fun, have a rewarding job, and make a lot of money."[3]

One of the great puzzles of the baby boom generation is how Reich's idealistic commune members of the 1960s became today's business-oriented competitors.

The answer seems to have two parts. To a degree, Reich was simply wrong. The people he wrote about were intensely competitive and materialistic. Blinded by the euphoria of Woodstock, Reich misread the generation. What he saw was "an extended family in the spirit of the Woodstock Festival, without individual 'ego trips' or 'power trips.' "[4]

In the years since Woodstock, it has become obvious that the baby boomers are not immune to either ego trips or power trips.

To a degree, however, Reich was quite right. Not all baby boomers, nor even a majority, are competitive and business-oriented. Reich's observations about the others, especially the pleasure-seekers, still have insight and value, almost two decades after they were made.

A man from Alabama described himself as business-oriented. "Five years ago," he said, "money wasn't important to me. It's a battle to the top now. I want to be at the top and secure financially. . . . Sometimes," he continued, "I can't enjoy my life because I'm too concerned about my work."

A woman accountant, thirty-four years old and getting divorced, told our interviewer, "At one point in my life I forgot everything else and just worked, worked, worked. I was missing out on life. Someone started shaking me silly to get out of it. I'm trying to be a little bit more like a pleasure-seeker these days."

An Ohio computer analyst, a thirty-year-old woman, said, "Ten years ago I thought that today I'd be raising a family, cutting the grass, and baking cookies. But now it's no kids, no grass, no cookies!

"I'm a competitor," she told us. "I genuinely enjoy my work. I excel at what I do and I like it. I think pleasure is overrated. Pleasure-seeking is a waste of free time."

The assistant news director of an NBC affiliate TV station in Florida told us, "It's funny. Just the other day I was with a group of my co-workers. . . . We realized that we all had the same stomach remedy in our medicine cabinets. I mean, we hardly ever take it; but maybe once a year the stress gets so bad that we take our stomach medicine. All of us were pretty freewheeling in college, but now we want to achieve something . . . we're not as happy-go-lucky as we appear.

"So many of us put so much pressure on ourselves to achieve what we're trying to achieve. There's a lot of stress trying to succeed at your job, seek pleasure, and support the family in the best way possible. We put a lot of pressure on ourselves, our loved ones put pressure on us. . . . There's stress in trying to get ahead and trying to have rewarding careers and the good things in life."

Finally, the thirty-three-year-old owner of a start-up business in Tennessee described himself. "I'm the business-motivated type. I've always worked very, very hard. When I worked at Burger King, I worked night and day. Even at the police department. Whatever I've done, I've usually done it twenty-four hours a day, seven days a week."

"What was your most exciting experience?" our interviewer asked him. "I guess it was when I first started working at Burger King," he responded. "I had two hundred and fifty employees and twenty-five managers under me. I learned a lot about business. I went all over the country to conferences and just learned a whole lot. Now, I'm trying to do it all over again."

One of the surprises in the survey was how many people said they knew not a single person who was a competitor—a person totally into his or her career, wrapped up in work, fully business-motivated.

"There's no one like that in this town," a man from Utah told us. "You can't be a competitor in this small town."

The work-obsessed competitors who are numerous in business and professional ranks in America's big cities may be in short supply in smalltown America.

THE COMPETITOR AS A MANAGER

Competitors are the most business-oriented of the baby boom generation. Hence, they are the most likely group to serve as managers and, in that capacity, to exert considerable influence over the lives of everyone who works for American companies and other organizations. What kinds of managers do these competitive, business-motivated baby boomers make?

I have discussed this question with older managers, with the boomers themselves, and with employees in many American corporations. As should be expected, the managers who are baby boomers differ a great deal in their style and behavior. Nonetheless, a few generalizations can be made based on my conversations and experiences with them. In many respects, the younger generation is much like that which preceded it, but there are some differences, which I will identify below.

Many managers from this generation are quite sensitive to other people and are aware of what motivates them. There is great misunderstanding among older people about this. They think boomers are insensitive and inept with people, and they do not understand that the problem lies in a difference in values between the generations. Younger managers are very sensitive and attuned to others in their own age group. Callous they may sometimes be, but they are not blind to others or to their concerns. When they choose to be, baby boomers can be sensitive, insightful, and caring.

Do they choose to be caring less often than the managers in the generation before them? Is the reputation merited which some younger people have acquired for being sensitive only when it is to their direct benefit?

It is hard to answer such questions, dealing as they do with very personal matters into which it is difficult to inquire. My impression is that baby boomers have the impatience and abruptness of youth, and in many situations evidence the characteristics of that stage of life. But so did the older generation at the same stage of life. I do not see anything unique to the younger generation in this trait, and I expect their interpersonal behavior to become more polished as they age.

Baby boomers are a more imaginative group than their predecessors— more willing to do things differently because they are less confident of the usefulness of traditional methods. Many have been iconoclasts all their lives and will continue to be far more flexible than most of their elders were.

They are much more into fun and play on the job than their predecessors. Only the most extremely business-oriented fail to mix some enjoyment into their work. They are also far more tolerant of this behavior in others who work with or for them than was the previous generation.

They are direct, honest, and demanding. They want an opportunity to show what they can do. They ask when they can expect promotions and complain when they don't receive them. They tolerate similar kinds of demands from their subordinates and are likely to tell the people who report to them to measure up or move along.

They generally lack what is often referred to as a social conscience, being deeply attached primarily to their own careers. However, they are not, by and large unethical. Most boomers consider themselves more honest and willing to accept losses, to hold to contracts, for example, than their elders. To be self-centered and ethical, too, may seem a contradiction to the older generation, but it is not to baby boomers.

Will the baby boomers who become managers modify the American workplace? There is no doubt of this, but the subject will be treated in a later chapter.

THE INTERNAL STRUGGLES OF
BEING A COMPETITOR

It is the competitors who have given the baby boom generation its reputation for being into trendy clothes and cars and other expensive possessions. To all outward appearances, the competitors are very materialistic.

It bears repeating that many in this generation have always been very competitive. In the sixties its members were into what other people were—rock music, drugs, protesting. In the eighties they see what other people in their generation have, and they want it themselves. In this sense the generation, and particularly the competitors among them, deserves the reputation it has.

But our interviews suggested that there is a deeper side to the baby boomers' materialism, in which goods are not so much an objective as a means to an end, at least to many of the competitors. It is not things they really want, nor even the status which possessions tend to bring in our society. Viewing the competitors as primarily pursuing material goods for the goods' own sake is to project onto them the values of the preceding generation.

Instead, they're looking for a competitive edge. They think the way they dress or where they live or what they wear will give them an advantage over the competition if they can get just the right thing and get it first. This interpretation doesn't necessarily redound to the competitors' credit. They are so competitive that to many people they seem like sharks.

While working on this book, I received a letter from a former student who had finished graduate school and now worked for a large financial company. He wrote that what has surprised him most in business is how many "slimy and disreputable"—to use his words—people there are. "School leaves one with a very naïve view of the world," he wrote. "In the real world there are very few generous people, just some who are less grasping than the others. My problem," he concluded, "is how much to be like them."

This issue arises continually in discussions with the competitors. They often seem to ask themselves what the standards are to which they and the people with whom they compete, should be. They are afraid that if they hold themselves to higher standards than others do, they will lose out in the contest.

One young executive told me the following story:

"My company was one of a consortium that put up some money for a new venture. The company had a hot product, but like most start-ups, it was doing great one day and down in the pits the next.

"In its second year the company got into a cash squeeze. It couldn't pay its bills, and so something had to be done. Something like this happening is very common with new companies, and people who are used to developing new businesses expect it. But for the people who haven't had experience and just have a dream and hard work, it always seems to be a shock. They never seem to have anticipated it or to have made any provisions for it. That's what happened in this case. So when the company ran out of cash, the people whose idea it was, and who had been running it, suddenly found themselves at the mercy of their creditors or of the bank. They were also at the mercy of my company, which was their partner and which had more money it could make available—if it chose.

"It looked to our top management like the new company was going to do well in the future, even though now it needed more capital to keep it going. My company had additional funds to put in, as did other investors, but the guys who had put it together and had done all the work had very little left. So when the company refinanced, the outside investors, including my company, took over full control and forced the founders out. They ended up with little or nothing for their ideas and efforts. The new company did do well, and my company eventually sold its interest for a great deal of money."

He continued. "We were out drinking, my friends in the company and I, and we had a big argument about what had happened. I felt like we'd been a bunch of sharks. It wasn't right to take the guys' company away from them, even if they'd made a mistake or two.

"My friends disagreed. They said we had another manager all set to run the company, and since it couldn't have two head people, the founder had to go. And if he went, his close associates should go, too, so the new top guy would have an opportunity to bring in his own team.

"They said that we, the investors, had the legal right to force the founders out. They'd made the best deal they could when we'd financed them, and it was the deal that the founders had thought would be most lucrative to them. So when it went sour for them, and we used our rights in the contract to expel them, then it was just what they should have expected. So my friends insisted we'd been fair. It was a very hot argument.

"I still think competition among people, even partners, should have some limits, but lots of people think the only limits should be legal ones." He paused. "I guess some people don't even stop there."

Many baby boomers have great aspirations and set high goals for themselves. But it's tough to be a competitor. There's a lot of pressure, and it's a rough world. Many competitors seem to think that if they really want to, they can go back to a more simple life. At least, that's their hope.

They say, "I could live on less. I could make life more simple. I know I can do it because I did it in the sixties; I lived more simply."

But very few people are really doing it. The competitors are run by their competition.

I recall a discussion one of our interviewers had with a woman. She owned an advertising agency in Los Angeles. She said she wanted to return to New England, to a simpler life.

The interviewer could see how well she was dressed, and asked her about it. She acknowledged that her tastes had changed. She said she knew she needed lots of money to be able to afford the fine clothes and antiques and art she wanted.

She talked about her baby-sitter. She said she had become very dissatisfied with her. She was a person without ambition, she said. She wasn't the kind of person she wanted her children to be with. The sitter was her age, but nothing was important to her except to be able to buy clothes for her own kids and to go to the Amvets with her husband on weekends. "I can't talk to her," the woman said. "I want my children to be with someone who is more aggressive, more competitive."

Yet this woman still longed to escape the business world and live a simpler life.

There seems to be among the competitors an element who wish they were pleasure-seekers. They are in a constant mental struggle. In their self-searching, many competitors recognize implicitly the philosophical superiority which the pleasure-seeker insists is his or hers.

This attitude is very different from that of the business executive of the previous generation. For that person there was no question that the hard worker had the moral and philosophical edge. It was the business executive and the entrepreneur who were building and accomplishing things, not the pleasure-seekers. To business executives of the previous generation, the person who didn't devote himself or herself primarily to work had to justify his or her priorities.

But for the competitors among the baby boomers, the moral and philosophical situation is very different and much more difficult. To them, it is the pleasure-seeker who really knows what life is about. It's not about the rat race, and the competitor knows it, even if he or she is not able to get out of the competition itself.

A competitor says, "I've got my career. I've got to keep at it and build it up. But my friends are all off in Tahoe and I'm not there. What am I doing with my life?"

However, many competitors remain competitors, even when they try to be less compulsive about work. Hence the internal struggle. So when a competitor takes time off and goes out to Tahoe, then that person says to him or herself, "I'm here at Tahoe, having a great time, but John and Doris are back in New York getting rich. I'm as good as they are; at least, I think I am. Maybe I ought to be back there. I don't want them to get too far ahead of me. Anyway, I need lots of bread to pay for this skiing. Maybe I should get back in the rat race."

4

THE TRAPPED

"What should be our next category?" Gary asked. "Have we gotten to Susan yet?"

"We could go to me," Susan said with a smile, "but there is another category which comes to mind which we might want to do first. As I think about it, there are a lot of people in it. I guess I usually put those people out of my mind because I feel bad for them. I think they're unhappy."

Gary nodded. "I've met people in your generation who are very unhappy," he said. "At least, they seem unhappy to me. I think they're trapped."

"What?" Bif asked. "What did you say? Trapped?"

"Yes, trapped," Gary answered.

"He's right, Bif," Susan said. "I know people who are caught in situations they don't like. For example, a job with a big company can look very appealing at first. It seems to promise security and a person always thinks he or she will advance up the ladder fast. Then it doesn't work out that way, but a person stays there just the same. Or someone gets married. At first it's all moonlight and roses. Then things get more complicated. Maybe the two people grow apart. Things aren't like they used to be. Maybe they don't love each other anymore. Maybe they don't even like each other. But they both stay there, and they become more and more miserable.

"Some people think they can run into the trap and still get out with the bait. They think they can make a lot of money in big business, or enjoy their marriage, and for a while it works. But then they get stuck. They're unhappy, but maybe they don't really realize that they are trapped. It crosses their minds, but they don't want to think about it. They say, 'I ought to do something different,' but they don't. They say, 'I want to get out,' but they can't.

"One of my friends at a big company where I used to work said to me, 'Gee, you got out of here and started your own company. Why didn't I think of that?' It was as if she were saying, 'I am just as smart and capable as you. I could do what you've done.' But the point is, she didn't, and she's still trapped in that job. People like her kind of know they're trapped, but they don't take any steps to get out."

"I never thought about it before," Bif commented, "but I see what you mean. Still, I don't think I know anyone who is trapped. No one ever talks about being unhappy."

"Not to you," Susan said.

"What do you mean?" Bif asked in surprise.

"You don't look like you would be sympathetic," Susan responded. "Competitors like you aren't sympathetic to people who aren't going great guns. So people don't talk to competitors about feeling trapped."

"I don't know if this should be a whole category," Bif said. "There may be a few people like that, but not many."

"I disagree," Gary interjected. "I think there are a lot of people in that category. What makes someone trapped is not the situation that a person is in—some people are happy in situations in which others feel trapped. What makes a situation a trap is that he or she wants out, deep down, but can't seem to do anything about it.

"I told you," Gary continued, "that I had met some people in your generation who I thought were trapped. One is a manager for a big company located in California. I went out to see him once on a business deal. That night he and I got together with the people who worked for him and had a few beers. We were at a nice resort, which overlooked the ocean. I remember the conversation so well because the setting was so beautiful—the night was bright and starry—and the discussion was so out of context with the evening.

"This guy had had a lot to drink, and he'd shift moods unpredictably. One moment he'd be the most gracious person you'd ever meet. The next he would be vicious. He'd ask about my life and seem very interested and admiring; then he'd suggest that I was kind of a fraud and a crook. When he was being gracious, he'd say how much he'd like to work for himself like I do, and how he thought he could do it very well. Then he'd attack me and my motives and seem very hostile. I could barely keep up with the switches. He did the same kind of thing with the people who worked with him. One moment friendly and the next bitter.

"I was determined not to let him make me angry, and I wasn't. But I thought about the whole thing afterward and I decided that he was just very unhappy in what he was doing. He thought he could do better things and he resented people who were doing what he wanted to do. So he took it out on his subordinates, and sometimes, like when he was drinking, he couldn't even conceal his feelings from people with whom he was doing business. I decided he was trapped in his job and was very frustrated. He wanted out, but somehow he couldn't get up the courage to do something different."

Bif objected. "I don't see why a person would get into a trap in the first place."

"No one gets into a trap on purpose," Susan said. "A person does something because it seems the best thing to do at the moment. Later it becomes a trap.

"I think that each person goes through a series of phases in life when the intensity of a particular relationship is high. When you're young, it's the relationship with your parents. When you're in your teens, it's with your peers. In your late adolescence and twenties, it's with potential mates. Later, it's with your spouse, if you have one, and maybe with your children. For some it may be a relationship with people in your business or in your profession.

"The danger is that you get stuck in one of these relationships at a time of high intensity, and then you're trapped and can't move on. You think, 'I can't leave this person. I don't know what else is out there. It's too late for me to try something different. What will other people think of me if I leave?' So a trapped person talks herself or himself into staying in the trap."

"That reminds me of another example," Gary said. "She's the wife of a friend of mine. She's about forty, so she just makes it into your generation. She's one of the first baby boomers. Anyway, I was talking to her once about her life. She told me she's not as positive a person as she used to be. 'Little things bother me a lot more,' she said. She told me that she had stayed home to take care of the kids for many years, and now they were going out on their own. The house was almost paid off and she hoped to have more opportunity to travel, she said.

"Then she started talking about her friends, but I think that was just a cover for talking about herself. She said she thinks too many women her age aren't doing as much as they could or would like to. Many of her friends feel inadequate, she told me. Not enough of them want to start something new at this age. She said, 'We're too old to start something.

" 'I feel I ought to be doing something more with my life. I feel that I ought to be more productive. I'd like to leave some part of me on this earth. I'd like to make a contribution that will be noticed by someone. That's what happens when you've been married for twenty years,' she said. 'My family has been my whole life.' "

Susan was frowning as Gary finished. "I know women like that," she said. "One of my best friends from high school is like that. She loves her husband very much. I remember once when we were talking and I said something about her being like someone else, she got mad and snapped at me, 'David and I aren't like anybody else!' It struck me at the time that she didn't limit her comment to herself. It was 'David and I.' I thought that was very romantic.

"But David won't let her work. He wants her to stay home. So I ask her how she spends all day and she says, 'Just goofing off. My prime hobby is going shopping,' she says. 'My friends and I go to McDonald's for lunch. We always find ways to do something while David's at work. Oh, we rearrange the house or wallpaper, or take a walk around the block. I try not to make the high point of my day cleaning toilets.'

"I think it's a very sad story. For some women, staying home and taking care of the kids is all they want to do. But others think that will satisfy them and when it doesn't, they're very unhappy."

"But shouldn't people accept," Bif asked, "that a woman who stays at home does just as much and makes just as much of a contribution as one who has a job outside the home?"

"If people did accept that," Gary answered, "then a lot of women would be better able to respect themselves, I think."

"That's the heart of it, to my mind at least," Susan commented. "For some women, staying at home is all right; they don't have any problem. But for others, the question of what a woman's role in society should be has trapped them. The real problem is not what others think of a housewife, it's what she thinks of herself."

WHY PEOPLE GET TRAPPED

People become trapped for a number of reasons. Some are trapped because they dropped out early and the world passed them by. They don't know how to get back into the world, and their defense is to say that they're happy where they are. These are the people who say they are content while they overeat and smoke continually. All the body signals such a person sends, all the signs of the actual psychological state indicate the exact opposite of being content.

There are people who are trapped because while they were making their way up in a corporation and were working fifty or sixty or seventy hours a week, they also took on a marriage and two children, and now they can't handle it all. Some recognize that they have to make some choices. So they drop out of their jobs or their marriages.

A tragic example of the trapped was an unemployed forty-year-old man in Indiana. Our interviewer wrote on her interview record form, "Not a talker and not cooperative. I think he was holding back a lot." It appeared that he had a great deal to hold back. Asked what his outlook was on life, he responded. "My outlook? It went from twenty-twenty to twenty-four hundred. I went blind."

What did he think he would be doing now? "I thought I'd be working," he replied. "But now I'm not."

What was important in his life? "I have no idea." What was he concerned about? "Nothing really." What was special about him? "Nothing really."

Here was a person trapped by a physical handicap, and suffering great bitterness from the situation.

There are also baby boomers who don't like themselves because they think they're too much like their parents. These are people who feel that they've become today's hypocrites. They believe that they stood for one set of values in their college years and have somehow been transformed into something else.

They are living out the greatest fear they had as college students: that they'd become exactly like their parents. They spent a large part of their years of emotional development revolting against what they now see they are becoming. They are constantly looking back and saying to themselves, "I can't believe I heard myself say that to my child. I sound just like my parents."

This is a difficult group of people with which to deal because they are very unhappy with themselves, and so are extremely negative about everything. We encountered people of this type in our interviews. One is a salesperson for a computer company. She is a most unusual salesperson because of her negative attitude. She is continually regretting things she has or hasn't done.

"We don't want to stretch ourselves too far," she said. "We are becoming complacent like our parents but some of us still have a lot of the sixties attitude left in us. We are rebellious just so we won't become like our parents. We are not wishy-washy. We have very definite strong attitudes left over from the sixties."

A thirty-year-old female computer scientist living in California told us, "I'm trapped, because I'm apprehensive. I have some of the qualities of my parents but I haven't been able to sort them out yet."

Most baby boomers have accepted that as life goes on a person's priorities change. They don't think that means they have sacrificed their values. They recognize that people's interests, concerns, and commitments can change without meaning that they are hypocrites or traitors to themselves. But some are trapped in their own conception of themselves and are bitter because they can't live up to that conception today.

"I grew up in the middle of the country," one thirty-year-old woman told us. "When it was time to go to college, my friends split. Some went to the East Coast, some to the West. Many of the people who went to the East went heavily into political issues and movements. My friends who went west became hippies and flower children, or went into the media. They were into defining a life-style more than into politics. Later I think the people in the West were more true to the vision we had when we were young. They were more true to the relationships and the values. They weren't drawn off into the mire and ultimate frustration of politics. I think my friends who came east, at least many of them, became the trapped ones."

ADMITTING THAT ONE IS TRAPPED

Respondents to our survey were prepared to tell us about their friends and acquaintances who were trapped, and they knew many people like that. But people who themselves were trapped found their own situation more difficult to discuss.

People who are trapped often do not recognize that they are. Or if they are aware of it, they find it very difficult to express openly. To admit to oneself that one is trapped is usually a step toward doing something about it, and some people fear the unknown and change. Many people who say that they are contented with their lives are in fact seething emotionally in very undesirable situations.

We did find some people who were prepared to admit to us that they were trapped. One was a thirty-two-year-old woman from Minnesota. For eight years she had worked at a job she didn't like. During that time she had married and had a child. She grew to hate her job and felt trapped in it. She was now preparing to leave work, "even though it is a large socioeconomic step back," to go to graduate school. "I want to see what the next level of education will bring me as a career," she said.

To a twenty-seven-year-old Iowa farmer and graduate student, our interviewer described someone who was worried about being too much like his parents. "That's interesting," he responded. "That's something I think about, but I don't discuss it with anyone. I feel that way sometimes."

"What are you most concerned about?" our interviewer asked a woman. "Health, money, and keeping everyone happy. Scheduling our lives to make everyone happy," she answered. "Except for my mother-in-law, she complains about everything. She thinks I shouldn't work and spend my time driving her around. She doesn't drive. She doesn't work. We are the only ones she has to bother. I don't know. I'm not sure. His mom always says we will have to take care of her properties when she dies. If she goes, I will have to quit my job and take care of the properties, if she doesn't blow it all in Las Vegas."

"Trapped by a mother-in-law," our interviewer observed.

A thirty-five-year-old insurance salesman in California was having trouble placing himself in a category. "Do you have anything for the disgruntled and frustrated?" he asked. "People who are not satisfied with their lives but who don't have an answer for how to change it. It's not the 'Let's Get Highs.'. . . It's an interim step before one gets to the drugs and alcohol. They either can't make a change or are unwilling to make a change, but they're not into drugs or alcohol." Was he one of these people? our interviewer asked. "Oh, no," he responded. But he left the interviewer with little doubt that the person he had been so eloquently discussing was in fact himself.

5

THE CONTENTED

There was silence at the table. Gary waited awhile, and when no one spoke, he asked: "So where are we now? We have been talking about people who are trapped, but by different things. Some are stuck in bad jobs or bad marriages. Others are stuck in the past or in their own conceptions of themselves which they can't live up to."

"The trouble with this," Bif said, "is that there's no reason for a person to stay in this category—to stay trapped. If my first wife were trapped, as Susan said she was, by me, then she got out of it when we got divorced. That's what I don't like about this category," Bif said. "A person can always get out."

"Some people can get out," Susan said. "I agree. Some do get out. But lots of people don't. Still, you have a good point. I think that many people who are essentially satisfied in life, and who lead fairly well-balanced lives started out as trapped and got out of the trap."

"Then maybe that gives us another category," Bif suggested.

Bif's comment surprised Gary. "What do you mean?" he asked. "How could we make a category out of that? Why do you say a person can always get out, even if he or she is trapped?"

"Baby boomers know they have a lot of options," Bif responded. "We know we're not stuck. A person might get into a bad situation sometimes, but there's no reason to stay there. That's the point with baby boomers. We know there are always options."

As Bif paused, Susan spoke: "That's what you mean, isn't it, Gary, when you say that people my age are independent? I think Bif is right. Baby boomers have a series of options in the back of their minds and draw them out as things change in their lives.

"Almost everyone is potentially trapped at some time or other," she continued. "I think that I've been trapped more often than most. There's almost a cycle in which a person gets trapped and then gets out of the trap. If she doesn't get out, then she just remains in the trap. There are traps in jobs, in families, in relationships, in health. There are clubs that turn into traps; there are diet fads and sects that turn into traps—all kinds of traps. Some people say, just accept your lot. Stay in the trap.

"I've always tried to get out. It's just what Bif said. There are always options for our generation. When I'm in a job I can't stand, I go do something else. If I get caught in a diet that's too much, I just exercise more to keep my figure. When I find myself in a relationship I don't like, I look for another man."

"I wonder, Susan," Gary asked cautiously, "whether you are really content with your life?"

Susan eyed him with surprise. She didn't think that she had said anything to provoke such a question.

"I mean," Gary explained without waiting for her answer, "you seem always to be looking for another man. I sometimes wonder whether or not that is just a cop-out on your part? Maybe you're afraid of a lasting relationship."

Susan was shocked. She started to make a joking response to divert him from the issue, but then she hesitated. He had asked the question seriously, and she was by nature both an honest person and very interested in her own psychological makeup. She sat thinking about how to answer him while both men waited silently. Bif knew she was on the spot and was curious to know what she would say.

"Maybe I am afraid of a lasting relationship," Susan finally admitted. "I don't think I'm afraid of loving a man," she said, looking directly into Gary's eyes, "although I've asked myself many times if I am. What I'm afraid of, I think, is that a relationship will turn into a trap for me. I'm afraid that a man will want to put me in a box and keep me there, and I won't have a chance to do different things and grow and change. The men I've lived with have often done that to me. You wanted me to keep house, Bif, remember? And the man I lived with after you did, too. He got very mad at me when I decided to go to graduate school and then start my own company.

"I think I am afraid of a long-lasting relationship," she said, "because men so often want me to fit into some mold. I'm afraid of getting trapped in a relationship. If a person could have a relationship which is supportive and still be free to change and grow and do things differently, I might change my mind."

From the inflection in Susan's voice as she ended the sentence, it was clear that she had finished.

Bif spoke now, picking up the line of thought which Susan had interrupted several minutes before. "We don't have a category for people who are just satisfied with their lives."

"You mean we need a category for people who have gotten out of being trapped?" Gary asked.

"Yes," Bif answered. "That's what I think."

Bif paused, then continued. "I know some people who would fall in this category," Bif offered. "My sister is one. She got married during college and didn't finish. But the guy she married turned out to be a real jerk. He left her and is now living with a girl friend. So my sister is in the process of getting a divorce.

"I was worried about her, but she seemed to feel better about herself because she had gotten out of a bad situation. That's why I said before that people can always get out of something like that. They can always take up some other option. I encouraged my sister to get rid of her husband rather than to just keep in the same old situation.

"Anyway, in the past five years I think she's become more secure with herself. She seems less threatened. I think she understands herself better. She's been setting goals for herself. For one thing, she decided to go back to college. Since she's over thirty, that took a little courage. But she even hopes to go on to graduate school after that. She took the CPA review and did quite well. She's a person who has overcome a trap and now is pretty contented with herself."

"You know," Susan observed, "I feel that way, too. I feel kind of content with my life right now. I'm in the job I want to be in, working for myself. I'm living in the house I want to live in. I can come and go when I want. I can go down to the beach if I want or go sailing, or even go out west to the mountains.

"I think that category we're talking about," she continued, "would be people who came out of a bad situation. I think I belong in it."

"So how do we put this?" Gary asked. "We say that some people are content with their lives. They've achieved satisfaction in their jobs and acceptance in their communities. They're happy in their relationships."

The others nodded in agreement, but as they did so, Gary began to have doubts himself. "I'm troubled by having a category that says people are happy," he said. "I haven't met a lot of really happy people in my life. I think no one is really happy except momentarily.

"I think people are always trying to grasp a little more. They're happy when they get what was next in line for them, but then they're unhappy again when they set the next goal. Look at the groups we've already talked about. The competitor is always worried that the competition is gaining on him. He can't be happy long. Each day or each project is a new contest. If he allows himself to be happy, he'll relax and fall behind.

"Then the pleasure-seeker is always trying to find some new and enjoyable diversion. Anything he or she does consistently becomes familiar and boring. A pleasure-seeker tends to get jaded, and so has to keep on the alert for something new all the time. Pleasure-seekers are not happy either except momentarily."

"But then I don't think I'd call myself happy exactly," Susan continued. "It's as if everyone had something that kept her or him from being really happy. There's always something you can't have or can't get. I'd say I'm contented rather than happy. I'm contented with my life."

"Is it just because you've overcome the traps you felt you were in?" Gary asked.

"No, I don't think that's all there is to it," Susan replied. "Maybe there are even some people who haven't been in traps at all."

"I know people," Bif said, "who have a good family life, and who do a lot of things, but nothing overmuch. They like material things but don't go nuts about them. I think most of them are reasonably content with their lives. One friend of mine doesn't have a lot of money but gets along fairly well. He told me once that he allows himself to buy one thing spontaneously each year—one big item. Everything else he budgets for and buys according to a plan. He's kind of a together individual—at least I think of him that way."

"Is he different from the people we've been talking about?" Gary inquired.

"In some ways he is different, I think," Bif responded. "I don't think he's ever been in a trap, or gotten out. He hasn't changed jobs; he's still married to the same wife. He's an ordinary person. I think he'd say he's happy with his job and his family and his hobbies. I think there's lots like him."

"He's another kind of contented person," Gary suggested. "Susan was talking about people who are contented because they've escaped a bad situation. You're talking about people who are content because they're satisfied with their lives; isn't that right?"

"I think so," Susan responded. "The people I have in mind were trapped, but got out. The trapped are the people who say, 'I should have; I should have . . . but I never did.' The contented people say, 'I should have; I should have . . . and I did! I got out of the bad situation.' It was an accomplishment to have overcome the situation. They are pleased that they did it; they are relieved to be out of the trap; and they are contented with their lives as a result."

"I'm glad we came up with this category," Gary said. "I think we would have missed a lot of people if we hadn't. Not everyone is trapped, or a competitor or a pleasure-seeker."

"When you really think about it," Bif observed, "we probably each know a lot of people like that. I have two friends who have decent jobs. They just had a baby. It took seventeen years of trying and the woman had five miscarriages in the process. To have a child was very important to them. Now they have their child and they are very content."

Susan had sat, quiet and unsmiling, while Gary and Bif exchanged stories about contented people. Her silence began to trouble them.

"What are you thinking about?" Gary asked.

She shrugged.

"You don't like contented people?" he asked.

"I think they're boring," Susan answered. "I mean, the people you're describing—they're boring people. They don't have goals; they kind of sit and vegetate. They're not interesting people."

"Now wait a minute, Susan," Gary objected. "You were part of the contented group yourself just a little while ago."

"They're not the same group, really," Susan insisted. "The people I was talking about are not boring. They do different things. They try out new things. If they get into a trap they get out of it.

"What I worry about is, Am I making the right decisions now, so that when I'm older I'll feel that I lived my life the right way?

"The people I'm talking about are active. They make choices, and when they work out, they're content. I think the people you two were discussing are not interesting."

"But interesting or not," Gary said, "they're contented, too. The result is the same, no matter how you get there.

"Maybe you'd be more tolerant of these people if you thought of them as trying to achieve a balance in their lives. They try to have a family or a relationship and a career, and some time for themselves. That's what you're like, isn't it? Isn't that what you were telling Bif—that he ought to have a better balance in his life?"

Susan nodded, reluctantly.

"So what we should say is that there's a category of people who are balanced, or content. But they get there different ways," Gary concluded.

REACHING A BALANCE IN LIFE

Many people who are content say that they have achieved a balance in their lives between competing influences. Others say that they were trapped once, but have found their way out. We found many people who described their lives in both of these fashions.

One of the most interesting was a forty-year-old homicide detective in New York's South Bronx. "I enjoy what I'm doing," he said. "It's stimulating. I really go around playing cops and robbers. It was always a dream with me to be a policeman. There's a lot of satisfaction. I have a seventy-four percent clearance rate in my homicide files. I'm very proud of that."

But he also expressed some doubts. "I really wonder why I do it sometimes. I've stopped in many a urine-stenched elevator wondering if when the door opens up, some mother is going to be standing there with a sawed-off shotgun. I wonder if the next thing I'll see will be blue and red lights, or maybe not even that.

"It's a trip," he continued. "Maybe that's my high. But I can't make any mistakes in my line of work."

He described himself as having a more serious approach to his family life today than he had ten years ago. "Financially, what I do is crazy work. We don't get paid that great. If I was as smart ten years ago as I am now, I would probably have been able to do a lot better for myself.

"Still," he continued, "basically I'm content."

In Nebraska we encountered a thirty-three-year-old man who told us the following story: "Ten years ago I got caught up in the tail end of the Haight-Ashbury crowd in San Francisco. Then after that, my only purpose in life was to make money no matter how. I know it doesn't make much sense, but I just wanted to make money.

"I taught high school and my wife was a legal secretary. But after a few years we decided to quit our jobs and move to a farm. We pushed for a more simple life. I could have been coaching basketball, but we really didn't want to deal with people anymore. We wanted to be somewhere where we could be happy with ourselves. We felt a farm was a good place to do it.

"What is important to me is being at peace. Being happy with myself and where I am. We don't have a lot of money but we're buying some land. We consider ourselves sort of the second wave of the agricultural era.

"We're enjoying it. People ought to be happy with what they're doing whether it's hauling garbage or something else. If a person is happy and if he feels he's doing a good job with it and if he's lucky, he'll get paid well. Like me . . . I'm happy with my seventy-eight Buick. I shine it up and take care of it instead of buying a new car. . . . I don't worry that my car is getting too old. Or the people who just enjoy life because the sun is out . . . they enjoy people enjoying themselves . . . being at peace with oneself. I'm not there now, but I'm working on it constantly. I'll be there yet! There are a lot of happy people in this world."

Are these people really content? Are they happy? None of our respondents described living without some difficulties. Perhaps no one *is* truly content except momentarily.

"A lot of my friends are contented," a midwestern woman told us. "My husband was laid off once. He went out and found another job right away. When I didn't have a job, the opportunity arose and I took it. It's different from our parents. When they grew up, there wasn't the same relationship in the family. The mothers never worked. I think now my husband has a better relationship with the kids. He shares the home responsibilities and raising the kids. Women then didn't drive, have checking accounts, or such. They just stayed home and took care of the kids. I don't know how they could be so dependent on the husband.

"What makes me content?" the woman asked. "I'm not a pleasure-seeker anymore. I'm busy with my kids and family. I'm busy with my work. The most exciting time besides my wedding day was the two days I had my children. It was more exciting than buying a new home or cars.

"I've held everything together where my friends haven't. Either their marriage or relationships with kids have fallen apart for them. I've been married for twelve years and I have a close family relationship."

After our interviewer described the contented to her, a thirty-four-year-old California homemaker responded in the following way: "My husband and I are like that. We've felt trapped. I was married for twelve years. It took me all that time to make the decision to rise above a bad marriage.

"Last year my oldest children's father died. [This was her first husband.] It was hard for them but very hard for me, too. When you're married for that long, there's still a feeling of caring 'cause it's another human being. I felt very bad. It was sudden—he was only forty-two. It was a hard thing for the kids to get through. My mother has emphysema. It's a condition we take one day at a time. She's very young—fifty-nine. Now she's just a shell of the original. She used to be spunky. We've had our share of bad situations that we've had to overcome in the past several years."

Where did this woman get her strength of character? "Since I've moved to California," she continued, "I've met a lady in her sixties . . . she's got cancer. I respect her greatly. She's such an inspiration. She doesn't talk about her illness. She gets on with living. She's such a unique person, and she's all alone. She has a daughter, but she seldom sees her. She lives in a mobile home. She's so independent. When I feel bad that I'm living in a strange city, I think about her being all alone. She's alone and happy and has a great sense of humor. I feel very lucky to know her."

A thirty-two-year-old chemist in Texas told our interviewer that he was content. "Five years ago my wife and I planned our life situations and that's what we're doing. We overcame a few bumps now and then. I would say we're never quite contented with our jobs, but we strive for job changes. I took a new job several years ago and made a change. Now I'm in a much better situation."

One of the striking features about the baby boom generation is its remarkable talent and capability. But often a person must escape a trap to be free to follow where talent leads.

"I'm business- and career-oriented," said a thirty-four-year-old Massachusetts man, "but I don't have blinders on. I'm not going after the almighty dollar. There's more to life than that. I'd say I'm part career-oriented and somewhat contented. I've gotten myself out of some bad situations that I felt trapped in. The first was changing careers and the second was going through a divorce eight years ago. I managed to turn two bad situations around totally.

"I'm a real estate broker now. I was a teacher, but no one respects teachers. I sing, too," he added. "The most exciting thing I've done is that I've just finished a master tape in New York. I've been going to different record companies to see if I can sell it. Doing the tape was exciting and rewarding to me. I'm waiting to hear what a record company will say."

The woman who interviewed this budding recording star mentioned to me that she found him a "very exciting guy. I put a star by his name. Maybe I'll call him back," she said.

"I'm like the contented," said a twenty-seven-year-old homemaker in Washington State. "I'm trying to better myself by getting out of a very bad experience growing up. I didn't let the situation I grew up in dictate the way I would live the rest of my life.

"The most exciting time in my life was when I decided that I could go to college," she continued, "that I could get grant money to go. As I said, I grew up in a terrible environment. My parents had no money to send me, and they were alcoholics. I did not want to be a product of that environment. My brothers and sisters did not fare as well as me. I came out on top! As maybe you know, the prognosis for children of alcoholic parents is not good. Many follow the same patterns as their parents. We had a very bad experience growing up, but I finally realized that I could get over it and make it."

Said a thirty-two-year-old secretary in Kansas, "Someone you can be happy and peaceful with is very important to me. I stress peaceful because my first marriage was extremely violent.

"I got out of a bad situation," she continued, "by getting a divorce. I was an abused wife. If I didn't get out, I was afraid my daughter would grow up thinking that's the way life is. Plus, I didn't like living in fear. So for those two reasons, I called it quits!"

Contentment also comes from independence. "The most important time in my life," said a twenty-two-year-old homemaker and baby-sitter in Arkansas, "was when I went for my first job. It gave me a feeling of independence. My husband and I were on the verge of divorce and it was a time of my feeling intimidated and scared. The job showed me that I could stand on my own two feet when all my husband ever told me was that I'd fall on my face.

"The job was selling furniture. I felt a great deal of accomplishment in being able to support my family. "Now I'm contented," she said.

"I'm contented," said a thirty-six-year-old woman in Missouri. "I guess you'd say I'm kind of a workaholic. I'm a production supervisor for a printing company; I'm a bartender for a private millionaires' club; and I do housecleaning.

"My independence is special. I've been divorced for seventeen years. Most of my friends have been married three or four times just to avoid being alone.

"Why do I work so hard? I'm worried about my daughter's education. She's eighteen years old, but has a learning disability."

Our interviewer asked her how she can be contented when she has to work so hard. She answered, it was the most exciting thing that ever happened to her.

"I struggled for years to make ends meet and I was full of self-pity. But as I sit back and look outside, I see it's not so bad. I've come up from all of that in the past ten or fifteen years.

"I got to buy my house. None of my family ever owned houses until one sister got married and her husband had a house. I'm the oldest in my family. Not even my mother had a house."

Finally, "The important thing in being content," said a thirty-year-old New York man, "is to have the right formula or the right mixture in life. People like that are half and half. They're career-oriented and family-oriented. I'd call them equalizers. I'm one of them."

6

THE "GET HIGHS"

"There's still another group," Gary said. "One we haven't talked about yet."

"What?" Susan asked in surprise. "I thought we'd covered pretty much everyone."

"No, I don't think so," Gary responded. "There's a group of people who destroy themselves in your generation. There always has been."

"What do you mean, 'destroy themselves'?" Susan asked.

"I mean people who commit suicide or kill themselves with drugs or alcohol. The writers and poets of your generation often end up that way. I remember in the mid–nineteen-seventies when Richard Brautigan killed himself."

Bif looked puzzled.

"He was a poet," Gary said. "He wrote 'In Watermelon Sugar' and 'Trout Fishing in America.' "

"I remember those," Bif said.

"Remember how Allen Ginsberg's poem 'Howl' starts?" Gary asked.

Bif and Susan said nothing.

Gary smiled, enjoying a minor triumph. "It starts, 'I have seen the best minds of my generation destroyed by madness, starving, hysterical, naked . . .' " He continued. "Still, I wasn't thinking so much of people who kill themselves one night as much as I was thinking of people who kill themselves more slowly."

"What do you mean?" Susan asked.

"I mean people who use drugs or drink too much," Gary replied.

"Gary," Susan said, exasperation in her voice, "no one 'uses' drugs. People 'do' drugs. Drugs are an event, an experience. They're part of the social scene. Or maybe if you're square or from the older generation, people 'take' drugs. But nobody 'uses' drugs."

Gary looked provoked. He didn't relish being put down by Susan, especially in front of Bif. But he held his anger and merely responded, "I'm sorry. I don't know much about drugs."

"I don't think you know anything about drugs," Susan said to him, more gently this time, as if to a slow learner.

Her tone made Gary even more angry. "Okay," he said, "I don't take drugs. I'm afraid of them."

"But do you drink?" Susan asked.

"You know I drink," Gary answered curtly, exasperation in his voice.

"Most people in my generation who do drugs also drink," Susan said.

"I know that," Gary answered. "It's a generational thing, I think. People in my generation are usually uncomfortable with drugs and don't know much about them. I told you, I'm afraid of them. I'm not afraid to say that. Isn't it true that a lot of people really get in trouble with drugs?" Gary asked the question with an edge to his voice.

"You're right," she answered. "There are people who get addicted and can't handle drugs. I think many of them are very sensitive people who can't handle the contradictions of everyday life. They try to escape from it all by getting into drugs or alcohol too much. There's more and more pressure in the world. And it's especially hard for our generation. Our expectations were so great. Drugs are a way of relieving the tension of not achieving your expectations. When I was in school, people were always turning to alcohol or drugs for relief from the pressures of school."

"I think that's right," Bif said. "There was so much pressure that people had problems because we felt we needed to succeed. Some people handled it poorly by turning to drugs. I think one lesson we learned in my generation was that we could have prevented lots of damage that drugs have done if there had been less pressure put on us."

"I know there was a lot of pressure," Gary said, "and that there still is. But I guess I really don't understand why go to drugs. It isn't just to get lost, is it? I mean, just to hide from the pressure?"

"No," Bif answered. "People do drugs for other reasons. They do drugs to heighten their awareness, to cope better, to have more energy. Whatever you're doing, it increases the intensity. It makes you feel good. It lets a person escape reality, because there are contradictions and difficulties in life. It makes sex better, too. People in our generation think they can handle it.

"You talk about people destroying themselves," he said to Gary. "When people start with drugs, they don't think of destroying themselves. People do drugs for social reasons or to expand their knowledge. Drugs are mind-enhancing, so a person takes drugs to do complex math. He can do in half an hour what otherwise takes him three hours. Or people do drugs to alter their minds, for insight or for a spiritual experience."

"Drugs are about entertainment and sex," Susan said when Bif paused. "They are a recreation, a diversion. When I went on a trip to a resort in California, my friend brought along 'Ecstasy.' She said to me, 'I want you to do these drugs.'

"I didn't know the drug, and I was wary of it. So I said no. But she insisted. And I thought, 'If you have a friend you trust who is in your network, then you know nothing will happen to you.' Your friend says, 'Come on. We've done it and nothing bad will happen. This drug costs thirty-five dollars a pill and you won't use it. I got this expensive drug to be part of an occasion. I went out and spent that money and you say you won't do it! Come on!' "

Susan paused and thought for a moment. "I think it matters a lot how you are introduced to drugs," she said. "When I was young I'd go out in the woods with my friends. I was usually the only woman. Often I'd go with Bif and his friends. I wasn't scared because I knew them all and I trusted them. They would hand me a mushroom or a pill and they'd say, 'Take this.' And I would. I knew they would take care of me if anything went wrong. So I'd take it, and nothing ever went wrong. I never jumped out of any windows in tall buildings or anything like that.

"That's why people do drugs," Susan continued. "It's the peer pressure. The same reason you sleep with a strange man, right? But my friends don't do coke. We're afraid of it. It's too easy to become addicted. We like coke too much to do it."

Susan paused, then she added, "A friend of mine calls coke 'the white leash.' "

" 'The white leash'?" Gary asked.

"Because it leads a person around," Susan explained.

"A lot of people use . . ." Gary stopped in midsentence and, with a sharp glance at Susan, corrected himself, "take coke?" he said, asking for confirmation.

"That's true," Susan acknowledged. "It's available in bars, or at weddings. People sniff it at dinner."

"One night when it was snowing and the airport was closed, I had to take a bus from New York City to Washington," Gary said. "I was sitting on the bus in the terminal, waiting to leave. The last thing the bus driver did was to open the door to a guy who came through the bus selling packets of coke to the passengers. When he'd made his sales, he got off the bus and the driver closed the door and we left.

"I talked to a woman on the bus," Gary continued, "who used . . . I mean, did coke. She told me it made her smoke pack after pack of cigarettes, three packs a day, and she drank everything, her mouth was so dry. She said she'd feel dead afterward."

"It didn't affect me like that," Susan said, shrugging. "I gave it up because I liked it too much."

"Your friend," Gary said to Susan, "he's an airline pilot, isn't he?"

"Yes."

"Does he do coke?"

"No."

"Does he do any drugs?"

"Not anymore. But his friends who are pilots do. They don't do coke, any more than they drink before they fly, because they know it affects their functioning. But I know they don't think that a joint affects them at all."

"I know an MD," Bif suddenly put in, "who is high on coke all the time. His friends can't understand how he doesn't get caught."

"Doesn't this worry you?" Gary asked his companions. "The media say that more and more people are worried about what drugs are doing to the country, and the government wants to test everyone to see if they are using drugs."

"I think it's exaggerated," Bif said. "Sure, a lot of people do drugs, but there are a lot who don't. And there are all kinds of drugs. Some are good and some are bad. Some are good for some people, and others are bad for those same people. I don't think you can generalize."

Bif was warming to his subject. "I think lots of the concern about drugs is just a media hype. They're stirring it up, creating a public outcry. It's a form of persecution of people who think like we do, like they used to do in the sixties. But it will go away. They'll lose interest and have to find something else."

"But surely there is a real problem," Gary insisted.

"Yes, I guess so," Bif agreed reluctantly. "There probably is a real problem for some people who get addicted to some drug. But you shouldn't deny something to everybody just because some people can't do it properly.

"The people who can't handle it are self-destructive," he continued, "just like you said, Gary. But it's not only drugs that people get high on. They get high on booze, too, but your generation doesn't create a crusade about that. And they get high on religion."

"On religion!" Gary exclaimed in surprise. "How can you connect drugs and religion?"

"Well, maybe not religion, exactly," Bif admitted. "But people get into sects and get high on what they do there."

"What do you mean?" Gary asked.

"I think people who get addicted to drugs, who give them to their children, are people who go to extremes. They get overcommitted to something. There are people in our generation who get overcommitted, and it can be to lots of different things. Some people are overcommitted to their social life; some to work. Some people are so overcommitted to play that it becomes work to them. For some people, when they get overcommitted, then they get dependent in order to be able to handle it. They get dependent on drugs, or on a cult, or something."

"I don't see this exactly as Bif does," Susan continued. "I don't think it's people getting overcommitted as much as it's trying to raise consciousness. At least, that's how I see the people in the sects. I have a friend who came to see me last year. I used to date him when I was in college. He came to my door. He didn't even know I was living there. He was selling books. He had this book about where Christ was during the years that were missing from his life. The book said Christ was in the

Himalayas. It's kind of interesting. Anyway, my friend came in to talk. He lives in Colorado with the people who believe like he does—they have some name for their religion but I can't remember what it is—and he travels around the country with some of them, selling the books and trying to make converts, I guess. He didn't get to stay long, but he said he might be back.

"Anyway, what he said was that he was convinced that we are put on earth for a higher purpose than just to live. So he thinks he now knows the purpose and is helping other people to find it as well."

"You know, you're right," Bif said to Susan. "I went to a wedding the other day. At the wedding we took communion. After I came back from the railing, a woman came up to me. She said, 'I saw you take communion.' Then she added, 'You know, don't you?'

"I didn't have a clue as to what she meant, so I just looked at her.

" 'You *know*, don't you?' she said with greater emphasis—now more an assertion than a question. That's all she said, nothing more. But I guessed that she meant that I knew something of a spiritual significance. I didn't."

"So what did you do?" Susan asked him.

"I decided I had to get rid of her. So I said, 'Yes, I know.' Then she smiled and went away."

"You were lucky she went away," Gary said. "You might have made a friend for life."

"She sounds like a higher-purpose person," Susan said. "I think that they really are a separate category. Maybe they could be combined with people who do drugs to excess, but higher-purpose people shouldn't be confused with people whose goal in life is to be wealthy or to be pleasure-seekers.

"I think a lot of these people have been influenced by the Far Eastern religions," Susan continued. "They are into enlightenment and seren- ity. They're concerned with metaphysics, and with the overall quality of life."

"But what distinguishes them from other people who are religious?" Gary asked.

"I guess it's because they go to an extreme," Bif answered. "They get high on their sect. That's why they're like the people who are too much on drugs or alcohol."

"There's something good about their approach though, isn't there?" Gary asked.

"What do you mean?" Bif responded.

"Isn't there something admirable about believing that there's more to life than pleasure-seeking or being a competitor?"

Susan shrugged. "I guess you could say that," she answered. "But they're still people who get high all the time."

"Are our categories exclusive?" Bif asked. "Can a person be in more than one?"

"I don't think so," Gary answered. "At least, I don't think we should think of a person being in more than one at any single time. A person could have characteristics of more than one category, but must have some dominant set of priorities which put him or her in one category."

"But a person could move among the categories over time, couldn't she?" Susan asked. "I mean, I know a lot of people who have moved among the categories as their lives changed."

Gary and Bif agreed that a person could move among the categories and that people do. In this sense, the categories are not exclusive.

HINTING AT DEEP PROBLEMS

Finding people into drugs and/or alcohol, and therefore are Get Highs, who would acknowledge it to us was difficult. But some people would hint at it. A woman who is now thirty-seven said the following to our interviewer:

"I remember when I was in college. We had a drug culture. Most of us who experimented then wouldn't mess around with what people are messing around with these days. I don't know what the answer is. My sister is three years younger than me and in college they used drugs more heavily than we ever did. But drugs and the culture of the sixties were very influential on my experiences in life. I was one of the liberals . . . we experimented with everything and more. In college we had two groups, the liberals who experimented and the conservatives who didn't experiment with drugs.

"It was a fun time to be in college then. I look at the kids in college today and they don't have the causes that we did back then. It was more exciting then with the Vietnam War and the civil rights movement. There aren't any more good causes that college students are going after. I feel bad. They're losing out on that experience. Maybe you ought to ask some questions on drugs . . . but you know my name, don't you? I don't know if I'd be straight with you."

This response was typical. In general, our interview respondents said that they knew people who fit into the Get High category. But few would identify themselves that way. Two, however, stood out in our interviews as fitting into the category.

One was a twenty-nine-year-old man who designs race-car engines. "I'm a thrill-seeker," he said. "I guess I'm a little bit of a competitor and even a pleasure-seeker as well. I fluctuate among those groups often to the extreme. Sometimes I get real caught up in my work and nothing else matters. But I don't stay that way for long. I take time off and I play too hard . . . so hard that playing eventually becomes work. My problem is that there are too many things to do. When you make money you overwork and overplay. I have my pilot's license, I race cars, I have a lot of friends, and party a lot. I've never almost gotten killed, so I don't know what to say about what would really be exciting in my life."

What underlies the drive this person has to risk his life? In the interview he offered some reflections that threw light on the question.

He spoke slowly and sadly as he said, "I never really had a family. I really feel I missed something growing up. We never had family get-togethers. I think most of this generation had family they could count on and share things with. But I never did. And today my family lives too far away to have that now. I'm too distant.

"The thing which made the biggest impact on me in my life was my divorce. My wife and I couldn't communicate. . . . I want a partner that can grow with the decisions I make . . . a person who can keep up with me both in education and in a career. My ex couldn't keep up. She was from the old school . . . stayed at home and wasn't accomplishing anything with her life. I want someone who can keep up with the changes. I've been changing so fast right now. I'm currently living with someone. What's hard for me right now is that a lot of people I know are having families. I don't want to consider having a family because I feel if you don't have the time to spend with children, you shouldn't have them. My dad didn't spend any time with the kids. He always traveled so much."

A deep sense of disappointment and loss seemed to drive this man. But he was also exciting, as many Get Highs are, to other people. He was the second man beside whose name one of our interviewers placed a star. He may get another call; this time for a different reason than for a survey.

It may seem strange to include people who are involved in religion with the Get Highs. At first I hesitated to do so. Certainly, many people who identify themselves as religious, and among them those who are born-again Christians, do not belong in this category, and so I did not include it in the survey. But our interviews disclosed a group of people who are extreme in their religious orientation. When we asked other respondents about the Get Highs, and included those who get high on religion, our respondents laughed approvingly at the suggestion, and many answered, "Yes, I know people like that."

"I have a friend that is high on religion," a thirty-year-old dental assistant from Wisconsin told us. "And I have one that gets high on drugs. When she's off drugs, we get along. She gets real erratic and goes back on them. Then we can't get along."

One respondent in our survey, who is a Get High in the religious sense, is a twenty-nine-year-old man now living in Arizona. The interview with him went as follows:

"When I was growing up I went through a lot of changes. As a teenager I was more confused and I didn't know what I wanted to do. My father is a minister. I was brought up with God. I went through a lot of things. Finally, I had a nervous breakdown and found the Lord. Now, I understand the Lord. Young people are tormented by Satan himself. If people don't know Jesus, they should get down at the altar and pray to Jesus and find the Lord. Sometimes God has children that he has certain things he wants them to do. He has plans for them. Sometimes they rebel, and things happen to them in order to get them to do what he wants them to. I'm happier now serving the Lord. When Satan puts his powers on me, I get to the altar and get his powers out of me."

At this point in the interview he stopped and, with suspicion in his voice, asked the interviewer, "Are you a Christian? Because if you aren't, I . . . ."

"Oh yes," replied the interviewer. She then noted on the interview form; "I am. But even so, I was afraid to answer otherwise!"

This man from Arizona is a Get High. However, many Americans are religious without falling into this category.

A fork-life operator in an Indiana factory, who classified himself as contented, said to us, "The most exciting thing in my life was the day that I got saved. I accepted Jesus as my savior. Our best work in his eyes is only dirty rags. Without accepting Jesus, and knowing and understanding that he died on the cross to save us, I would not be saved by Jesus like I am today."

Another young man told us, "Before my family and loved ones or friends, I'm a born-again Christian, so I would place my relationship with Jesus Christ before anything."

He also classified himself as contented.

Religion plays a very significant role in the lives of many Americans, but they are also able to function on a day-to-day basis and to converse with others without the only subject being their religious beliefs. The religious Get Highs are extremists who, as both interviewers and respondents told me, are high on religion and are erratic and frightening to others.

How MANY IN EACH CATEGORY?

Respondents placed themselves among the various categories. In each case we reviewed the categorizations and the entire interview, and in a few instances placed a person in a different category than he or she had suggested. This was done only where there was a clear inconsistency between the overall interview and the self-categorization.

The contented can be broken down into two categories: First, those who are contented because they have escaped from traps, and are therefore survivors, are the largest single group. This demonstrates the crucial role which change—whether of jobs or spouses or careers—plays in the lives of baby boomers. Second, those who are content because they have achieved both variety and balance in their lives.

Those who identified themselves as Get Highs are very few. Finally, there were a few who refused to categorize themselves, and whom we were unable to place in a category with sufficient certainty.

Are these figures likely to represent the generation as a whole? The answer is broadly yes—but with two qualifications.

Our responses included an underrepresentation of housewives, many of whom feel trapped. Also, since people were reluctant to acknowledge feeling trapped, in the percentages cited above there is an underestimate of those who are trapped and an overestimate of the contented.

It is unreasonable to say that we reached the Get Highs in proportion to their importance in the overall population of baby boomers. Those who are drug- or alcohol-dependent (or both) were not readily available, and would be unlikely to identify themselves as such. The religious Get Highs were easily identified, but there are not many people (in proportionate terms) who are so extreme in their religious orientation as to be labeled Get Highs. In contrast to the Get Highs, a very large number of Americans have significant religious convictions while being identified as belonging in another of the categories.

The table below shows the baby boom generation distributed among the five categories on a judgmental, but not arbitrary, basis as well as on respondents' own self-choices:

CATEGORY	PERCENTAGE
Pleasure-seekers	25
Competitors	10
Trapped	15
Contented	48
Survivors (28)	
Balanced (20)	
Get Highs	2
ALL CATEGORIES	100

CATEGORIES APPLICABLE ONLY TO BABY BOOMERS?

Do these categories apply only to the baby boom generation? Many of the previous generation can think of people who are in their late forties, and older, who could fit into each category.

This is because differences among human beings tend to be in terms of degree, not of kind. Differences are matters of subtlety and nuance, but are not any the less important. Even though people could fit into the categories who are not baby boomers, a careful study of the previous generation would identify other categories. Where there is overlapping, the distribution of the two generations among the categories would be much different.

For example, if there are pleasure-seekers in the previous generation, they are far fewer, have a different philosophy, and play a different role than those among the baby boomers.

People in the previous generation are driven more by duty; by concepts of obligation to others. They are driven more by concerns about what they owe to others. There is less of a concept of duty among baby boomers. (There are, of course, exceptions, especially those baby boomers who fought in Vietnam, as we shall see in the next chapter.) They seem driven more by their own desires.

Yet there is an explanation for this. Baby boomers have had an opportunity to make choices. They have asked questions and tried out different answers. Their parents didn't have choices, or at least didn't think they had. They felt driven in certain directions by necessity. They had to make a living; to find security by being employed in a big company. It is possible to label this duty, or say that being in such a situation is being driven by duty. But to baby boomers, their parents' situation was dictated by necessity—like not having any choices.

Baby boomers know they have an opportunity to make choices: to select one thing and give up others. When they make a choice and then try to carry it out, it may seem as if they're being selfish. But it's largely because they have choices their parents didn't have.

Still, the lack of feeling of duty among so many baby boomers does matter a great deal. There are pleasure-seekers in the previous generation, but they lack the influence which pleasure-seekers have among baby boomers.

When there's no concept of duty or obligation, and a competitor is asked, "Why do you work so hard?," he or she has trouble giving a satisfactory answer. A competitor can't say, "Because it's my duty, my obligation," as people in the previous generation could.

When a pleasure-seeker asks a competitor, "What's the point of working so hard? Why aren't you out enjoying life?," the competitor doesn't have an answer. What is he or she going to say: "I do it just because I like it"? Even if that's the truth, it sounds unconvincing.

Nor is it only a pleasure-seeker who asks that kind of question of a competitor. People who are balanced in their approach to life also ask the same types of questions to competitors. In fact, this is exactly what Susan asked Bif in their initial conversation about the priorities in each of their lives.

7

THE LEGACY OF VIETNAM

Although the Vietnam War is now more than a decade in the past, it remains a vivid presence for many people and has cast a long shadow over the baby boom generation. In the interviews done for this book, we talked with people about the war and its impact on them and on those they knew.

We found individuals who had been in Vietnam very reluctant to talk about it. Again and again veterans said they were trying not to think about the war. One person's response can serve as an introduction to the type of answer we got from many.

"I don't really want to discuss that," he told an interviewer when asked his opinion about the war. "I was over there for twenty-six months. I don't even like to think about it. It gets me real upset. I had to go . . . and I didn't complain. It was my duty to go.

"I guess what really bothered me was that I didn't like how the people back here were reacting to it. That's what really ticked me off.

"I think the politicians went about it the wrong way. My superiors over there were really good. But I was in combat and the people back home didn't really understand what was going on."

When this man was asked how the war had influenced the lives of people he knew, he answered, "I don't know. I never thought about that. I try very hard not to think about that. There was a lot of fighting and many of my friends got killed. So many sad things happened over there that I try to put the whole thing out of my mind because if I think about it, I just get upset all over again."

Other responses from vets were similar. "I'll tell you about Vietnam," said one, "but I have to be very drunk. I can't talk about it otherwise. If I get drunk enough, I'll tell you about it."

Another said simply, "I still can't visit the wall" (the Vietnam Memorial in Washington, D.C., where the names of the dead are inscribed).

A Special Forces officer in Vietnam, now a high-level executive of a major American firm, was better able to talk about his experiences. A younger man was asking him about the war.

"Most of what I know of the war," the young person said, "I learned from Hollywood. I saw *Apocalypse Now*. Was it like that?"

"Like what part of it?" the veteran said.

"Like, say, the helicopter attack on the village, with the music on the loudspeakers and the colonel, who I guess was high, sending men out to surf while the battle went on."

"I took part in many assaults like that one," the older man answered. "That part of the movie was very realistic. There were some things that were Hollywood, but it was mostly accurate." Two other men, both also having been officers in Vietnam, quietly nodded agreement.

"We used music blaring from the helicopters all the time," the Special Forces officer explained. "The rotors of the helicopters created air currents which dispersed the sound and on the ground made the noise seem to come from all directions. It disoriented the enemy gunners on the ground when they were trying to shoot down the 'copters.

"We did bizarre things to keep sane. All of us had something we tried to keep the same—for example, a radio operator from your home state. Something to touch. A constancy. Something that remained the same despite the war and reminded you of your home.

"When we were in combat we were high all right, but it wasn't from drugs or booze. We were high on adrenaline. We had to be to stay alive."

The Special Forces officer was unusual in that he could talk about the war without substantial emotional difficulty. Whatever emotion he felt was deeply bottled up inside him, just as it had been during his years in Vietnam. But for most of the vets we talked to, the war was too painful a subject.

Many of the Vietnam vets belong in the category of the trapped. They are psychologically trapped by the experience of the war. Because they are not letting their Vietnam experience come out, it affects their lives.

When we discovered that vets were so reluctant to talk about the war, we made special efforts to encourage them to do so and to draw them out as painlessly as possible. By these efforts we were able to get some of them to open up, and we then checked their opinions with others who would not have volunteered much information otherwise. We were after insights into the impact of the war on them today.

We also asked questions about the war and its influence on people who were not Vietnam veterans. The youngest respondents in our survey were in grade school when the war ended.

Some of them told us, "I don't know anything about it." Others asked us, "When was the war?" or "Who was the war between?"

As one would expect, the war had a very different effect on the youngest baby boomers than on the older people in their generation. Without doubt, the significance of the war was much greater for those who were directly affected by it, or whose loved ones were directly affected.

When people asked when had the war occurred or who had been involved in it, we gave them a brief rundown: the war was between the South Vietnamese and the Americans on one side, and the North Vietnamese on the other. The American involvement in the war began to grow appreciatively in the early 1960s and reached a peak in the late 1960s. It declined until the American troops were withdrawn in 1972 and 1973. After American troops were withdrawn, the North Vietnamese took over South Vietnam.[1]

With this assistance, some of the youngest baby boomers were able to put their own views into words. Some continued to have no opinion about the war. Others who had opinions had them shaped by Hollywood's version of the war, via films like *The Deer Hunter, Coming Home, Apocalypse Now,* or *Platoon.*

However, the older baby boomers remembered the war well. Some had strong views about the war, and we took down their responses.

How does the experience of the war affect the vets today? We had certain expectations from the media's discussion of the issue. The media suggest that the war emotionally crippled many veterans because of the horrible things that they had seen and in which many had participated. As a result, they are said to be ashamed and mentally unstable, and therefore unable to cope in ordinary society.

Our survey provided ample evidence that Americans who did not go to Vietnam share the media's view. We asked respondents whether or not the war had affected their family members, their friends or acquaintances. If they answered affirmatively, we asked what the impact of the war had been on these people.

We received scores of comments, most often of the following type:

"The war screwed up my brother royally," a blue-collar worker from the Southwest told an interviewer. "His personality hasn't been the same since he came back from Vietnam. . . . Before the war he was a real loving person. He had a lot of friends and was very sociable. Today he is very cold. He's not a person with feelings anymore. He doesn't have any friends and he won't talk about it."

Another person told an interviewer, "My brother was stationed in Thailand during the war. That changed his life totally. He didn't come out too good. It wasn't because of any fighting because he wasn't in combat, but because of all the drugs. He got too involved in drugs. It wasn't good for him. The drugs really influenced his life. He's totally different now because of his dependence on drugs."

"I had a brother who served in Vietnam," a thirty-two-year-old supervisor from the Midwest told us. "I wasn't aware at the time of what he was going through emotionally and psychologically. It was a real upheaval for him. He suffered a lot."

"I was a child in grade school during the war," said yet another person. "But my uncle who was in the war talked about it. They shot at anything that moved, then later looked to see who or what it was that they shot at. Sometimes it would be a friend on their side. They had to fight that way to stay alive."

A thirty-five-year-old woman in Ohio told an interviewer about her brother. "My brother was in Vietnam. We never discussed it a whole lot. He's gone now. He had a massive heart attack. The war had a real effect on him. It was hard to reach him after he returned. They didn't have any of the counseling when he was alive like they do now. I think it would have helped him. He went to alcohol after he came back."

"My brother-in-law had a drug problem from over there," a woman from Missouri told us. "He came back addicted and started going to a shrink. He abused the drugs that the psychiatrist gave him. He ended up in prison and that ended the marriage with my sister. He wasn't the boy I had known six years before."

A man from Nebraska who had been a high-school student during the height of the war told us this story:

"The younger guys around my hometown heard all about the war from the big guys who had fought over there. They told us that America didn't fight to win.

" 'They're just playing a game over there,' we were told. 'They're dealing out people's lives like in a card game.'

"They said to us, 'We'll break your legs before we'll let you go.'

"The older boys said it was all a big joke over there. Vietnamese would sell coke to Americans during the day and kill them at night. Of course, in Nebraska, if you were called up, you went. We didn't think about going to Canada or anything like that."

"I was one of the lottery boys," said a New Yorker, now thirty-five years of age. "We had to go through the days of picking numbers and worrying if our own was going to come up. I saw friends go away, but I was lucky. My number wasn't drawn. In some ways it was fair, but in others it wasn't."

Other people talked about friends who had been in Vietnam and now seem strange to them. A thirty-three-year-old man who lives in Pennsylvania told the following story: "My wife and I went with five other couples to the Pocono Mountains last year to camp. We were all sitting around the campfire when someone threw a beer bottle into the fire. It exploded and one guy just went berserk on us. He thought he was back in Vietnam. It was just crazy."

He added, "The ones I know who went, only half returned. They came back extremely different. It changed them dramatically, for the worse for the most part."

"Most of the people I knew came back rebellious," said a young Massachusetts man. "The people hated them for fighting in the

Vietnam War. They thought at the time that they were doing something good. They came back and they didn't fit into society anymore. They were on drugs. I had a friend that was blown up pretty bad by a rocket. He was shell-shocked. He is now anti everything. He blames everything bad on the U.S. government. You can forget talking to the guy."

Certainly it must be true that the war left some Vietnam vets mentally and emotionally handicapped. We heard that message from many of their relatives and friends. Yet we also talked to scores of vets, none of whom told us that Vietnam had damaged them so drastically. These vets said that they were angry, but not so much at themselves or at what the war had done to them as people. Instead, they were angry at the American public, which either misunderstood the vets' views or simply disagreed with them.

"I was in Vietnam," a veteran, now forty-one years old, told an interviewer. He had been an infantry private in the war, and was now a blue-collar worker. "It was an exercise in futility. That's the nice way of putting it. My biggest gripe was that they wouldn't let the military commit themselves. We were there. They should have let us go and do our own thing. We should have been able to do what the military is paid to do. I'm not going to argue whether the war was right or wrong. But damn it . . . we should have been able to do it the right way and stop playing around with it the way we did. We'd have objectives; then they'd make us walk away from them. It was very frustrating to the men who were there.

"Vietnam really influenced my life," he continued. "Let me put it this way. I was eighteen years old, coming off a farm in Wisconsin. That experience taught me that taking a life isn't as sacred to me as it might be to you. I don't think I would feel the remorse an average person would. And that would be true of most combat soldiers. If push comes to shove, a soldier does things that an ordinary person wouldn't do.

"A friend of mine was walking towards me in the rice paddies, and the next thing I knew he was a corpse cut up into pieces. That has a terrible impact on you. Life in a sense is cheapened. The life of another person isn't sacred. It's either the enemy dies or you die, so you shoot.

"I hope something like that never happens again. I hope we've learned something from it. I don't worry about Nicaragua because I think we'll do it right this time. It will be flash-bang there. The American public won't let us stand still next time. We won't let fifty or sixty thousand men get killed. We'll either go in there and do it right or we won't go in there at all."

Other survey respondents echoed this man's words. "We'd get all psyched up to go take out a target," one said. "We'd head in, then some bigwig would pull us out. It was all games and pretense and dishonesty. They wouldn't let us fight the war with dignity."

A thirty-six-year-old skilled tradesman employed in a New York factory told us that his outlook on life has changed quite a bit in the last few years. "I'm a Vietnam vet," he said, "and I've changed primarily because of people's outlook towards the vets. The stereotype is that the vets were all crazed. The only ones who lost were the dead ones in the war. I've gotten less confidence in the government. I've learned too many things that go on because of the operations I went through.

"I received fourteen battlefield citations," he continued. "We had all-American dreams until we got over there. We had to turn out to be dirty fighters in order to stay alive. We had our own lives to save. We were all hurt either physically or mentally. We had to come back and justify ourselves. We had to fight the dirtiest damn war there was, and we had no one to meet us and tell us everything was O.K. That we love you. They blamed us for participating in the war. Everything about the war back home was negative. The songs were negative. I remember the Beatles singing, 'Love, love, love . . .' while we were being trained to kill. And the media coverage was all negative. We weren't looking for a pat on the back—just a little compassion is all. The next war will be even worse."

Why do so many vets refuse to talk about the war? We asked this question of all the vets we talked to, and those who would say more than it was too painful to talk about gave us the following answers (composite paragraphs assembled from interviews with several vets):

"People in the States think we won't talk about the war because of the terrible things we did. They think we're ashamed. But that's wrong. We don't talk because no one who wasn't in the war wants to hear what we really think. Most who are screwed up got that way after they came home. They got messed up as a result of what happened here.

"I think we should have let the military do its thing in Vietnam. But in this country I can't say that. It's offensive to people who weren't in the war. It's too crude. It's not offensive to a soldier, though. I know how to kill, and I'm not afraid to.

"People who weren't in the war think it was a baby boomers' war because it was young people who fought it. But it wasn't our war. It was the older generation's war; they were the higher-ups who were in charge. It was a dishonest war. They were dishonest with themselves. It was all evasion and show and lies. If it had been our war, we'd have done what had to be done, or we'd have gotten out. It wouldn't have been just the pretense of a war in which thousands of decent men got killed.

"So many other people avoided the war. We went. We felt it was right. Today we can't say anything without a big argument. So we don't say anything."

Being silenced by a public attitude is very difficult for Vietnam vets. They are largely baby boomers, members of a generation which prizes honesty, openness, and mutual respect. Because they have a view which the majority in the country doesn't share, they are silenced or treated contemptuously and pitied. This kind of treatment is a very difficult burden for them to bear.

PART TWO

THE CHOICES BABY BOOMERS FACE

8

THE IMPORTANCE OF VALUES AND RELATIONSHIPS

Despite the different groups among members of the baby boom generation that have been identified in the preceding chapters, there are also very substantial similarities. People in this generation overlook the similarities and tend to focus on the differences. But to their parents, the similarities among baby boomers are as striking as the differences. Baby boomers as a group are very different from most people in their parents' generation.

ARE BABY BOOMERS LIKE THEIR PARENTS?

"A lot of my friends have a very negative feeling toward their parents," a twenty-six-year-old woman clerk in California told us. "My friends have a feeling that our folks sent us down the tubes. I don't feel that personally, but my friends think our parents ruined it for us. Pollution, toxic waste, and other problems all started with their generation and they never bothered to solve the problems. Most of the problems today people say were a result of their parents' generation. Of course, our children may say the same thing about us one day."

A thirty-year-old Pennsylvania attorney told us, "No one I know feels that they are like their parents at all."

But others identified with their parents and were concerned about it. "I worry about being like my parents," said a thirty-one-year-old bank manager from Kentucky. "I want to be a pleasure-seeker; I want to be different from them."

There were some exceptions. One young woman told us how much she admired her mother, and that she wanted to be like her. Another person told us that her parents had raised several children on very little income and that he hoped he could do as well.

For the majority, however, to be different from their parents was a significant objective in life.

HOW BOOMERS ARE DIFFERENT

Baby boomers are fiercely independent and certain of their uniqueness as individuals. Nevertheless, our surveys identified a group of key values which they share and which can be contrasted with those of the older generation. Some values which are common to both generations have been the subject of other studies and will not be commented on here. However, those studies have been far less effective in identifying the differences between the generations.

Possessions versus Experiences

Material possessions and advancement up a corporate ladder are more important to the previous generation than to baby boomers. By comparison with their parents, baby boomers feel that experiences are more important. It's what a person is, what experiences and challenges he or she has had that are significant, not what a person has. At least, these are their values.

When boomers get together, they are more likely to exchange stories about what they've done—whether travel, or drugs, or relationships, or jobs—than talk about cars, homes, art, decorators, swimming pools, or stereo systems.

For example, one young woman told me about an Outward Bound trip she had taken.

"I remember one night in particular," she said. "They—the people who ran the trip—took us into the forest—it was in central Oregon—and left each of us at a different place. I was alone, in a clearing, in just the clothes I was wearing. It was summer. They told us they'd pick us up in the morning. When it got dark, I was so scared I wanted to run away, but I didn't know where to go—I didn't know where the others were. I thought they'd come back to get me; but they never did. I spend the night curled up under a tree, with my back to the trunk and my chin on my knees. I don't think I slept at all. At dawn they came for me."

She referred to this trip as a high point in her life, and I asked her why.

"Because that night," she said, "I learned that I could do things I never before believed I could do. That even though I was a woman, I could be out on my own and take risks. It gave me self-confidence. It taught me that I could be alone and survive."

It would be possible to multiply examples like this many times. Surveys pick up the same phenomenon on a larger scale. The army, for instance, after years of advertising military service as a way for enlistees to develop job skills, discovered that baby boomers think military experience is more valuable for personal development than for the job skills they might acquire.[1]

Suspicion of Authority versus Acceptance of Direction

"It was twenty years ago," the woman told me, "but I remember it vividly. . . . I was at a national television-news network where I kept the 'morgue'—the file of old newspaper clippings. Each day I read *The New York Times* cover to cover, to clip it up. This was in 1965, just around the time of the Tonkin Bay incident, and I'd see brief announcements appear in the middle of the newspaper and then move forward day by day. When they got to the front page, it was usually because the press had discovered someone in the government wasn't telling the truth.

"When I realized that the government was lying, I was horrified. This was my government and it wasn't supposed to lie. Then in the next nine years it seemed as though everyone lied—the president, the military, the large companies. Today, when the military points to what may be a real threat from the Soviet Union, I'm not sure I can believe them."

This woman's comments were echoed again and again in our interviews.

An attorney in Philadelphia, now thirty years old, commented about the Vietnam conflict.

"It made me enormously distrustful of the news media and very skeptical of the abilities of American politicians. With the people I know, I think the war caused a cynicism about the truthfulness of American public officials."

A retired registered nurse in Michigan, now thirty-two and raising a family, said that during the Vietnam War, "I think we finally realized that it is *not* my country right or wrong! The war gave you a different outlook on authority. We couldn't just accept things anymore, even if your parents, government or society said, 'this is right.' Well, I felt that I wasn't going to let anyone pull the wool over my eyes. Do you remember Nixon? Nothing was true anymore. I learned that what you read or listened to on TV was just not necessarily true."

"Having lost friends in Vietnam," said a thirty-four-year-old Massachusetts woman, "I developed an apprehension about the people running this country. I had always thought that the president was infallible, but I realized that this guy is not infallible. He's an ordinary person like me. And he's running the country! I lost my friends in a war because this guy didn't know what the hell he was doing."

"As far as I'm concerned," said a thirty-two-year-old man in Nebraska, "the whole war caused me not to trust politicians and not to put stock in the national news."

Said a man from Missouri, "I was against the people who protested against war and their tactics, even though I was against the war. In the end, however, the war turned me against the government."

"The war made me more pessimistic about the ability of our leaders," said a twenty-five-year-old woman. "I can't believe we were involved in it the way we were. I can just feel the bad feeling of it sometimes, you know. I don't think it will ever happen again. I'd pay a pretty high price to keep it from happening again."

"Well, the war certainly had an impact on our generation," said a California insurance salesperson. "We won't get involved in another situation like that again. It was certainly good for business but it wasn't good for people. It weakened our trust in government tremendously."

These many comments, so similar in tone and content, were aptly summed up by a thirty-one-year-old woman in Minnesota who spoke about her generation as a whole. "The war in general just caused us to mistrust our government. That's all."

In place of the older generation's acceptance of authority, this generation developed a deep suspicion of it. The woman who had worked in the TV network morgue went on to tell how her suspicion extended beyond the government to other large institutions, like the church and business.

"We were trying to choose a new minister for our church," she said. "So I was thinking, what are my values in terms of an authority person? I realized that I respond to other people in the congregation. It's those people, my friends, who hold me. I don't respond to the church as an institution—and I reject its claims to any control over my life. I don't look beyond the individual or my close associates to the institution. I don't have any loyalty to the institution. I think my rejection of my parents twenty years ago, and of the government at the same time, has extended to all institutions."

Various opinion surveys taken by the national media show far more distrust of the leadership of major institutions among the baby boomers than among older people. For example, a *New York Times*-CBS poll showed that baby boom Catholics were twice as likely as older Catholics not to approve of everything the pope has done.[2]

Also, polls show there has been a dramatic erosion of confidence in the leaders of our major institutions (educational, medicinal, military, religious, governmental, etc.) since the late sixties. Although it is widely believed that confidence in America has been rebuilt, the recovery of trust in government and other institutions has been quite modest. If anything, recent polls indicate that baby boomers are less trusting of government and big business than they were previously.[3]

Probably it's not surprising that baby boomers don't trust institutions. They grew up with a bad war, drugs, a rising divorce rate,—maybe it makes sense that they put emphasis on their personal lives, not on what big organizations do.

Fun versus Duty

People of the older generation looked upon work as an obligation, something they had to do in order to gain a better life. They worked to provide for themselves and their families. It was a burden, but one of which a person could be proud if he or she carried it steadfastly. A person did not expect to enjoy work. To look for enjoyment in work was to misunderstand what it was about.

Baby booomers have a very different attitude. They will not accept work solely as drudgery. Whether they are professionals or blue-collar workers, they want work to be enjoyable.

"Our employees want us to provide eight hours a day and forty hours a week of interesting, enjoyable, personally satisfying work," the president of a large industrial company told me. "Because we can't provide what they want, our people turn off and our productivity and quality are awful."

In place of duties, obligations, and chores, young people want activities that help them grow, gain new experiences, and feel good about themselves.

This is the first generation in American history to insist that work be fun.

The possibilities for baby boomers to have fun while making money working, and the difficulties their parents have in accepting this turn of values, are illustrated by a story told to us. The man is a very handsome thirty-five-year-old who worked for several years at an electric-equipment supply house. One day at a shopping mall, a three-hundred-pound (as he tells it) woman, who was in advertising, stopped him and told him he had a very marketable face. She gave him her business card and told him to call her if he was interested. He was, and a few days later, he did call.

Soon after, he quit his job at the electrical supply house and became a male model. He travels, makes a good bit of money, and enjoys himself.

However, his mother, who lives in a moderate-size southern city, is very unhappy with the change. She keeps asking him when he will go back to his job at the supply house. He isn't suffering at his new job, so she cannot be convinced that what he does is actually work.

When people are young, they like to travel, to see the world. So baby boomers often put a premium on jobs that involve travel. As they age, they get bored and want diversion. Baby boomers look for new challenges, changes in assignment as they move into their thirties. They like the company of the opposite sex, and they look for jobs in which there will be an opportunity to meet others their own age. The workplace has become a social occasion. Visiting a company that employed many young people and had a very informal atmosphere, one television reporter blurted out in surprise, "People like to work here. You can see it in their faces. All those meetings would drive me crazy, but they really enjoy each other."

Not all baby boomers find challenges, social interaction, and diversion in their jobs. Perhaps most do not. But virtually all look for these features and aspire to them. Denied something fun to do, they turn off and devote their imagination and attention to activities outside the workplace.

A revealing example of young people's attitude toward work was recounted by then Secretary of Labor William Brock at a conference in Washington, D.C.[4]

Secretary Brock had visited a successful automobile assembly plant in California, managed by Toyota and producing a car in cooperation with General Motors. "I walked up to a young man on the assembly line," Secretary Brock related. " 'How're you doing?' " I asked him. 'I'm having fun,' he told me. I'd never heard that in a manufacturing plant before. You might hear it from your children at home—but not at work."

With the older generation, duty extended beyond work. Professional people got involved in community activities because it was their duty. Housewives did volunteer work for charity because it was an obligation—as well as a quasi-social activity.

Today the younger people who do volunteer work feel it is more a matter of what they get out of it personally; how it helps their personal development; how it makes them feel about themselves.

The young minister of a church was asked by his bishop to accompany him to Mexico City in the aftermath of the great earthquake of 1985. At first he refused to go because of other plans. The bishop insisted, and finally he went—spending a week in the ravaged city. When he returned he told his congregation that he was very glad he had gone. Why? Because he had done some good for the earthquake victims? No, although he probably did provide assistance. What had been meaningful to him was the experience he had had personally. He had seen suffering and death, and yet in the face of tragedy he had also seen the expression of religious faith. He had felt his own faith deepened. He had himself grown and benefited from the experience. This was what mattered most to him. "I almost missed a very meaningful experience," he said, reflecting on how close he had come to refusing the trip. Duty occupied a far lower place than personal growth and experience in his value system.

The traditional values were about society, about duties and obligations to others—to spouses, other family members, fellow employees, employers, the community, the nation, the church. Boomers' values are personal—they concern relationships among individuals. Baby boomers are looking for what's in it for them—not what they can do for someone else.

One of our respondents, a twenty-six-year-old man from Illinois, put the matter this way. "If I were doing research about our generation, I'd be interested in the sense of responsibility people have. How seriously do they take their responsibilities? I think our generation has a different view of what it means to be a responsible person . . . I think something is happening in that regard."

Put down on paper, these observations about younger people may sound far more negative than intended. Note that work is still being done, and assistance is still being provided to the needy. But the motivation has changed because the underlying values are different.

If work is still done and the needy cared for, does it matter that the motivation has changed? Yes, it matters a great deal. Unless a charity can appeal to the baby boomers in formats that satisfy their needs and interests, then it will receive little from them in contributions. Recent reports from the nation's major charities are that baby boomers are small givers. "Cheap," said a newspaper headline.[5]

However, an alternative explanation is that the major charities are continuing to appeal to baby boomers in a fashion similar to that with which they appealed to their parents—and it is an ineffective approach. As the rock concerts for African relief have demonstrated, baby boomers, when appealed to in a way that is consistent with their values and life styles, will respond generously.

Similarly, unless an employer tailors jobs to what young people are looking for, his company will get the least capable people and will find they become dissatisfied and will perform poorly. In fact, the search by baby boomers for occupations they can enjoy often leads them away from big organizations.

A man comes to mind who is now thirty-six. Years ago, he started working as a probation officer in Connecticut. He worked for the state for about four years, and then for the feds for seven years. His life had become frustrating; he was trying to induce change in the lives of people who didn't want it. He said he had a nice office, good pay, and benefits, and could have been secure for his whole career. But he left. His father was amazed when he left, since he had a "nice job" and "a good pension." But the fellow told me he could no longer compromise his values. He said he knew he was in bad shape when he would refer to his clients as "chumps" and "creeps." He valued his leisure time and hated his work. He took his salary and invested in real estate and finally resigned. He and his wife now own a year-round first-class guesthouse on Martha's vineyard. He says that his highest priority is leisure time.

Another man had a college degree in accounting, but he wanted to be in the sports world. He was offered a job with a Big Eight accounting firm, but knew that if he tried to work his way up to partner, he would have no time for sports, and might never get to follow that aspect of his interests. So he took a job doing accounting for a big corporation. But he works only eight hours a day. He spends the rest of his time going to sports events in order to meet people. What he is preparing to do is to set himself up as a financial manager for sports stars. That way he'll combine both of his interests, and he'll be continually stimulated.

Opportunity versus Security

The generation which grew up in the Great Depression and in the Second World War absorbed from the events of its childhood a deep concern for security and a desire to avoid risks and disasters. It is a security-conscious generation—always calculating the risks and trying to avoid them.

There is very little of that attitude among the baby boomers. They seem obsessed instead with change and opportunity. They seem rarely to count the risks.

In Pennsylvania a thirty-year-old attorney explained the generational difference this way: "To our parents' generation, security was more valuable than to people in my age group. Our parents experienced the Great Depression. They wanted secure jobs and a home. Our generation has no appreciation for that at all . . . of what it is to be out of a job when you really want one. I don't think many of us have been unemployed for long periods of time."

Another boomer described his generation in the following way: "My generation is more risky, more innovative. We're willing to take long shots in our decision making. We may not be as stable in our approaches, but we make quicker decisions. We do it. We act. Then we read the situation afterwards. That's it!"

I recall asking a manager in his thirties, "How many jobs have you had?"

He paused while he counted. "Four or five,"he answered.

"And you're getting ready to look for another?"

"Yes," he said.

"Didn't you ever stop to think that you might fail at one of the jobs?" I asked.

"It crossed my mind," he replied.

"But never caused you to hesitate?"

"Maybe hesitate, never to stop," he answered.

"What did you think you'd do if you failed?"

The puzzlement in his face caused me to rephrase the question. "I mean, what would you have done if a job hadn't worked out?"

I should have recognized, I thought to myself, *that he doesn't believe he could fail.*

"Oh, I'd get something new," he answered. "I could get unemployment for a while; or my wife's job could support us."

"So what matters is the potential ahead—not the risk?" I asked.

"Yes."

"No insecurity?"

"None."

This is another thing that's very different from the previous generation, in which only a very few do not carry a very deep feeling of economic insecurity. In contrast, many baby boomers have little or no sense of economic insecurity.

Individuality versus Sameness

In this survey, baby boomers were asked about their close friends. In general, they were drawn from four areas—work, the neighborhood, the church, or high school or college.

"Are you mostly like your friends, or different from them?" the respondents were asked.

Almost half told us they were quite different from their friends. And those who initially answered that they were alike often reconsidered and told the interviewer about how they were different. Fully 88 percent of the entire group of respondents said they were quite special and different from their friends, and told us in what way.

"Animals," a woman from Michigan told our interviewer. "I'm hot and heavy on animals. My friends aren't like that."

"I am crazier, more inclined to take risks," one woman said.

"I am more imaginative," said a man. "I'm always the one who comes up with new things to do."

"I'm more stable," answered another. "I have my life well ordered. I've not been through a divorce like my friends."

"I'm a unique person," one man told us. "I'm not like anyone else."

This theme of uniqueness and individuality runs deeply in the generation. We encountered very few baby boomers who expressed any concern about fitting in with a group. Instead, they seem to have chosen their interests and then either found a group of friends with similar interests, or they kept to their interests despite a divergence from their peer group.

Baby boomers do not seem to put a very high premium on conformity for its own sake. They do not look at a group and worry if they are being left out.

What they do, however, is look for new diversions, and they watch each other for clues as to what is new. As a result, they often all seem to be doing the same thing at once, and this is often mistaken for conformity. It isn't. It's a search for diversion and change.

This is very different from the previous generation's preoccupation with "keeping up with the Joneses." The fear then was of being left behind. Among the baby boomers the competitors are the most likely to have concerns very like their parents' in this regard. Even so, for the previous generation, keeping up with the Joneses was a search for status, not to prove that one was just as good as the others, as it tends to be for baby boomers who are competitive.

What baby boomers want is to feel good about themselves, and to achieve it by doing their own things. Because there is a limited number of "own things," lots of people do similar activities. But to each person, it is his or her own, and all believe they are somehow unique in doing it.

This value of individuality has deep roots in American life, of course. But the baby boomers are far more deeply individualistic than their parents. Probably the Great Depression, with the insecurity it entailed, caused their parents to band together to protect themselves. This was a major factor in the attitudes which the trade unions came to embody. And the Second World War contributed to a regimentation of people, which also resulted in a sameness that is alien to the baby boomers.

To the previous generation, fairness is sameness. To the baby boomers, sameness is of little value. Instead, to them fairness should include an opportunity to achieve individualism and uniqueness.

Relationships versus Possessions and Status

Baby boomers place a very high value on their relationships and continually are concerned about them. But they are very diverse in what they are looking for in a relationship. In general, they see a relationship as an experience, and to many, this must involve learning and growth if it is to be really good.

"What I look for in a relationship," a thirty-three-year-old man from Ohio, recently divorced, told our interviewer, "is someone I feel comfortable with—someone who has the same values but not necessarily the same opinions. I look for someone I can talk with and sort of share mutual understandings with."

A twenty-five-year-old woman, who lived in the Northeast, was more cynical. "The men I meet don't often look for a continuing relationship," she said. "I think it's because they want a relationship which suits their needs and wants. They want immediate satisfaction. They don't have time to develop a friendship before having a sexual relationship.

The result is that there isn't much opportunity for growing and changing with a person. I have asked myself why they're like this. I think it's because they don't really like themselves."

But some men answered in a way she might have approved. One example is a twenty-six-year-old Illinois man who said, "I'd describe what I look for in a relationship as mutual affirmation. That's to have a relationship where you give the other person encouragement and build their self-worth."

In the survey the baby boom generation split nearly in half with respect to what is important in a relationship. Forty-seven percent stressed compatibility and security. Forty-two percent stressed trust, partnership, and support. (The remaining 11 percent placed great importance on lust, as they termed it, or were not sure.) The discussion the respondents had with our interviewers suggested that people who stressed compatibility and security were seeking a refuge of sorts from the tensions and pressures of the world. Those who stressed trust had a concept of a relationship that involved challenge and change, and sought from it personal growth, not protection. But whatever an individual's expectations of a relationship, virtually all baby boomers placed great store by it.

To a significant degree the previous generation focused on what possessions it had, more than on relationships. It tended to be more coldly logical, to be concerned about things and about position. Baby boomers are often more focused on how they feel, on emotion, not facts. They talk about how they feel about themselves—not about how they are. Some are thin because it makes them feel better about themselves; it creates more opportunities to meet people. They want to make money because it allows them to do more things and to feel better about themselves. They're business-oriented because then they can feel good about themselves.

Baby boomers are far more involved in personal relationships than their parents were. Their parents tried to form stable relationships so they could get on with the business of acquisition, ladder climbing in business, and raising a family. Most baby boomers seem to be willing to let relationships emerge and dissolve, regardless of the impact on careers and often even on families, in order to look for opportunities to feel good and have a good time.

Baby boomers interviewed for this book were asked what they

considered most important in their own lives. Because people tend to answer that the family is most important to them, and because the family is such a complex locus of emotions and concerns, we asked each person what besides the family was most important to him or her.

Eight percent of the group insisted that there was nothing of importance to them besides their families. But fully 42 percent said the most important thing was how they felt about themselves. For 26 percent, a job or career was most important. For 20 percent, religion or the community was most important. Finally, 3 percent were unable to decide what was most important.

What do people mean when they say how they feel about themselves is the most important thing? They seem to mean the sum total of their ability to achieve their set goals, the degree to which they have the relationships they desire, and finally whether or not they have experiences that add interest and meaning to their lives.

"What was the most exciting or satisfying part of your life?" we asked.

As might be anticipated, responses differed a great deal. One thirty-two-year-old man in New England, now a sales manager, said, "I was involved with a drum and bugle corps from the time I was six till I was twenty-six years old. We were always on the road in the summer . . . traveling all around the U.S., learning about people. It helped me a lot. Lots of times I don't know which way I would have gone had it not been for the drum and bugle corps. I never turned to drugs like so many of my friends did. I really benefited a lot from that. It was the highlight of my life. I was in it until four years ago. I met my first wife there. We've even formed an alumni association now. I still hang around with my friends from there. The whole experience really made my life."

A thirty-nine-year-old chemist from Pennsylvania told us about his last year in college.

"I was compelled to achieve a lot before I left academics. I knew it would be the last chance I would have to be creative without having a lot of responsibilities. I've never felt as challenged or productive since. I got a lot of internal rewards and self-satisfaction out of it during that time."

Asked what they like to do, baby boomers often respond, "Things that are challenging, that I learn from."

The learning experiences cited were not always enjoyable. "My parents separated twelve or thirteen years ago," a thirty-four-year-old man told us. "That may have influenced all my decisions in life. The first two years after their breakup really set me back. I had trouble figuring out what I was going to do. But it helped me mature a lot faster. Initially it was a bombshell, but I realized that it was far better in the long run."

A twenty-three-year-old man from Kansas told us, "I spent the whole summer working on an internship in southern California. I learned about my profession, about business, about people, and about myself. I really grew up and I realized that people in the Midwest can really get in a rut if they don't look around."

One man, in his middle thirties, helped build a company out of nothing over eighteen months, and it appears that he'll make a fortune. He told us that the most important thing in his life was when he left college and went around the world. He had been visiting in Australia and decided, "Why go back the way I came; why not go around the world?" So he took off, hitchhiking across the Outback, then by steamer to Java, and across Java by working on a riverboat. In Lahore, Pakistan, he met a fellow who put him up for the night. He awoke in the room at midnight to see the young man sitting in the middle of the floor, shooting heroin into his arm. He stayed awake the rest of the night in fear of what might happen to him. Nothing did, and he left the next day. He traveled through the Near East, into Europe. When he returned to the United States, it was Christmas and eighteen months after he had started.

Two years later he spent fourteen months traveling from Detroit to Tierra del Fuego by foot and by whatever rides he could pick up. He had been up and down the world as well as around it.

Those experiences had taught him three things that made him successful in business, he said. First, they had given him great self-assurance; he knew he could accomplish things. Second, they had shown him that he had courage and could take big risks and survive, even prosper. Finally, he had learned how to get to a far-distant goal by working at it one step at a time.

The baby boom generation has traveled. Rich or poor, they have seen more of the world than their predecessors. They are outgoing; they have found some mechanism to get out and meet people: school, or a drum and bugle corps, or bumming around, or the military, or work as a truck driver. One way or another most have developed a wider perspective on the world than previous generations.

Most importantly, the baby boomers are more complex in what they want out of life than their parents.

"I feel that my generation's outlook is so very different from my parents'," a thirty-two-year-old midwesterner told us. "We seem to have so much more opportunity. We're not as confined as our parents were. We were brought up thinking that if we don't want to do something, we don't have to and we don't have to feel guilty about it. We want more self-fulfillment instead of satisfying others' needs. Our parents are concerned about doing what should be done, and we're more interested in making something what we want it to be."

Candor versus Tact

One of the most disconcerting things about the baby boom generation to older people is its candor about human relationships. While the previous generation preferred to conceal true feelings behind vague allusions and indirect references, the younger generation prefers to speak out plainly.

In personal relationships younger people insist on honesty, even when they get hurt in the process. "If you no longer care for me," a young woman says to her lover, "tell me. Tell me the truth, I can take it. I've been hurt before, but I can't stand to be lied to."

Members of the previous generation would rarely say that and mean it. They had been brought up to disguise their emotions; to mislead others about bad news in the belief that they would be hurt less; to send oblique messages clothed in pleasantries until finally someone got the message and drifted away.

What is tact to the previous generation is often considered dishonesty by baby boomers. The result is that in relationships that cross the generation gap, when a person is making the greatest effort to be considerate, he or she may be risking the greatest misunderstanding. When an older person tries to change a relationship by subtle signals, the younger person is infuriated. When a younger person tries to modify a relationship by a direct statement, the older person is deeply offended.

In both cases the hurt is occasioned as much by how the other person approached the matter as by what was actually said.

A man in his fifties told me how his approach to handling a relationship had been altered by the influence of a woman in her thirties whom he had been dating. "Once, I decided to break a date with her," he said. "So in my mind I went through a whole set of excuses—lies, really, about sickness, business conflicts, and others—to see which was plausible.

"Finally," he continued, "I stopped looking for excuses and tried to figure out the real reason in my mind—the reason that had to do with the relationship. In fact, I thought she was putting too much pressure on me. Then I told her. It worked out much better than a lie would have because when we talked about it, I realized that I had misunderstood what she was doing. That's what I had learned from her—from the baby boomers—to be direct and honest. That's the difference between the generations."

It's hard to overestimate how important honesty in a relationship is to baby boomers because in their set of values it has largely replaced what used to be considered sexual morality. When they are asked how another person ought to behave, they rarely talk of fidelity or purity, but they say instead, "I think a person ought to be honest in a relationship."

Honesty can encompass fidelity, if that is what the people involved want. But it need not. What the baby boomer wants is that whatever another person prefers to do, he or she should be honest about it.

Yet this value is often violated in practice. "I don't tell you when I sleep with another man," one young woman told a man with whom she had a longstanding relationship. "No one does that anymore. We all play the game to some degree."

"But you don't think that's right, do you?" he asked her.

"No, I guess it's not really right not to tell you."

What is striking about this conversation to someone brought up in the traditional morality is that both people involved agree that what is wrong is her deceiving him about other lovers, not her having them.

In the course of our survey, an interviewer asked a twenty-seven-year-old Massachusetts man what was important to him in a personal relationship.

"I haven't found out yet," he answered. "I'm seeing someone new, but I don't think I could marry this person, so I've told her that. I don't think opposites can get along very long."

In general, baby boomers have concluded that it's necessary to be open with other people to feel good about oneself. This is one of the basic explanations why the gays have come out of the closet, as well as for the candor about human relationships in general that so shocks the people of the previous generation.

Baby boomers are equally direct at the office. One day, an older manager called in a young subordinate at an advertising agency. He had asked her for a memo, and she had prepared it.

"I don't like the tone of this memo," he told her. "It's threatening. I think it's inappropriate."

"I didn't intend that," the young woman told her boss. Later, as she reflected on the incident, she became very upset. The memo had been direct, but she certainly didn't consider it threatening or inappropriate. Her older colleagues told her not to do anything. "Don't rock the boat," they said. "He'll forget about it." But she wanted to know what was wrong. Finally, she decided to confront her boss about it.

"I'm really upset over this," she told him. "Would you show me what was wrong?"

Her boss, surprised again at her directness, looked away. "There was nothing wrong," he admitted. "I was out of joint about something else. There was nothing wrong."

The young woman left his office, convinced that she had done exactly the right thing by going directly to her boss. She had insisted on direct and honest communication. The older people in the office would have just let the matter sit, as they had advised her to do. If she had followed their advice, she would have suffered in silence, never knowing what she had done wrong and never being told that her boss had made the mistake, not she.

Baby boomers are generally candid even when it isn't self-serving. A man in his mid-twenties applied for a teaching position at a major university several years ago. He was an alumnus and had outstanding academic credentials. Still, he was not offered a job. He sued the university on certain grounds. In court the university's dean was asked by the applicant's attorney why the man had not been hired.

"Because he led a student strike against the university when he was a student in which there was violence against officers of the university," the dean explained.

The applicant's attorney was thunderstruck. He had heard nothing of this.

"How do you know it was my client who led the strike?" the lawyer demanded.

"Because he told us so in his job application," the dean answered. "He listed it as one of his achievements on his résumé."

9

BELONGING

"One of the things that surprises and impresses me, I admit," Gary said with a smile, "is how you two keep in touch. Even though you developed different interests and entered into different relationships, you seem to have kept in touch."

Susan and Bif exchanged glances.

"We want to know what each other is doing," Bif answered.

"And how each other is doing," Susan added. "I keep in touch with Bif because I really care about him."

"You seem sometimes to push him a lot," Gary ventured hesitantly.

"But only because we know each other well and I care about him," Susan insisted. "He knows that."

Bif nodded in acknowledgment.

"I guess to an outsider it could sound as if we're not really close and don't support each other," Susan said, "but we are close. We're a little like brother and sister. We may sound matter-of-fact with each other, but underneath the surface there's a real bond."

"It's not just each other we keep in touch with," Bif added. "We have other friends who are close also."

"That's right. There are lots of people I hear from or who call from time to time," Susan said. "I value relationships and I don't want to lose my friends, so I stay in touch. But I also want to know what they're doing because I'm searching for new ideas for things to do."

"I think everyone has his own reason for keeping in touch," Bif said. "I like to go out to dinner, or for a drink, or to a ball game with my friends. That's my relaxation—it's a very important part of my life."

"You're not into hobbies or that sort of thing?" Gary asked.

"You mean, do we do things with our hands, like make things?" Susan asked with a smile. "You know I hate that sort of thing. Maybe some people in my generation do that, but I think most of us are into something we do with friends.

"But that's not the only reason Bif keeps in touch," she continued, "is it Bif?"

Bif looked at her with a puzzled expression. "What's she driving at?" he wondered.

"I think you call me and your other friends to find out if you're keeping up. You want to know if other people are making more money or have a bigger house. You want to know the fashion—is a Mercedes out of favor? Should you be going for a BMW now? Does one of your friends have his own company? Are you losing ground? You're so competitive, you have to keep tabs on how everyone else is doing."

Bif's puzzlement had transformed itself into a smirk that seemed to acknowledge the truth of what Susan was saying.

"Even with me," she continued, "the reason you keep in touch is to be sure I don't get ahead of you. It's not because we socialize anymore. It's not even to stay together from time to time."

Gary winced a little at her directness, but neither Susan nor Bif noticed him or gave a similar reaction.

"What made you nervous, and kept you interested in me," she continued, "was when I set up my company. You wanted to know how successful I'd be. You didn't want to fall behind. You wondered if I'd do really well, and it made you uneasy."

Bif shrugged in acknowledgment.

"Bif, are most of the people you keep in touch with competitors?" Gary asked.

Bif thought for a moment. "I guess so," he answered.

"Do pleasure-seekers and the other groups we talked about each have their own special reason for keeping a network going?" Gary continued.

"I think so," Bif responded. "The competitors want to see if they're keeping up; the pleasure-seekers are out to get new ideas for activities; the trapped seek to measure how far short of their ideals they're falling by looking at others; the contented are usually curious about the others. The self-destroyers are often driven to search for help."

"But they continually reject help," Gary objected.

"It's a yes-no relationship," Bif said. "They want help and they don't—but they keep in touch."

"I wonder," Gary asked Susan, "if you'd stay in touch with me?"

"What?" Susan asked, surprised at this turn in the conversation.

"Not long ago you said you thought your interests were changing again. That you are on a three-year cycle or something, and that as that time limit approaches, you begin to feel fidgety unless you can develop new interests. I took that to apply to me."

Susan looked down at her glass. However, she didn't object.

"When you lose interest in me," Gary said, "you'll not see me anymore?"

"Oh, I'd keep in touch," Susan said with disarming candor. "I never drop anybody. I just move on to the next one."

"Sounds pretty calculating," Gary observed.

"I don't think so," Susan said. "People change and move on. But I keep in touch because I want to be a quality person and it's important to me how I affect other people."

HOW NETWORKS SUPPLANT
THE FAMILY

When Bif and Susan describe the network to which they both belong, they are talking about one of the most significant social innovations of the baby boom generation.

People used to see themselves belonging to a spouse or to a family. Belonging occurred in the family, and people related to the rest of the world in a rather formal way.

But the baby boom generation belongs first of all to a loose grouping of companions with whom they form an attachment, then continue that relationship through separations and reunions. It may seem like a family, but the people in it aren't related. For many people, groups are often stronger than family ties. A person gets married, and the group accepts the spouse as a member. They find support and companionship in the network.

For some people in the older generation, networks existed but on a reduced scale. There were networks of old high-school or college chums who got together once in a while to keep in touch and to socialize. There were also people in the same business who helped each other get things done or advance each other's careers. These groups tended to be of only one sex, and were related primarily to school or jobs.

Both the school-chum and business-associate networks still exist for baby boomers, but they have carried the concept much further, converting it into a close support group to supplant the family.

The new generation has constructed networks of both sexes who share a cluster of priorities, who are competitors or pleasure-seekers, or who are trapped or contented. It is very different from the way it was in the past.

Baby boomers lead complex lives requiring support from others. If a person is single and his or her parents die, the support family system is gone. In the past a person would have been pretty much alone. In today's difficult and hectic world, to be alone can be devastating. So people turn to their network of friends for support.

A network isn't a family—it is no stronger than the family used to be many years ago—but it is stronger than the family is today. Years ago the family was strong when the members would sit together on a Sunday afternoon and share their experiences. But nowadays people have dispersed, and the family isn't there anymore as the basic support system.

Many baby boomers have parents and siblings, but the network is stronger. "You always call," people say about others in their group. Someone calls to find out how the other person is, but also to see if he or she can help, if something is wrong, or to find out what's new.

Even for those who are married, the network is as important as the family. People who are married often stay in the group; and if they are divorced they turn to the group for support. In today's world the group endures when marriages dissolve.

For most baby boomers, a network is not just a group of people with whom to socialize. It exists to meet various additional needs. It provides support when things are difficult. It allows communication in greater depth with casual acquaintances. It permits a person to judge where he or she is in reference to peers—in business as well as in one's social life. The group also provides diversion and, in some instances, sexual relationships.

People sometimes belong to more than a single network. Some of the networks are loose, involving school chums or business associates, and are not really a person's key support group. Because of such loose networks and because people belong to several, there is a lot of overlap. Networks interconnect. Sam may use Sally's friends, without having met them, by getting their names from Sally; and vice versa. When someone in a network wants help that isn't available from his or her friends, he or she asks others in the group about their connections, and eventually tracks down the assistance needed. In talking to baby boomers about their networks, I have sometimes thought that if you traced all the interconnections, everyone in the generation could somehow be reached through the networks.

Networks are especially significant to people who are trapped. They are a source of broadening experiences that provide alternatives to a trapped person. A trapped person can sometimes break out of his or her prison by learning of other opportunities from the group. It is also a source of the courage needed to make a change.

For baby boomers the office plays a major role as a place where they can meet people and build networks. As is usually the case, baby boomers often do not make a firm distinction between the social and business aspects of their lives.

People meet at work, and at business-related endeavors like meetings or conferences or on airplane trips. Now that men and women are both in the work force, work is where people socialize.

Yet it would surprise a lot of business executives to realize that many employees see the office as a substitute for a health club as a place to meet people.

Most companies lag almost ten years behind the life-styles and personal interests of the people they employ, especially the better educated and more imaginative and innovative. In the 1960s people started encounter groups and sensitivity training. In the 1970s many businesses started sensitivity training. But by then people were into sports, running, and fitness. Now, in the 1980s companies are into wellness and are building spas. But now people have moved on to social-purpose rock concerts and the spiritual side of life. Though it may seem unlikely today, business will probably adopt some of these things in the 1990s. By being so slow to pick up current trends, many companies miss a major opportunity to work more closely with their employees.

By and large, business isn't tuned in to the networks its employees belong to. Managers don't listen well. People do things that would be of value to companies, but companies object because they take a long time to get accustomed to new ways of doing anything.

The major exceptions are start-up companies, which have made a business advantage out of adjusting to employees' changing interests, including the desire for informality in the workplace, and have thereby attracted especially creative and productive professionals. By trying to put the office at the center of each employee's own network, and by positioning the work environment as part of that employee's social contacts, these firms have attracted a disproportionate part of the best talent in the baby boom generation.

10

THE COMPLETE PERSON

"Sometimes people in my generation think your generation lacks balance," Gary said unexpectedly. "You have values and objectives, but for most of you, balance isn't one of your goals. I remember that we mentioned some people in your generation who try to be balanced, and we put them in the contented category, but I think most of you tend to excess, whether it's in business or in enjoyment. People who lack a goal of balance tend to go too far in their lives—they develop too great expectations and, as a result, encounter too great disappointments.

"Once when I was in Japan, I heard an old man—a business executive, as it turned out—describe life as a tapestry which each person weaves. Daily he or she adds threads which are harmonious, or which are shocking in color and disruptive of the pattern. All aspects of life add to the tapestry—all aspects are interrelated parts that create a whole.

"But your generation substitutes for this vision of life as a single tapestry an obsession with each moment. You are only interested in where your head is at now. You accept change from minute to minute, but without seeing the overall pattern. Impatience blinds you to the pattern of change and to the possibilities in it. Independence keeps you from learning from anyone except your own network. Individualism insists that everything you do is new and unique, no matter how commonplace it really is. You seem to stumble continually into what could easily have been foreseen."

Susan and Bif were stunned by Gary's condemnation. He had not been so critical before. A lengthy silence ensued until Bif responded.

"I don't think that's fair," he began, "or true. I think the older generation clings to values like loyalty, persistence, and single-mindedness. To me, people who hold on to those values seem one-dimensional and uninteresting. They remind me of the advice given by one of his father's friends to Dustin Hoffman in the movie *The Graduate* about his future. Do you remember what he whispered to him? 'Plastics,' he whispered, 'plastics.'

"As if choosing a line of business was all there was to life. Someone who could only say 'plastics' was a very shallow person.

"This kind of total focus on a product or a job is out of date. I'm not like that and neither is Susan. And I like the work I do. I get pleasure from it and I'm self-motivated. For me, being a professional gives expression to my desire for autonomy, recognition, and uniqueness. I would do what I do even if I didn't have to work. But since I do have to work I decided to do what I like.

"For a while I was satisfied simply to do it well. But at one point I decided it was time to find a way to make what I did more lucrative.

"I had to change my activities a little and get a different employer, but making more money has made it easier for me to do other things with more enjoyment."

Susan had sat looking troubled as she listened to Bif. But it wasn't what Bif was saying that upset her. She was still angry at Gary, even beginning to regret having brought him along.

But she waited until Bif finished speaking before saying anything to Gary.

"I think you are way off base," she said. "I think what you said is true of your generation much more than mine.

"I have a friend who got a Ph.D. and started teaching in a college. But he got bored, so he went into administration as a student dean. When he tired of that, he took over the student-housing functions. There he learned a little about housing, so when a job opened selling condos at a big resort development, he applied for that. He was likable and casual, so they hired him. After a couple of years he had learned a lot about tax law—which you have to know to sell real estate well—so he became an investment adviser.

"I said to him, 'You can't stick to anything. You just want constant change. Every few years you have to learn something new from the ground up.' And he agrees it's true.

"I think a lot of people in my generation are like him. If someone in your generation," she said to Gary, who grimaced at the reference to his age, "follows a career path like that, people say he or she's unstable. But my generation admires his continuing to learn and the variety he has in his life."

"When I was less into business," Bif said, "like when I was in college, I spent a lot of time in sports. But I had to study as well as do my sport. If I just trained, then I couldn't be happy. Part of me wasn't satisfied.

"That's how I tried to keep all of me satisfied. I couldn't be happy if I left something out. I couldn't feel good about myself."

"I know people who think of themselves as self-actualizers," Susan said. "They do Outward Bound to develop the physical aspect. They do Forum, Lifespring, or Time Management to develop the mental aspect. They're into primal scream or psychotherapy to build up their emotional capability. And they go to retreats or use drugs or get into religion to do more with their spiritual side."

"I'll bet they don't have any time for business," Gary put in.

Susan was startled by the interruption. She hesitated a moment, then had to admit that Gary had a point.

"You're right," she agreed. "Actually, most people don't realize how costly it is to a person to make a business go. It can be all-consuming," Susan said. "You set up your staff, you spend all your time dealing with problems and opportunities. The motivation is all economic. You think of people in terms of boxes they fit in, in the company. I know, because I've been in that scene. I'm still in it to a degree.

"But the rest of you doesn't change. It doesn't grow. You know nothing about other people outside of the business, and nothing about other organizations. You kind of hide from the world in your business."

"When does a person stop working? When should the brakes be put on?" Gary asked. "If your generation wants to be complex people with lots of interests, where do they put the brakes on business? As a rule, are people content when they have enough money to pay for their life-style?"

"I used to be satisfied," Bif said, "but I'm not sure now. It's beginning to seem as if a person never has enough money."

"I think the problem," said Gary, "is that lots of people in your generation don't know what life-style they want. So they can't get enough money. And they can't be happy."

"I think what it is," Susan said, "is that a person's priorities keep changing. As she changes and keeps growing, she needs more or less money. It's not that she doesn't know her life-style. It's that she keeps changing. I keep experiencing new life-styles that require more money. As I get more money, I do more things with my friends. If someone in my group can't go to San Francisco because she doesn't have the money, I pay for it. I don't accumulate power and wealth.

"But other people I know who are my age want to go back to school. That's another option. So they have to accept being broke for years."

"If you can get people away from TV and spectator sports, because these things are too passive, and into the outdoors and sports and games, then they've got a chance," Bif said. "That's how business and other activities fit together for this generation. If you're doing outdoor things, then you're active and you take that energy and activity into business. You're not passive—whether at home or in business. So the one side of your life helps make the other side better.

"I'm not as narrowly business-focused as Susan says I am," Bif continued. "I'm interested in people, not just in financial accounts, and I can see the people in an organization as more than cogs in the machine.

"When I look at a company I can see not only its balance sheet and income statement, not only its wealth and riches, but also the people who compose it—their talents, hopes, fears; their lives, emotions, successes, opportunities, failures, even lovers and families.

"I know this is much richer than the financial aspect—it's 'rich' in a different sense. When you're aware of the human aspects of an organization it makes the numbers shallow, bland, and almost uninteresting. I know that the people who overlook the human richness in an organization and see only the dollars are really the poor ones, because they're poor in spirit. To see only the dollars is a tasteless, insipid life, even if a person becomes financially rich in the process.

"You see, Susan," Bif concluded, "I'm not just a money-hungry monster."

"You're not money hungry?" she asked.

Bif paused, then gave her a keen glance. "Not just a money-hungry monster," he repeated.

"I think you should keep trying to develop a concept of the whole person," she told him. "You ought to keep up with your travels and adventures. You shouldn't surrender it all to the business. Those aren't the values of our generation.

"There's one final thing about this," Susan went on. "Single-minded people are too specialized. They want to control their own area and exclude others. Everyone else is forced into a supporting role.

"Because your generation is so single-minded," she said to Gary, "it has tried to force mine into supporting specializations. We're supposed to devote all our attention to doing this or that thing super well. We aren't supposed to have time for much else or for our careers, if we decided to have careers, to be varied and interesting. But we won't accept that. We won't consent to being excluded from key business and political roles just because we are more complete people who don't give up our entire lives to a particular role.

"When the older generation chooses to be single-minded, and the younger chooses to be more complete in its approach to life, it seems to me that the stage is set for a major conflict."

SCARED LIKE MAD

During our interviews we talked to a man in his late twenties who works for a very large company. He is a manager and has been getting promoted rapidly. Once he was invited to visit the company's headquarters with a group of other fast-trackers. They had cocktails with the company's top man and his staff, then went on to dinner, where they had a chance to ask questions. The first seven or eight questions were about various aspects of the business. It's a complex company with many different lines, but the CEO was on top of every one. He showed great versatility.

He knew all aspects: marketing, production, strategy. He was confident and gave superb answers.

Then the manager, who was one of the younger persons there, asked a question. "I'd like to know more about you as a person," he said. "What are you interested in? What do you believe in? What is important to you as an individual?"

There was a long pause. The CEO looked stunned. His staff people said later that it was the first time they had seen him speechless.

Finally, he answered. "Well," he said, "I like what I do. I like the business. I enjoy my work."

He didn't have anything more to say. All his life was tied up in the business. Without it, he was an empty person. There was nothing else there.

The top man had also missed a major opportunity to perform a service. The reason the young manager had asked him about his personal life was that he himself was under pressure from his friends who were pleasure-seekers. They were asking him, "Why are you working so hard? What's the point? You're wasting your life. You ought to stop it."

So the young manager was actually asking the company's chief executive officer for help. He was really saying, "Tell me what I can say to convince them that what I'm doing is right. You're successful. You're the boss. Tell me why you do what you do. Tell me about your life so I can tell my friends and get them off my back."

Our interviews produced an intriguing perspective on baby boomers as they try to get a lot out of life by doing different things.

For example, a forty-one-year-old man, who is a construction inspector in a large midwestern city, told about the other things he was doing besides his job. "I've been on the auxiliary fire department for eight years," he said. "I've run for political office. I've directed plays. I'm currently directing a murder play. It's a form of interactive drama.

"I want to do something different from the job I have now. I've always wanted to have my own detective agency. But changing jobs scares me like mad. Still, I'm going to do it. I'm going to get into something else."

However, the danger with having too many opportunities available is that a person won't be able to make up his or her mind about which to choose.

Still, many boomers seem to keep only loose attachments to others, relying on networks rather than on family, and using the phone as a way of staying in contact with people. They believe it is a great advantage, especially if they have to move to a new location, to be without ties to a family or a business, because then they can do what they want.

This rootlessness, which is still an influence among baby boomers as they grow older, was well-expressed a quarter of a century ago. Even as children, baby boomers seemed to engage in an unending series of experiments and explorations, each readily abandoned in favor of something new. It's a psychological state they are after—a state of excitement—all the time.[1]

Many Americans over the generations have had a deep involvement with nature, but the baby boomers have given that involvement a slightly different cast. In the past, Americans who were nature lovers saw nature as mystical, a semireligious experience that helped them understand the basic place of natural things and man in the world. The conservation movement was an example.

But though some boomers see nature as a source of enlightenment, a larger group treats the outdoors as if it were a sport. To them nature is a pleasurable experience, not a source of enlightenment. The result is the same, however, because nature is valued, sought after, and preserved—for the beauty and pleasure it provides, if not for its religious or mystical significance.

11

A NEW MEANING OF SUCCESS

Gary resumed the conversation. "I've heard about a lot of studies recently that seem to show that baby boomers aren't doing that well financially."

"Just the other day," Susan said, "I was talking to one of my friends. He told me that he couldn't believe that he was making the salary he gets, but still couldn't afford to own a home. He said that if he'd been told that years ago, he'd have laughed at whoever said it. 'I was raised the American way,' he told me. 'I believe that to own a home is the most important material possession a person can have. But I can't afford it!' he said."

"I've heard that," Bif responded. "But our parents didn't make most of their money when they were our age—they made it later. I know many people who aren't doing that well now, but they haven't given up, and I think they'll do very well in the future."

"You're right about that," Gary acknowledged. "I read that young people are far more optimistic about the future than are older people."[1]

Bif and Susan were silent, as if the things Gary had said did not apply to them personally. Finally, Susan commented thoughtfully: "Even if what you say were to turn out to be true, does less affluence mean people are not successful? Or is it a choice people have made?

"I think it's a choice people have made. They have chosen to change the standards of success. People want the environment to be good; they want to have fun at work; they want to have time to have meaningful relationships. If the result is that people don't make as much money, then they accept that. A few years ago the government and the big companies were all telling us how much cleaning up the environment was going to cost, as if that would persuade us not to do it. But we wanted it done, even if it cost a lot of money. The same thing is true about nuclear power. The utilities spent all this money building nuclear power plants, so they want to use them now. But nuclear plants aren't safe. So we say don't use them, even if it costs a lot of money not to.

"I feel the same way about Social Security. I know I have to pay a lot of taxes now for it, and I'll have to pay a lot more in the future. But I want my parents to get Social Security. I don't want to have to take care of them myself; and I don't want them abandoned. So I'm willing to pay taxes to Social Security to help them be cared for.

"I think you have to realize that if the environment is cleaner, and if you are not in danger from nuclear power plants, and if your parents are taken care of, then your life is better, even if your income isn't as great as it might be otherwise, and even if you pay somewhat more taxes than otherwise.

"The older generation always measured how well it was doing on the basis of how much money it made, even though the air was poisonous, the rivers polluted, and the wilderness was being built up into housing developments. They were making more money, but the quality of life was getting a lot worse. The economists and the people in government who put together all those numbers don't seem to understand that. Today we may make less money, but our life is actually better, and if you could measure quality of life accurately, you'd see that."

Gary sat absorbed in thought. "Maybe," he said finally, "but my generation didn't measure success by money alone either. It also measured success by how well a person did in advancing up a career ladder."

"But that's different, too," Susan answered with a touch of exasperation in her voice. "We've been trying to explain that to you. There are so many of us in our generation and such a large population of us are working that there isn't as much room for upward mobility, and so people have found other ways to be successful."

"Money and career advancement are still important," Bif said, "but there's more to the story now than that. People want entertainment; they want to feel good about themselves; they want the opportunity to do different things and to pursue their real interests."

"I think," said Gary, "for my generation, success is almost completely measured by comparing yourself with other people. You're successful if you make more money than they do or if you attain a higher-level job than they do. It's how we motivate ourselves to work: by offering more money and promotions.

"But as I listen to you, success seems to have a somewhat different meaning. It's more doing what you want to do, having time and money to do your own thing. It's much more individualistic, not connected to how the other person is doing."

"That's largely true," Susan said. "But remember, there are many different kinds of people in our generation. The contented and the pleasure-seekers fit what you just said exactly, but the competitors are more like your generation was—I mean, is."

"Yes," Gary agreed, "but even the competitors in your generation have more of the pleasure-seeker in them than did my generation. They tolerate the pleasure-seekers—and want some of the experiences and diversion for themselves. In my generation people who pursued variety and stimulation seemed frivolous."

"Susan, when you think of a successful person," Gary continued, "is it one who has created an interesting and challenging life?"

"To me, yes," Susan said. "But other people think it's someone who has the time and money to do what he or she wants—even if it's just to lie on the beach. For me that wouldn't be interesting or challenging enough."

"And the person who works hard and climbs a corporate ladder, making lots of money?" Gary inquired.

"Thats O.K.," Susan responded, "if he or she also has time for the other things in life."

"And if they don't?"

"Then they're not successful at all."

Gary changed the subject. "I saw a survey in a newspaper recently in which people were asked about their travel and job fantasies. Most men said they wanted to go on a safari. Most women fantasized about owning their own companies—more women than men had that desire."[2]

"It's just what I said," Susan insisted. "People want to have adventures, and they want to have independence."

"But it also showed," Gary continued, "that two thirds of Americans acknowledged that they didn't do these things, but got their greatest pleasure and satisfaction from watching television."

"That's the sad thing," Susan agreed. "People want to do things, but don't. Still, that's everybody, isn't it—the survey is everybody, and so it's your generation and mine, both. I'll bet there are more TV watchers in your group than mine."

"Well, they're older; so maybe they're less active," Gary conceded.

"But that's not the only reason," Susan argued. "It's also because my generation has different values and wants to be more active and is. That's what we've been talking about."

"It seems to me," Bif put in, "that there are clusters of meaning in people's lives—the things they organize their lives around. For some people it's material possessions; for some it's social status. These are the clusters that meant most to the older generation.

"But for us it's personal accomplishments—in sports, or adventures, or business—and it's also professional respect—what your peers think of you.

"I think that part of the difference between our generation and yours is that for yours, success is a concept of the most or the best. For most of us success is as much a matter of balancing several dimensions—home, work, outside interests—and it doesn't require a person to have the most or the best in any.

"A person isn't a success," Bif continued, "unless he has a balance between family and career. I think I can make a lot of money now, so I'm really pushing for it. I can have a family and spend more time with it later.

"To me money represents independence and freedom. It's not just materialism. Money makes other things possible—experiences, security, freedom. It's an instrument, not an end in itself."

"Now you sound like a balanced person yourself," Gary said to him.

Bif was pleased, and smiled triumphantly at Susan.

"Not so fast," Susan objected with good humor. "He may talk like a balanced person, but he really isn't one. He says he wants to do other things, but all he does is work. It's a matter of emphasis, and while he aspires to having a balance in his life, he's really still a competitor.

"I look at your shirts and pants and shoes, so carefully selected to complement each other," she said to Bif, "and I remember that you used to say that trendy consumption is just a cheap path to social status for people who lack the strength of character to be what they really aspire to be. They look sharp, and put on like they feel great, but deep down I think they don't feel good about themselves at all."

"It's a matter of priorities," Bif answered. "I still think that a person can carry looking good too far, but in business you have to dress well." Even as he said this, Bif looked uneasy, as if his explanation didn't entirely convince him.

After a pause Susan resumed the conversation in a less provocative tone. "I sometimes think about the ideal job. It's what I would do if I didn't have to work for a living. I don't want to see a career as an instrument to something I enjoy—I want it to be fun itself."

AN OPPORTUNITY FOR EMPLOYERS

Why do baby boomers care less about success in a traditional sense than their parents did?

In part the answer lies in the greater number of options they have about how to live their lives, and in part in the lesser degree of economic insecurity they have experienced. Both these matters have been discussed earlier in this book. But an additional element has to do with their understanding of the causes of success.

"People succeed in business—or sports, entertainment, or politics, for that matter," a thirty-two-year-old woman told me, "because of greater advantages, greater natural endowments, better luck, or even harder work. But none of those things make them better people.

"The better people are those who have done what is best for their own lives—who have been true to their values—who have made the most of themselves—with or without success as other people might define it. To know if you're successful in my generation," she concluded, "you must identify correctly your own aspirations and life-style; then success means attaining them."

In accordance with this view, many baby boomers are trying to identify what they really want. The experience of one thirty-eight-year-old executive, let's call him Bill, provides a good example.

The founder of Bill's company was famous for the hours he kept and the relentless pace he expected of his staff. He died a few years ago—of a heart attack—and within a few months everyone had nearly forgotten him. Power was temporarily passed to his own chief financial officer, who is expected to retire in a year or two.

The board of directors has made it clear that they expect the next chief executive to pick up where the founder left off: hundred-hour weeks, travel three days out of five, relentless pressure, and selfless devotion to the company.

Bill is one of three candidates for the CEO spot, and chances are he'll get it. But right now Bill is asking some tough questions and saying to himself,

"Wait a minute! I don't really know if I want this. I have a family. I don't know if I want to work myself to death and be carried out in a box. Then a few months later everyone has forgotten about me. It would be as if I never lived at all, and I never knew my family or did anything else with my life. If that's success, I don't think I want it."

Bill's concerns seemed to be merited. It appears that you don't have much time to yourself if you run a company. A recent survey showed that the average CEO spends more than sixty hours a week at work, and that is more than CEOs spent just a few years ago. Most of them said they spent insufficient time with their families.[3] These are people whom others with traditional American values would label "successful." But baby boomers have their reservations.

The new concept of success, which Bif and Susan expressed, is an opportunity, not a problem, for employers. If companies want to keep people productive throughout their lives, and if they want their employees to live fulfilling lives while being associated with the company, they should accept and even reinforce this new concept.

At present, most companies stress promotion up a management ladder as the primary, if not only, measure of a person's success. Promotion carries both financial and status rewards, but the pyramid swiftly becomes more narrow as higher-level positions are reached. People who do not get promoted feel their failure acutely, and often cease to work with the same initiative and commitment as in the past.

Also, as the younger baby boomers emerge from college and graduate school with special skills, and soon outstrip other baby boomers who are already climbing promotion ladders, those who are passed over often turn off on the company.

What does a corporation gain from this phenomenon? The answer would appear to be, very little. For years scientific and engineering companies have struggled with the problem of demoralization that the emphasis on climbing a management ladder brings to especially valued technical employees. Because status and pay are associated with management, technical people aspire to management jobs. But when a valued scientist or engineer takes a managerial job, the company often loses his or her technical contribution; or, alternatively, finds that the technical person is a poor or incompetent manager. Either way, stressing the management hierarchy is counterproductive. There are more than enough competitors in the baby boom generation who will struggle to advance up the corporate ladder, and therefore no need for a company to try to motivate everyone to do the same.

So there seems to be no reason why a company cannot recognize the baby boomers' concept of success. People can be afforded an opportunity to develop in multiple dimensions. At the core of this effort is a recognition that success in a corporation can involve having an interesting career with varied challenges, even if one doesn't make it very high up the corporate ladder.

To provide these challenges, companies must be more prepared to vary job assignments. And employees ought to be able to initiate changes in assignment by requesting them and by taking training courses for them. Not everyone will want to do this, of course, and their wishes can be respected as much as possible. But variety, choice, and challenge will open up "success" to many more people.

Another advantage of accepting a broader definition of human success is that it may increase the respect which American managers have for their employees. Because success today is defined so narrowly in terms of managerial advancement, those who achieve high positions tend to look down upon those who do not. There is a sort of pervasive disrespect for the contributions of the rank and file, extending even in many cases to professional employees. Many managers insist on prerequisites solely because they are managers.

In our survey nonmanagerial people spoke almost unanimously of the lack of respect and uncaring attitude shown them by managerial personnel.

A chemistry researcher with advanced college degrees said in an interview, "Overall management may say that they're concerned with their employees, but it's hard to see any sensitivity from them."

A bakery worker reported, "Upper management couldn't care less about the employees a lot of the time . . . If the economy is bad, we (the employees) take the blame for it. They don't blame it on poor products or high costs . . . they blame it on people."

An electrician from California said, "To the employer I'm with now, you're a number, not a person. They don't care what you think. They just want all they can squeeze out of you for their eight hours. I feel a person will give more if they would just communicate and listen to people. Upper management blames the little people in the trade for the things that go wrong when essentially it may be their fault. They just need to be courteous and care for us as human beings. They would be happy if there was a machine that wouldn't talk back."

Despite what many managers seem to think, most Americans build successful lives without climbing to the top of a managerial hierarchy. If managers would recognize this and respect the success of others, they might be surprised how responsive employees would be. In the words of a professional engineer employed by a Seattle metal-design firm: "My company was bought by a Japanese buyer a few years ago. It's interesting to see the changes. The unions were thrown out in the street and the employees were given a sense of belonging. It's the little perks that help. Like the manager who gives the little person appreciation for doing work even if it's a menial task. The personal dedication makes work quality much better. Interest opens the mind."

This engineer is a success now in his own eyes, in part because his new employer recognizes the merit in what he does and sees him as a whole person.

Managers who do recognize the new concept of success are effective at helping employees achieve success. These managers understand what success means to others, and are able to define careers that help employees feel good about themselves. Since feeling good about yourself is one of the baby boomers' values, managers who follow the new criterions are following a good path to a well-motivated workforce.

12

CHAINED BY CONVENTION

Bif was not surprised when Susan appeared at their next meeting accompanied by Gary. He had hoped Gary might come along, despite clinging to the hope that one of their meetings might end in himself accompanying Susan back home. Now, with Gary in tow, Susan would have no interest in Bif later in the evening. For a while they talked. In the course of their conversation, Bif mentioned his current wife, and Gary made references to his marriage, which ended in divorce about two years ago, and his children. As Susan listened, she grew uneasy. Both men had been married, and Gary had children. She had never married, had no children, and wondered if she had missed out on something.

Because both men were her close friends, she felt more comfortable being honest and open with them than she would have felt with casual acquaintances. She began to talk about her own career and the choice she had made to remain single.

"Before," Susan began, "if a woman worked, she was looked down upon. People said: 'She can't find a husband, so she works.' Or they said, 'She works because she's mannish.' Or if she were married and had a job, they said, 'She married the wrong man; he can't support her.'"

"Now it's the opposite. There's a taint if a woman stays home. So if a woman gives in to the traditional ideas and stays home with a child, she risks not having her own or other people's respect."

"I think you're too hard on women who stay home," Bif said to Susan. "A lot of people respect women who take care of a family."

"You're such a traditionalist!" Susan responded. "All you want is a woman who stays home."

"Yes," Bif answered, "and I don't think there's anything wrong with that. Children need to be brought up by their mothers."

"Even if their mothers are unhappy and don't feel good about themselves?" Susan asked. "Won't that get communicated to the children?"

"I talked to a young woman recently," Gary said, "who told me, 'I don't regret getting married, but I wished I had waited a few more years. We started going into a recession when we first got married, and all our hopes and dreams went down the tubes. We should have waited until we had more money so we wouldn't have had any financial problems.' "

"That's my generation all right," Susan said. "There are women who get married too young; who get married and give up their careers; who want to get married and don't; and who could get married but don't want to. There are all kinds."

Gary continued. "This young woman also talked about how very fast-paced her life is. She said: 'Whether you want to be a go-getter or not, you're forced into being one. I didn't think my life would be this hectic when I was young. I like being busy, but I also like to enjoy myself. Things can get very confusing.' "

"There was a time," Susan said, "when I thought maybe I ought to get married and have children. My parents wanted me to. My brother had just had a child. It was my turn.

"Their expectations made me very uneasy. I didn't want to just go out and start looking for a husband. But I felt the pressure. I began to feel uncomfortable about myself. They made me wonder whether I was doing the right thing with my life. I even began to wonder if I could find a husband if I wanted to. I felt like I had to do something.

"When I went through that stage, I decided to get away. So I went to California one summer to find people who were looser, more accepting. It made a big difference. Out West I could get outdoors. When you do something exciting, you always meet exciting people—and you build your confidence all over again.

"I'm a very weird person, I guess, because I'm now very comfortable with myself. I enjoy men, but I don't need someone to tuck me into bed at night.

"I think many women get married in their twenties and thirties when they are often alone and don't know what to do with themselves. Then they can forget the singles thing and don't have to worry about what to do with their lives."

Since Bif and Gary still sat silent and listening, Susan went on.

"In real life women decide to go the route of family, children, love, all that—and give up the outside world. Why do they do it? It isn't that women are different from men and want these things more; it's that the social pressures overcome them. Domestic responsibilities interfere with having a profession.

"To cope with all the additional requirements of a home and family, a professional needs a wife. She needs someone who does for her what the wife of a professional man does for him. But it couldn't be her husband. She wouldn't want that in a husband. She wouldn't respect him.[1] Perhaps she needs a maid.

"Thats the professional woman's dilemma.

"We want the female to be different than she has been, but not take the male role. That's hard, because there are only two sexes.

"It may seem risky not to marry and to depend instead on yourself. But is it really? Is it less risky to tie yourself to a man? You might outgrow him and be unhappy. Or he might divorce you and leave you without a career or money. He might get rich—but he might not. Either way you're tied to him.

"I think the message to women ought to be: 'It's all right to get married, and it's all right not to get married. It's all right to have children, and it's all right not to have children.' Then there wouldn't be a lot of pressure."

As Susan took a long breath, Bif jumped in: "At our first meeting you insisted that my life wasn't very good, because I was too much into work and didn't have time for other things.

"But is your life really so good? You say it is, and you knock people who are married and have kids. But are you really comfortable being alone? I know you're able to be with a lot of men, and you still travel and have a variety of experiences, but don't you miss a home and children?"

Susan was disturbed that Bif would attack her so roughly when she had admitted that she was troubled by the idea of marriage and a family. Now she seemed nervous.

"As I get older, I say to myself, 'Why haven't I gotten pregnant? Maybe I can't have children.'

"Before, I thought, 'I'm career-oriented so I won't have children.' Now it's 'am I career-oriented because I'm afraid to have children?' There's deep anxiety—a self-doubt.

"It's very hard to know what to do," Susan continued. "Suppose I decide to have children and drop out. But I'm business-oriented and I love my life-style. I certainly can't bring myself to give it up for children and a husband except if I could say, 'It's only for a few years, then I'll be back to my career.' Perhaps then I could maintain my self-image. Sometimes I think I'm becoming like a trapped person.

"Other women want children, but can't find a husband. They're too convention-bound to get artificially inseminated or to have a child by a casual relationship.

"The saddest of my friends are the ones who want children and marry late, only to discover that there are fertility problems. This crisis extends to work, of course, because it diverts their attention from work."

Susan laughed briefly and continued. "Maybe you're right, Bif. Maybe I should think about getting married and having a family. Maybe that's what's happening. Maybe everyone is giving up fooling around and settling down. Maybe AIDS has everybody scared out of fooling around."

"What I want to know," Gary said, "is whether women who decide to leave work now and have children will want to stay in that situation. A man and a woman get married, and they say they want to have children, and they want their children to be raised by a stay-at-home, full-time mother. The woman thinks she'll be happy for years hence. But will she still have the respect of her husband and her friends? Will she still have her own self-respect? Will she feel good about herself, or will she feel trapped and no longer interesting?"

"I had a call from a friend of mine the other day," Susan said. "She's married and has two children. She said, 'Susan, you've got to come over. I've got to talk to an adult. I can't stand it anymore with these two kids! I've got to have an adult to talk to.' "

"Aren't lots of people in your generation deciding to give up their freedom to have families?" Gary asked.

"Yes," Susan admitted. "The pressures to do things like that, to assume traditional roles for women and for men, are very strong.

"There are all these pressures," Susan continued. "Get married, don't get married; have children, don't have children; have a career, don't have a career. People can't decide what's important to them. A person has basic values—which, we've agreed, most people in our generation share—and must decide his or her own priorities and make his or her own choices."

WHAT SHOULD WOMEN BE DOING?

Our interviews revealed there is a generation of women struggling with having to make basic choices about their lives. Certainly, what role women should take in our society is one of the most significant and burning issues that everyone faces.

"Our generation is so different," a thirty-one-year-old woman told us. "We face so many things that our parents didn't have to deal with: careers, relationships. . . . There are very few role models for us. You don't know if you should be married and have children or have a competitive career."

"I think women are overwhelmed by it all," said a twenty-six-year-old woman. "We have to deal with financial pressures, relationships, social life, children—whether you're going to have them or not! Perhaps we're beginning to find roles again, but they are very complex roles today. Instead of pleasing just one person, like our mothers did, we have so many people we have to please—children, our employers, our spouses, ourselves. There's so much more emotional complexity to deal with."

"I am in my thirties," a woman told us. "I'm on my second marriage. I have a career with a good-paying job. But my husband wants a child. So now I have to decide between a child and a career."

We asked respondents what women their age ought to be doing.

A twenty-three-year-old woman engineer answered, "Women should be getting involved in a worthwhile career. It's hard to depend on a husband now because there's so much divorce. They should think about a career so they could survive on their own if they had to.

"With all these pressures on a woman," she added, "what I want in a relationship with a man is just someone who can make me feel great about myself."

Men and women were asked about the role of women and the attitude of men toward that role. "What should women do with their lives?" In one of the few showings of near unanimity, both men and women responded, "Whatever they want to do with their lives."

In the generation as a whole, our survey suggests, almost three quarters (74 percent) say that women ought to be doing whatever they want to do. Five percent think they ought to be married and raising children. Six percent say they should be working. The remaining 16 percent say women should be raising children and not working.

Perhaps surprisingly, these percentages differ very little by sex. Men were only marginally less likely than women to respond that women ought to be doing whatever they want, and were only marginally more likely to respond that they should be taking care of children.

"They should have equal rights," said a twenty-eight-year-old offshore oil-rig worker from Louisiana. "They should have equal rights on everything, even fighting a war. I want a woman that's equal, not a subordinate. They should work and have equal pay."

A twenty-six-year-old chef from Pennsylvania said women his age ought to be "just doing what they're doing . . . working or whatever they want. All my friends' wives work. They enjoy working. It's the way of life now, even if you have children. With children it's rough, but that's the way it is. They'd probably say they want more than they have because they're not where they want to be yet in business."

"How should men respond to the choices women make?" was another question we asked.

"The men should let the women do what they want to do," was the most common reply. To this otherwise universal expression of tolerance, there was only one dissident voice. A young man of Chinese extraction, who had immigrated to the United States several years earlier, lives in New York, and now works as a computer programmer, commented, "I think women in this country are too self-centered. They have got a good thing going, much better than in Asia. They are getting the upper hand."

In his voice was resentment, and he refused to discuss the topic anymore.

It appears that in today's society women are given a difficult range of choices, but that by and large, other members of their generation, women and men both, are prepared to accept whatever choices they make. This, of course, only puts the burden more heavily on each woman to make the right choice.

A LOWER PRIORITY FOR CAREERS?

Among the older baby boomers, many women are falling into the trap of waiting too long to decide to get married and are now giving careers a lower priority while trying to find husbands.

We interviewed a woman about thirty-nine years old, who for years had been completely into her career, and never wanted to get married. She dated a man she had met in college for fifteen years. Repeatedly he asked her to marry him, but she refused every time.

When he dated other women, she was crushed, but she never consented to marry him. Finally, he married someone else.

"Now I'm almost forty," she said, "and I want to marry. I've gotten older but I've gotten better. I'm in better shape. I take better care of myself."

On the negative side, she says she has only 1 percent chance of getting married now.[2]

"I see it all as a single woman," a twenty-four-year-old woman told me. "I think I'd like to get married, but it's so hard to know who to trust. A person talks to you and you think, 'What does he want?'

"I tell my friends I'd rather stay home on Friday and Saturday nights and read. I don't want to go to the singles clubs. It's just a meat market. People get drunk; people do drugs. I stick out like a sore thumb. I say to myself, 'What am I doing here?'

"The clouds never seem to break open. I never see the light. I look up and I say 'Give me a sign!' But the clouds are still there."

Another woman told me about when she got married for the second time. She had been married when she had just finished high school, and it hadn't worked out. Then she worked for almost twenty years. She was nearly forty when she met a man who had two children by a previous marriage. She had no children.

She said she had wondered whether she should get married again or not. "Marriage is just a piece of paper," she told me. "I know it isn't any more than that. I was married before and when he wanted to leave, the marriage contract didn't hold him at all. So it's just a piece of paper that can be torn up at any time."

She had a big wedding in a city in the South. "I was so much in control," she said. "I planned everything and was the calmest person there."

She is very proud of her husband, a handsome man, well built and in very good physical condition.

His children were there for the wedding. So were a few of her friends, women about her own age, not married, very attractive, and deeply into their careers. But they wanted to marry, she said. They had refused offers earlier, but now thought differently about it.

"I decided to get married again," she explained, "because it would make our parents feel better. Also I wanted to get out of the office, to have some new experiences. I figured that after a few months I'd do something different, like start a business of my own."

What she said made sense. Her concept of marriage was that it would liberate her, not tie her down. A year later, she had begun to look for a business opportunity and the marriage was a very successful one.

The conflict women have over the issue of marriage or career was dramatically illustrated by two contrasting comments made by young women to our interviewers. Said one, "Sure, I'd like to be married. But if I were married, I'd be bored."

Said another, "I'm forty. I put off marriage for my career for many years. Now I have two children. I simply wasn't prepared for the fulfillment and love which the children have brought me. I've loved a lot of people before, but nothing has ever been like the experience of love with my children."

U.S. Census Bureau data indicate that about one fifth of all people never marry. At age thirty-five, about 20 percent of men and 14 or 15 percent of women have never been married.[3] In 1986 the ratio of unmarried women, ages twenty to forty, to the total female population hit an all-time high. Baby boom women are staying single to a far greater extent than their mothers.[4]

Also, today almost one half of all adults live in single-parent households, live alone, or are single and live with other singles.[5] The predicted return of the traditional family is not occurring.

Finally, the most recent data show that of all women now in their thirties who get married, six out of ten will become divorced.[6] This is a far higher frequency of divorce than among their parents, but it is too soon to tell whether it will be higher than the rate for women in their twenties today.

SHOULD A COMPANY BECOME INVOLVED?

People are trying to get part-time jobs because they think that will allow them to have both children and a job. However, there aren't a lot of good part-time jobs, many women told our interviewers. One of the reasons parenthood is such a hard choice for professional women is that it makes it very difficult to get a part-time assignment.

"What should a company do, in your opinion," we asked boomers, "when a professional woman tells her boss that she is going to quit her job to raise a family?" If a woman is going to quit her job because she wants to have a family, should the company ask her, "Is this really what you want? Will you like yourself later?" Should they say, "We've invested a lot in you and don't want to lose you"?

Most answered, "I don't think a company should get too involved. It's a personal decision. If the company can't provide part-time work that fits a woman's schedule, it should just tell her it appreciates her and wants her to stay if she wants to, and let her make her own decision."

On the other hand, as young people struggle with the question of marriage and children, they want their companies to provide flexible schedules so that they need not be anxious about balancing family and work responsibilities. They want a day care, or referrals to day care, so that they can have a job and yet also have their children adequately cared for; and they want help in working out part-time schedules when necessary.

Companies that do not do these things appear to stand in the way of people having children, and it earns them a lot of resentment.

Employers can gain loyalty from employees by trying to help them balance home and work, but should not get involved in the choices they make about how to live their lives.

Already supervisors in many companies are making informal arrangements that permit employees to balance the office and the family. Most companies, however, do not formally encourage or even permit this. But they could. Supervisors also need to be cautioned about stepping over the line that lies between concern and helpfulness on one hand and interference on the other. Companies should provide this type of support to supervisors in their training programs.

Women also say that the same reasoning that applies to the office ought to apply to the home. A person who stays home ought to have flextime, just as if he or she were at work, and have time off to do other things besides take care of the children or do housework. His or her spouse can help provide time and opportunity to learn and grow and have interesting experiences. If a person is just chained to a desk or to the children, then it's clear few people respect her.

13

THE CONSEQUENCES OF PARENTHOOD

The baby boomers as a group are not unlike previous generations in setting the family as a higher priority than work or leisure activities. But their definition of the word "family" seems surprisingly broad to the older generation.

"I have a mother and father, and a sister, a brother, and three or four nieces and nephews," Susan said. "That's my family." Turning to Gary, she asked, "Why do you think a family is only children?"

"Because that's what mine is," he replied.

"My family is not my own children," Susan replied, "but that makes them of no less significance to me. When I was younger, I fought all the time with my brother and sister. Now we are friends and really enjoy each other. Also we get along much better with my parents than we used to. So we often visit my parents."

"That's not so unusual," Bif said. "Lots of my friends take care of their parents, or see them often. I heard the other day at work that in the next twenty years one of the fastest-growing life-styles in America will be parents living with their retired children."

He paused to let the thought sink in. Then he added, "I'll bet that when Susan retires, she'll find her parents living with her."

"I wouldn't mind," Susan said. "I hope they live that long and stay healthy. Anyway," she added, "by then I'll be so old they won't cramp my social life."

Gary changed the subject. "One thing I've noticed," he said, "is how often people in their thirties these days ask each other, 'What are you going to do when you grow up?' That's a question I used to hear addressed to children, but never to adults. I know it's a playful question to some degree, but there is also a serious element in it. I've even heard the children of baby boomers ask their parents, 'What are you going to do when you grow up, Daddy (or Mommy)?' I guess the kids pick it up from their parents."

"I've heard that question often," Susan agreed. "I've asked it of myself."

"So have I," added Bif.

"Is the reason adults are asked the question that, even in their thirties, lots of people have not made a real commitment to an occupation or a profession?" Gary asked. "I've heard it said that your generation has prolonged childhood—that is, the period of life before people make lifelong decisions—but to prolong it into a person's middle age seems silly."

"Are the thirties middle age?" Susan asked.

"I thought so," Gary answered. "Don't you?"

"Not really," Bif answered. "I think today that middle age starts about forty. People live longer, and can stay young longer, so I think middle age starts later."

"I think it's inevitable," Gary said, "that people begin to ask questions about their lives as they get to be forty: Whether they've done what they want. What should a person do with the rest of his or her life? What's important to them?

"If family is the number one priority for the baby boomers," Gary continued, "they are also the first generation to have such complete control over the decision to have children. Birth-control techniques have had a huge effect, and one result is that baby boomers are putting off the decision to have children until the last possible moment."

"There are different situations," Susan interjected. "There are always different situations. When they're teenagers, people experiment and they don't know a lot, and sometimes they get pregnant. But that doesn't happen very often when people are in their twenties and thirties. Then people have children because they've decided they want them.

"Children are a big commitment," she continued. "They make you change your whole life.

"A good friend of mine and her husband decided to have children. She says that if she had continued her corporate career, she would never have been able to raise a child. Only by running a business—which she and her husband bought—could she manage to work and raise her child. But even then, she said it's hard. Good child care is hard to find. She's been listed at the hospital's day-care center for six months, but hasn't gotten her son in yet.

"She's an interesting person. She thinks of herself as very traditional in that she wants to promote the basic values. But she also insists on having time for herself. When I ask her why she keeps working, she answers that a career makes you feel good about yourself as well as about your leisure time."

"One of the men at my office," Bif said, "has done something somewhat similar. He was one of our most effective people on the consulting side. So he was in continual demand and was traveling constantly. He has three young children and he decided to find a way to travel less. But he wanted to make a lot of money nonetheless. So he quit his job and joined some friends who had started a retail business. He agreed to run the administrative side for a salary, an ownership interest, and with an agreement on how often he would have to be out of town. It seems strange to go to a small but rapidly growing company in order to have time to spend with your family—but it has worked for him. He says the key consideration in agreeing to go with these fellows as a partner was the opportunity to be home at night with his children."

"When people my age were having children," Gary observed, grinning, "the key question was how to bring them up. For most people a strict upbringing was abandoned for a much more permissive one."

"The discussion was always about what was better for the children's emotional and intellectual development," Susan said, "as I've heard about those days. But I suspect that the children of my generation were brought up permissively because our parents didn't really want to be that involved with us. It gave adults free time."

Gary smiled. "Maybe so," he said, "but I wonder, what are the big questions that your generation faces in bringing up children?"

"We may not be the right people to ask," Bif responded. "Neither of us has children."

MAKING CHOICES ABOUT CHILDREN

In our interviews baby boomers talked extensively about the issues involved in having and raising children.

"I think the problem is how to have children but still keep time for yourself," one woman said. "I have an infant, and a three-day-a-week job. It's hard to have the job because it takes time away from home. It isn't that my job is more important to me than my personal and leisure life; instead, it provides a break from child-rearing. I delayed having a child until I was in my thirties because I wanted my own job and financial independence. Then I refused to have a child unless my husband would help raise it. He irons, shops, cleans, and does his share. We cooperate to find time to do the things we both used to take for granted before the baby—like being able to take a shower," she said.

"My experience with my children," said a thirty-eight-year-old man, "is that they reawaken parts of me that would lie dormant otherwise. As they grow, I live my own life over through their lives and experiences, and because I'm older, I have a different perspective than when I went through childhood the first time—I enjoy it more and get different things out of it. I can enjoy what I was too immature and inexperienced to enjoy before.

"Raising young children also allows me to exorcise certain demons by doing with my own children what I wished my parents had done differently with me. When I was a boy, my parents never stressed physical fitness, and it was years before I got straightened out and got into shape. I've felt much better since I accomplished that. So I've tried to help my children be fit from the start."

Two major issues kept coming up in talking to baby boomers about their children, or about the choice whether or not to have children. The first involved keeping time for oneself; the second, transmitting one's own values to the children.

In part the concern about transmitting values arises from the baby boomers' perception that their own parents were very unsuccessful in transferring traditional values to them. That so many of the previous generations' values were rejected by its children was among the most bitter things older people had to bear. The World War II generation had won wars; it had done well economically. They were a great success on their own terms, except many of their children rejected them as hypocritical.

Baby boomers remember the violent and wrenching scenes they and their parents went through years ago. And now they are beginning to have a big problem translating their values to their own children. For example, they believe in relationships, in sharing things, experiences, and thoughts; "let me share this with you" is a common expression. Children, in particular, require time, not just tending and support, for a relationship to develop. But the pressures of work and the multiple interests of baby boomers make it very hard for them to give much time to their children. Hence, the invention of the concept of "quality time," which seems, from our interviews to be as much derided as accepted by baby boomer parents. Many of them say that if you don't give time to your children, they aren't really your own.

Children, they say, take on characteristics and values of the people they spend time with: the parent who is at home and the baby-sitter, not the competitor parent who is always at work. People wonder how an absentee parent's values can get transmitted to his or her children.

Are baby boomers just as hypocritical as they accused their parents of being? The older generation spoke of human values, but seemed to be inordinately materialistic. Many baby boomers speak of values and priorities and the primacy of human relationships, yet have no time for their children.

Our interviewers talked to a woman in her early thirties who has a young son. We asked her if she worked and what was important to her. She answered that work was not as important to her as her personal life and leisure time—many baby boomers told us this in various contexts— but she said she needed to do both, about fifty-fifty. We asked why.

"Because," she said, "work is a necessity financially. Also, work fulfills me as a person. I want to be an individual, not just Rick's wife and Shawn's mother. I need another identity besides mother and wife." So she works full-time and finds what time she can for her son.

Like many baby boomers, this woman seems somewhat inconsistent.

She says her personal life is most important to her, but she leaves little time for it.

As committed to basic values as they are, baby boomers may be devastated if their children turn out differently and reject them. Yet this may happen because so many parents say that while personal relationships are very important to them, they don't have time to have them with their children.

Does that make them hypocritical? Will their children perceive that and reject them, just as so many baby boomers rejected their parents years ago? The possibility is there.

Baby boomers do ponder this dilemna. Some have even gone so far as to tell us that one of the reasons they hesitate to have children is that they are afraid of how they might turn out. But millions of baby boomers are having children. Will they be good parents or not? There seem to be two different views among baby boomers about this issue.

One view is that those who are having children at a relatively advanced age—in their thirties—will be very good parents. The argument for this view is that these people really want children or they wouldn't have them; it's a deep commitment.

Others ask, "Is it? Or are they having children because time is running out? They're not sure whether they want them or not, but they must have them now or they won't be able to later."

My own opinion is that, by and large, those who are having children want them badly. Because they are getting older, they must act sooner rather than later. Also, they are old enough to know what is important in life and what isn't.

On average, baby boomers will have fewer children than their parents did. They will have less opportunity to learn from experience about raising children. And people do learn from experience.

A woman in her forties told me what one of her children said to her. She has four sons, the youngest of whom is now fourteen. He said, "Mother, I've compared you to the other mothers, and I'm very glad you're my mother. You're not as strict as the others."

She was very surprised. His oldest brother, she said, used to spend weekends visiting neighbor's houses trying to find any other mother as strict as she was.

"But maybe my youngest son is right," she continued. "Maybe after three other children, some of the things that seemed so important before just aren't really critical. I relax because I know what is important and what isn't."

When people have only one or two children, as they do nowadays, by the time they learn how to raise a family by trial and error, they don't have any more children to raise. And the next generation will be made up exclusively of only and second children.

Still, baby boomers say they will profit from the greater openness and honesty they have with their children. They don't hide things like their parents used to. Many subjects were very hush-hush when the boomers were young. Topics that they could never discuss with their parents, many now discuss openly with their children.

Baby boom parents who worry about transmitting their values try a variety of devices. Some take their children to church. But churches teach primarily traditional values, and many baby boomers are uncomfortable with that approach. Many churches don't teach tolerance for the different ways people live, something many baby boomers believe in. Also, many churches teach submission to authority; many don't believe in this. Finally, churches teach organized religion, which boomers often think is outdated. Hence, many of these parents are unwilling to rely on religious institutions to help transmit values to their children.

In the end they are thrown back on their own devices, and their children's attitudes are largely shaped by schools, the mass media, and peer groups.

Ironically, many baby boomers who rejected their parents' concerns find that today they are concerned about the same things their parents were.

Some of them even flee back to the suburbs. "We can't afford to live in the city now that we have children." So they move out to the end of the commuter line and worry that they are regressing. Yet many seem relieved to be able to drop out of the struggle to have it all in the city.

The children of American baby boomers face a disturbing picture worldwide. It's not that they are bad children, but they are such a minority. They are a small, highly privileged group—with counterparts in every industrialized country—in an age in which nine tenths of the children live in the Third World, and most of whom are very poor by U.S. standards. Children in our country, at least a lot of them, are like the elite of the earth—kings and queens. They receive from their parents what by world standards is great wealth and opportunity—but also the isolation that comes from being in a minority.

"When I think about having children," said a thirty-year-old man, "I have a sense of powerlessness. In this country we do well with our businesses, but not with our children. I don't think I can protect my children or even have much influence on my children's education."

"The competition among parents to see that their children get ahead is really something," a woman commented. "My friends are putting their children into school six hours a day, five days a week, at two years old. This isn't only to get rid of the kid while the parents work or do other things. It's also to try to get a head start for the child. They say the children will be able to read and do addition before the first grade."

These, of course, are competitors trying to make competitors out of their children.

If a child starts school at age two, and has four years of schooling before first grade, as many now do, then someone who prepares for a professional career will spend twenty-two or twenty-four years in school.

What kinds of people will result from this excessive preparation? What values will the competitors transmit?

One parent said, "When my child comes to me fifteen years from now and says, 'We have this great new drug we're doing in college,' what am I going to say in response? I guess my response will be quite different from my parents' when I said that to them because I had the drug experience and they didn't."

The questions of having children and how to raise them are true tests of the values of the baby boomers. They decide whether to have them or not; and if they do have them, how to define the roles of husband and wife; and what to try to teach the children to believe. Yet, whatever the baby boomers do, their children are likely to be very different from what they expect, just as they themselves turned out very differently from what their parents had expected.

DOING MORE THAN IS POSSIBLE

When a couple has children, there is a big potential for trouble between them. In many instances when they both have careers, the man says, "You must care for the children because my job is more important," or "You must care for the children because that's the traditional role."

A woman in her early thirties told us that she was very unhappy about this. She and her husband had just moved into a new house; she had a professional job and a three-year-old son. She said she knew she should be happy. But she told this story:

"I was one of those women who had a child late in life. It's such a hassle getting him taken care of. I advertised for months to get someone to pick him up after day care, bring him back to the house and stay with him till I got home from work at six. Not a single person called. So finally I told my boss that I was quitting. I was giving up work. I'd stay home.

"He was very nice. He said that I could take a leave and come back later. Or maybe we could work something out part time next year. I can go talk to him about it when I'm ready.

"Yesterday I had five women over with their kids, all two- or three-year-olds like my son. We all agreed we'd got a raw deal. None of us could work. The men helped with the house and the kids, but it wasn't even. We still had all the responsibility. It isn't a fair system and we got the short end of the stick."

"It's like this," another woman said. "My husband told me, 'I'm more likely to be successful. So you,' he said, 'should care for our children. You should live with that in terms of your career, whether you lose your job, or slow up what you're doing, or fall off the promotion ladder, or take a leave, or whatever. You do it. I'm going to press ahead,' he said.

"This causes me a lot of bitterness," she continued. "If I give up my career, I risk not being an interesting person anymore. I also risk my husband no longer respecting me—despite what he says. In the end he'll act on what he feels, not what he thinks and says."

On the other hand, if a man and woman agree, as many do, to share the care of the children, then the companies they work for will often cause discord because the companies don't have a structure that permits such sharing to occur. Then the resentment of both the man and the woman turns against the companies.

This is a major problem, and it is rarely being solved. As a practical matter, many people cope on a day-to-day basis. Their bosses also cope by simply accepting their employees' family commitments, and by permitting informal time away from work for child rearing. This might generate loyalty and gratitude to the supervisor personally but not to the company.

Executives will generally acknowledge, if asked, that they are much more willing to make such accommodations for women employees than for men. Hence, there is another reason for a man to press a woman to care for the children—because more often her supervisor will permit her the flexibility to do so when his will not.

To some degree, many companies do try to accommodate the needs of families when both parents work. But a general social-support system that would make it easy for employees to work and have a family largely doesn't exist.

There seems to be a real crisis for the married woman who has a career and children. These women say they get worked to death, and that no one helps or takes their complaints seriously, a fact that was repeatedly brought home to our interviewers by women who are in this position. Recent studies show that a married woman works more hours than a single parent. A married woman with children spends eighty-five hours per week on job, homemaking, and child care. A single female parent spends seventy-five hours. A married male parent and a single male parent each spend sixty-five hours; and a nonparent of either sex spends fifty-five hours. So a married female parent spends half again as much time per week on job, homemaking, and child care than does a nonparent.[1]

Most baby boomers have children. Our survey found that 62 percent of our respondents supported at least one child. Many supported two or more, and a few had as many as six children.

It was often remarkable how parents were trying to take care of the children in their lives.

"I've gone through a divorce," a thirty-seven-year-old woman in New Hampshire told us. "Things have changed for me desperately. I work night and day. Besides raising a family, I work for an insurance company and I'm a private-duty nurse at night."

She added, "I think that although I'm working several jobs to keep afloat, I'm not interested in material objects. I'm not at all concerned with getting ahead. I'm just concerned with keeping up.

"I don't stand up with the yuppie attitude," she continued. "I think most women think they should be the Enjoli woman," she continued.

"According to the commercial, a woman is supposed to be a professional woman, mother, beautiful, and still have everything in hand. It's driving women mad trying to do it."

Probably women do have the hardest time coping with the multiple demands which family and work impose on them. But we also found men who were trying to juggle a great number of commitments.

A twenty-seven-year-old man in Iowa told us that he is "balancing marriage, children, graduate school, and a job. I think I'm doing pretty well," he said. "I'm moving upward. The effort's not hurting me too much financially. Most of my friends aren't married, working, and going to school like I am. I'm doing more juggling. I think what I'm doing is pretty cool."

One day I conducted a discussion among a group of male executives, many of whom were baby boomers. They began to discuss the pressures in their lives. They identified five key objectives. Then several of them advanced the proposition that the five objectives could be put in a certain order and pursued sequentially. That is, a man would pursue the first, then the second, the third, etc., as his life progressed.

Careers, advancement, position, and status had to be first, they argued, because if a person didn't build a career when he was young, then it would be too late because other people would be too far ahead.

Second in the sequence was wealth. This apparently meant a decent net worth that would give them some financial independence.

Third they placed their families. It wasn't, they hastened to explain, that they felt their families were less important than work. Quite the contrary. But they had to spend more time working while they were young because that was when they could advance most rapidly and build a nest egg.

Fourth was a contribution to their communities. This also would have to wait until their careers were far enough advanced.

Fifth was balance in their own lives. As they explained it, balance was to be achieved by pursuing the preceding four objectives in sequence.

Many executives in the room had thought out their life plans in these terms, and were firmly committed to carrying them out. But there were others who insisted that life could not be balanced by doing things sequentially. If a person commits himself primarily to a career between the ages of twenty and forty, they said, he will miss the opportunity to know his family. One day he will wake up and his children will be teenagers and he will never have known them. They said, "you will ask, 'Where did the years go?' "

Some of the men who stressed this point of view said they were speaking from personal experience. They had spent so much time at work when their children were young that they had never gotten to know them. Now they regretted it bitterly. There is no alternative, they insisted, but to try to do everything at once, somehow—try to find time for the family while building a career.

Baby boomers with children, women and men both, struggle to pour into their lives more than the vessel can contain.

PART THREE

THE IMPACT
ON INSTITUTIONS

14

THE LARGE CORPORATION: A GAME MANY PEOPLE DON'T WANT TO PLAY

WHAT BABY BOOMERS THINK ABOUT THEIR EMPLOYERS

"One thing I don't understand at all," a young businesswoman told us, "is how people in my generation can work for a big company. I don't see how a person can trust them. A big company is all politics."

In our survey complaints like these about employers, especially large companies, were continual. Finally, our interviewers asked respondents directly whether they thought companies were meeting the needs of people in their generation. Sixty percent answered that companies were not meeting their needs. Only 21 percent said there was a match of company practices and individual needs. Almost as many (19 percent) said they were unsure because they didn't work for private corporations or wouldn't answer the question.

We asked, What is the problem specifically? Responses were of the following type:

"I don't think employers are in contact with the work force," said a thirty-eight-year-old insurance agent from Virginia. "They see the figures; but we see people's attitudes. In my company there is a big gap."

An auto designer, who had until recently worked with one of the major automobile manufacturers, told us why he left. "In our company, management didn't seem to believe employees were accomplishing anything. . . . In my case I was offered a promotion and I still left. What angered me was that they took a benefit away. What I disliked was the way they handled it. I had a company car. The management made a broad-scale decision to take away company cars. They handled everyone as one big group clear across the corporation. They simply said, 'This will no longer be a benefit.' The management didn't care if individuals merited the cars. The company has gotten so big, they've forgotten about the individual. It was a hell of a reduction in pay I took, but I left."

A twenty-three-year-old man in Illinois told us, "People my age don't like a lot of things in the business world. First of all, this generation has been given the freedom to do as it pleases. Freedom is promoted in college. When you get to work, they want you to conform; they want you to show up at eight A.M., take a half hour for lunch at noon, and leave at five P.M. People my age want flexible time. Maybe employers should let people come in between seven-thirty and nine-thirty A.M. We'd work our eight hours when we want to. Even though someone else is the boss, we need some control and we want some say in the work that we do!"

To many managers, an attitude like this is the antithesis of what the workplace needs. To hear a young person insist on flexibility in work times, and also on some say in the business, is very provoking. Instead, many managers feel, they have to establish that the boss really is the boss.

From this very common management attitude, it should follow that a hardworking, long-hours employee is appreciated by management. Right? Unfortunately, many respondents in our survey say, "Wrong."

An advertising account executive in Texas told us about herself and her employer. "For a single twenty-five-year-old I'm pretty settled in my career," she began. "I'm very dedicated to my job, more so than most people I know. I'm farther along in my career, due to hard work and long hours.

"As for my company, I think as far as employee wages go, they are doing well. But everyone always needs little perks. An executive workout area would be beneficial. Employees where I work put in a lot of time, often fourteen- to sixteen-hour days. Managers should be aware what employees are putting into the company. They need to give a more personal touch to the workers. Upper management needs to get involved. We feel like they could get to know employees and treat them as human beings, not as a number. Just a thank-you would be nice. Let people feel important, whether they're a janitor or a manager. Managers should get more involved with employees; it would mean a lot. It would show they care."

Almost identical words were used by a thirty-one-year-old man in Illinois who works in a very different business. "In the construction business you are just a number," he told us. "Workers come and go. There is too little pride of workmanship. Companies should try to develop pride of workmanship. The auto industry is the same. Employers should get together with their employees and try to work together. Some companies do set up workout rooms and involve the employees in the company."

Said another young man, "I think that basically the workplace has gotten too large. People aren't treated as individuals. They're just a name. Nobody learns about the problems of each individual employee. I think employers should appoint someone to get to know people. The workplace is just too impersonal. People never get thanked for the good things. They only hear from the boss about the bad things."

A thirty-year-old New Yorker made a similar point. "A lot of employers are from the old school, so to speak. The turnover in the company I work for is incredible! The biggest thing is that they don't consider people's problems. So many managers are into their own career development, they don't take into consideration their own employees' needs. Employers, for the most part, don't communicate with employees. In the old school, they just told people what to do. That doesn't work anymore. Now they also have to say why we should do it. They must give some reasons why. They need to treat employees more like people."

These types of comments, which could be multiplied many times over in our survey, echo the insistence, reported in Chapter 11 on success, that bosses are disrespectful to their employees.

Note what the complaint is not. It is not about being made to work too hard. It isn't about pay and working conditions. It's about a lack of being treated as an individual and a lack of respect and care as a human being.

Were none of the survey respondents satisfied with their jobs? A few were.

"I'm very pleased with the company I'm currently working for," a thirty-six-year-old manufacturer's representative in Michigan told us. "I left a large company about eighteen months ago. I wasn't happy with the company I was working for because I wasn't being recognized for my skills and my needs weren't being met. I work for a much smaller company now. The firm I work for now has twelve salesmen and a secretarial staff of eight and two owners. From the first day I started working at this new firm, I was given an assignment and it was up to me how I was to handle it. What I do, and how I do it, are left entirely up to me. That's a real motivating factor. In a large corporation, everything is laid out for you. If you break from the traditional mold, you're labeled as a rabblerouser or a freak!"

There was even a woman who had good things to say for a large company where she was employed. She was a thirty-one-year-old bank manager from Kentucky. "I feel very fortunate to work for the company I do. They put a lot of value on the future of employees. They do career-pathing; we have stock ownership; and they have an excellent retirement plan for us. All those things make work more satisfying. The company really fosters employee growth. I've taken a number of training courses. I just finished the second Dale Carnegie course."

Favorable comments about employers were more often made about smaller companies. Said a cable electonics technician, twenty-seven years old, from Pennsylvania, "I work in a fairly young company. We have young executives as well as young employees. Our company offers a lot of benefits and incentives. They have schooling, advancement, and bonuses. The average age of the worker is between twenty-one and thirty years old. I have no problem with my company."

A twenty-five-year-old paralegal in Ohio discussed her employer, a law office. "The firm where I work is very nice. We call each other and the attorneys by first names, and we all interact as equals. Informality helps a lot. Also the willingness to take time with people of a lesser status. Employees are all in the same work area; you don't have someone sitting off in an ivory tower because they have more status."

For the most part, it seems that the age-old division between employer and employee continues in the United States, regardless of the change of generations. But the larger companies seem more unfeeling and undesirable, on balance, to baby boomers than do smaller firms; and the baby boomer is far more likely than his or her parents to make dissatisfaction known to management, and to leave a position he or she considers unpleasant. It is, after all, a very independent generation.

"My father's relationship with his company is a lot different from my relationship with my company," a thirty-five-year-old California insurance agent explained. "My father would stand up for his company, right or wrong. He'd do whatever they'd tell him to do. But my generation would say, 'No, we're not going to do it.' If the company insists, people in my generation would just go do something else. They'd find another job."

THE GENERATION GAP IN THE WORKPLACE

The very different value systems of the baby boomers and the older generation sometimes come into conflict at work. When this occurs, people of good will can get caught in the middle. A revealing example of this was once recounted to me by an executive in a large midwestern company.

"I sometimes think I've made my career trying to mediate between the two generations in our company," he began, "since I'm in my mid-forties and kind of fall between the two groups. I remember once I hired a young professional to manage an important new project for the company, which top management had agreed would take about eighteen months to get firmly launched. My new manager went to work with great dedication. Within six months the new person had attracted so much attention in top management ranks that my boss told me the new person was to receive a promotion and a transfer. I knew my young star would want to be asked—not told—about the promotion, so I suggested to my boss that I ask the new manager about it.

" 'What's to ask?' my boss said. 'It's a promotion and the company needs this person in this job.' My boss had been with the company many years. Long ago he and his wife had come to an understanding that when the company wanted him to take a new assignment, he simply asked what and where. Were he being offered this assignment, he would have nothing to consider. He was the old-style company man, now a high-level executive. 'What,' he asked me, 'would your young manager have to consider?'

" 'I don't know,' I told him, 'but I think I'd better ask just the same.'

"So I told my star about the promotion opportunity. The only response I got was request for time on the weekend to think it over.

"When I reported to my manager that our hot prospect had asked for time to think it over, he grew very angry. 'What is there to think about?' he said again, and he recounted once more how many different assignments he had accepted from the company without asking for time to think anything over. The more he talked about the situation, the angrier he got. 'If your young manager wants to think over this promotion,' he said, 'maybe we picked the wrong person to offer it to.' He instructed me to report to him the minute I heard from the young person.

"It was Monday morning when I received a reply from my star. Yes, the promotion and transfer were acceptable.

" 'If you don't mind my asking,' I asked the young manager, 'why did you want to think it over? What were you thinking about?'

" 'I wasn't sure that I felt right about leaving my project at this point, unfinished,' was the reply I got. 'I took this job because I was really interested in doing the work, and I wanted to think it over before I agreed to do something else, even if it was a promotion. So I talked to my staff over the weekend and I think that they can finish the project if I help them from time to time. So I think I'm free to take on something else.'

"I thought this incident was very revealing," the man in the middle told me. "My boss is an organization man, and he and the young manager are very different. But one is not clearly more valuable to the company than the other. Unthinking obedience is not necessarily more desirable than carefully considered commitment. My company needs both, and I think it may be able to operate in the future as effectively with people who think before they act as it has in the past with people who obey."

I told this story at a conference of executives from another midwestern firm. At the luncheon that followed, one of the managers told me that he had just been on the phone to his company's West Coast operation. The executive in charge had just offered management jobs to two of the company's best young people. One had said no. He had children in school and didn't want to travel as much as a manager would have to. The other employee said that he was already making just as much as a salesman as he could as a manager. So why should he take on the additional hassles and obligations of being a manager? He asked for time to think the promotion offer over, but indicated he'd probably turn it down.

The vice-president in charge of the western region was furious. "We made offers to the wrong persons," he fumed. "These guys are too dumb to be managers."

Why too dumb? Because they had a different set of priorities and greater independence than the older generation? This seems an unusual basis on which to conclude that a younger person lacks intelligence.

The independence of baby boomers is evident in many ways. For example, the attitude at college reunions is changing dramatically. When I first went to reunions twenty years ago, if a person told someone that he or she worked for a large company, it carried a lot of status. Other people were impressed by the security that a position in a big company implied; and they envied large companies for their size, success, and power. They respected the people who ran them and who worked for them.

Today it's very different. At a reunion I went to last fall, people were most impressed when someone admitted to owning his or her own company, and working for themselves. It didn't seem to matter how large the company was—or even if it were successful or not. What mattered was the sense of independence, of freedom, of being one's own boss. When someone said that he or she worked for a big company, people were very likely to respond, "Oh, that's too bad. It must be hard on you, working in that environment."

Even those who run big companies share a little bit of the same attitude. Even they don't think their firms are creative, innovative, or growing. I recall the chairman of a large company saying, "We aren't the ones creating jobs; we're not the entrepreneurs."[1] What is valued by baby boomers, and increasingly by society as a whole, is initiative and independence and entrepreneurship.

The surveys we have done suggest that the brightest baby boomers think big corporations are too bureaucratic; that the companies want people to follow rules, to stay in place and wait their turn, all of which baby boomers resist. The companies don't value initiative, they say;

companies don't let people exercise intelligent discretion or grow in their jobs. They don't let young people take risks or get large rewards if they do something outstanding.

THE CLASH OF VALUES

At the core of the generation gap in companies, especially the larger ones, is a clash of baby boomers' values with the managerial politics in large corporations.

In working for a large organization, the dynamics of interpersonal relations are as important as the ability to do the work involved.[2] Corporations are not just economic creatures. They are also stages on which human emotions are acted out: desires for personal success and recognition, jealousy, fear, greed, envy, and even rage. Managers and fellow employees have egos, fantasies, hangups, and racial, ethnic or religious biases. All these human aspects of the work environment have to be managed successfully by employees in large organizations.

The older generation developed a certain way of dealing with complex human interactions in a business. It accepted different standards for the corporate office and for nonbusiness relationships. People were expected to have two different faces: an organization face for the office, and a more human face at other times and places.

To be successful, a manager accepted that subordinates must be manipulated to do what the company wanted. People were enticed to stay in jobs by being offered promotions or other advantages that often never materialized. Ideas and creativity were solicited from people, and credit or rewards were often not forthcoming.

Subordinates tried to manipulate their superiors in order to advance up the corporate ladder themselves. People became "yes" people or "organization" people, agreeing with the boss so as to get ahead, suppressing their own individuality and desires, doing what the organization wanted.

These aspects of corporate life are very disturbing to many baby boomers, especially the more creative and individualistic.

I recall a discussion with some young managers. The experience of an older man with a large company came up during our talk. This man had been with his company for fifteen years, doing operations-type jobs. It was a big company, headquartered in New York. He'd been identified as a troubleshooter, a turnaround artist. He'd been getting promoted, but had never had any assignments at corporate headquarters. One day the company made an acquisition in the Midwest. This executive was sent there with three other managers to try to straighten out the newly acquired company because it was having difficulties. They were able to turn it around quickly and bring the company to profitability. But his company had left the previous management in charge of the acquired company, and the top executive didn't like the people from the home office. So slowly he forced most of them out—into retirement or resignation. The corporate office did nothing about it. Finally, the troubleshooter, who was still at the newly acquired subsidiary, complained to his old boss and was transferred back to corporate headquarters.

But there was no position for him there. "We can't force you on the president of a division," they told him, "but we're looking for a place for you." They told him what a good job he'd done for them in the past. He asked them for a different assignment, to get some experience outside of operations. But they told him, "No, we want the company to get the benefit of your expertise." In effect, they said to him, "You won't be good at anything else."

After six months of not finding a position for him, they told the man they were going to send him to some seminars outside the company. They said, "While you're there, look around a little. We think you're a great guy and we're still looking for a position for you, but you might find something better if you look outside the company."

He asked his friends, "Why do the guys at corporate headquarters who never handled a tough position get the promotions, while a person like me who has made the company millions of dollars straightening out troubled operations gets eased out? Why do political connections in headquarters count for more than performance? My company has a great reputation, but I think it's only for the TV cameras."

The company's top executives never told him he isn't wanted, or why they were dissatisfied with him, but they slowly pushed him out the door.

The group of young managers discussed whether or not they'd want to be told by management they were no longer wanted. "I would want some feedback," one said. "I think a company owes it to people to tell them where they stand. It may be good news or bad; hard to accept or easy. A person ought to know whether he or she has a chance to go up several levels, or will not move from where he or she is."

There was no unanimity on this issue. One manager disagreed, and defended the company. "I don't agree with the psychology of that," he said. "If you tell someone that in the judgment of the top brass, 'you're plateaued,' he'll be crushed and stop trying to get ahead. And conversely, if you tell a person, 'You're super; there are only two of you in the company,' then she'll go back to her office and put her feet up on the desk and sit back and slow down."

"I don't think so," the first responded. "If you have a twenty-eight-year-old person and you know he'll never go up, you have a responsibility to tell him."

"It's the same old game-playing," a young man exclaimed. "Corporate practices are just like the old-style interpersonal relations. They're not honest; they're exploitive; they're all games, not fair play; they're tactful. . . ."

"I thought tactful was good," I interrupted.

"I don't," he said. "I think tact is just a mask for being deceitful. I don't think people should pretend things are okay when they're not."

A basic value of the baby boom generation is honesty. With it goes a desire to know the score. Also, young people want to be one person with one face. "Like me as I am or don't like me at all," they seem to say. What they expect in their personal relationships, they think ought to apply to business relations.

This attitude is very threatening to the older generation of managers. It exposes their personal feelings to others. These managers simply don't share the same values and fail to comprehend how important honesty is to many younger people.

And so most companies will not share with younger people confidential assessments done for purposes of management-succession planning. The companies believe that there will be motivational problems if people are told the truth. They are also afraid of the internal political consequences of sharing the information.

Some managers hesitate to disclose promotion opportunities elsewhere in a large organization, either for fear of losing good staff or because they do not want to risk having to tell unsuccessful applicants why they did not get the position.

"At the company I work for now," a young woman once told me, "there was a vacancy for the job of manager of external communications. Two of us women in the unit applied for the job. The company president appointed a small task force to choose a person to fill the job. Because the company wanted to meet affirmative-action commitments, it solicited outside applicants and interviewed the women who applied.

"Meanwhile, the other internal female candidate was told she would not be selected. They didn't even give her an opportunity to submit a résumé or give her an interview. I was interviewed briefly. The task force, all males, offered the job to an outside woman applicant who was really outstanding, but it was a position and a salary far below what she would command in the marketplace. So she rejected the offer. The committee then hired a man from the outside.

"I was very much embittered by the process—more so than by its outcome. Neither of us women already at the company felt we got a fair opportunity to present our qualifications for the job. I think they couldn't figure out how to tell us we wouldn't get the job, if that was the decision they reached. So they tried to keep us out of it and selected someone else."[3]

Managers also resist telling employees when they are doing a poor job. An employee's poor performance may make the manager look bad for having hired that person, and the manager tries to ease out poor performers instead. However, from a baby boomer's perspective, a person who isn't told he or she is doing badly has no real opportunity to improve and may start a downward career slope without even being aware of it.

As a consequence of all this, many baby boomers turn off on large institutions. Because they often have economic freedom, they move away from big companies.

Recently top graduates from business schools have been going increasingly to investment banking houses and consulting firms. These young people get more money than people who take jobs at other kinds of companies, and they also get freedom to work on more significant projects. They know the jobs are killers, often requiring seventy or even eighty hours a week. It's like working at two jobs, which is why the companies pay so much.

Later in their careers, many go from the investment banks and consulting firms into a big corporate job. But even this move is often only a stepping-stone.

To many top business-school students the ideal career is to start out on Wall Street in an investment bank, brokerage house, or an investment fund, and specialize in a particular industry.

A person gets to know an industry from the point of view of financial analysis, then he or she goes to work for a company in that industry for several years, learning operations. Then, at thirty-five or so, he or she assembles a group of people and starts a company. By then, the individual knows the business—both financially and operationally; he or she can raise start-up money and knows how to run the company. Then the business is expanded rapidly. The idea is to have fun and make a lot of money.

A survey done by the Harvard Business School's student newspaper showed that out of sixteen hundred MBA candidates, about 40 percent want to work for their own companies by the time they're fifteen or twenty years out of business school.[4]

The result is that big companies that are not consulting firms or investment banks no longer get the best potential managers directly out of business school. They get some of them in mid-career, and keep some of them till they retire; but others leave to set up their own companies and become competitors.

One young man told us, "I think that in the next ten to fifteen years the younger people will get fed up with the big companies. There'll be a dramatic change because companies aren't meeting the needs of this generation. Everyone is asking himself, 'Where do I fit into this big organization for the next fifteen years? Don't I really want to get out of here and do something different?' "

"I know I'm thinking about that," a woman added. "I'm the tail end of the baby boom. My friends and I think that there are just too many people ahead of us. The numbers in the pipelines at the big companies are just too daunting. It's not realistic to think that we'll get to the top no matter how well we do. And anyway a big company is not such a great place to be.

"So my friends and I are all going to start our own companies. We're going to build down from ourselves. Rather than rise in a big organization, we'll start our own organizations where we're at the top and add people below us."

Because the big companies have lost their attraction for so many of the best talent in the baby boom generation, in the long term, they have only two major assets: They have the advantage of name recognition and brand identification, and they have the ability to raise significant amounts of capital. But most of them are so short of ideas on what to do with the capital that they have more capacity to raise money than to use it. This is one explanation why there have been recent waves of corporate takeovers: Big companies had a largely unused capacity to borrow, in part because they were too conservative financially, and partly because they have too few ideas for what to do with the capital.

The big companies no longer have the best young people; often they don't even have the most up-to-date technology; and they aren't innovative. The result is that they often appear to be sitting ducks for takeover artists or for competition from entrepreneurs.

If larger companies resist changes in style and practices to accommodate young people, then they will starve for the best talent and receive little of value from the people they already employ. Even top managers seem distressed with the style of leadership in large companies. For more than fifteen years, data have been compiled on how managers in American companies rate their own managers. In the early 1970s more than 70 percent of managers gave their own superiors favorable ratings. By the mid-1980s, only 46 percent gave their bosses favorable ratings. It appears that the young generation doesn't care for how corporations are doing things.[5]

There are surprising echoes of this sentiment among older managers, some of whom are aware of the attitudes of the baby boomers. I recall, in particular, the comment of an executive in his fifties when asked how he thought young managers whom he wished to hire perceived his company. "I think they believe we are not progressive, don't listen to young people, and aren't accepting any new ideas," he answered. Apparently, he had recently been in a top-management meeting to discuss why the company wasn't getting good young people to come aboard. "Young people want to get where there are younger managers and where they see an opportunity to advance," he told me. "And this company doesn't fit the bill."

15

HOW BABY BOOMERS WANT THEIR COMPANIES TO CHANGE

Baby boomers carry their values to the workplace and expect to be treated by their employers in accordance with those values. When aspects of the working environment and the aspirations of people are in concert, then employees are reasonably content and effective in their positions. When treatment at the job and values are not in concert, dissonance, discord, and a lack of comfort cause poor performance. In such a setting, people are easily turned aside from their tasks. Hence, companies that understand the values of the people they employ, and attempt to meet their expectations, are more likely to be successful than those which do not.

TREATING PEOPLE AS INDIVIDUALS

The major criticism baby boomers direct at the corporations which employ them is that they are not respected as individuals. In light of this criticism, it is not surprising that when asked what they thought ought to be changed, the largest proportion (46 percent) of our survey respondents said that managers needed to pay attention to employees' needs. But what do people mean by this in practice?

Among the suggestions for dealing with baby boomers that we gleaned from interviews are the following:

"I think older managers ought to talk less and listen more," said one woman. "Most of the people of my generation are very articulate and are willing to share their concerns and ideas."

Another woman said, "The hospital that I work for is really good as far as benefits go, but the working conditions are sometimes bad, i.e., they act like we don't know what we're doing even though we've been doing it for years. They don't consider our opinions at all, even though they usually end up doing things the way we would have. They should consider our opinions more."

This is the matter that causes the most complaints: a perceived unwillingness by managers to listen to the people who report to them. But respondents mentioned other problems as well.

"I think managers ought not to meddle with the activities of their subordinates," said one man. "People ought to be left free to do their jobs in their own way, so long as they understand the objectives and their project is on track."

"Companies need to know young people's threshold of boredom," said a thirty-four-year-old accountant in Massachusetts. "They ought to avoid boredom if they want my generation to be productive."

"It's a help to me," another suggested, "when my boss helps me set priorities for my work. I have a tendency to get diverted easily and sometimes I don't recognize diversions for what they are. Priorities and schedules are best based on experience, something older managers have a lot of."

In this and other ways, companies have an opportunity to adapt to the values and interests of young people. Since baby boomers value new experiences and the opportunity to learn and grow, companies ought to offer them frequent new assignments and challenges, though not every new assignment need be a promotion.

A serious problem is that people of the previous generation, who carry the legacy of the Great Depression, think it is dangerous to train and develop other people. They fear that a newly trained person may take over the job of the one who did the training. Many people think job security lies in making themselves indispensable by ensuring that the company will have no replacement for them.

But in a larger perspective, this type of thinking is self-defeating. If the company can't do without a person in his current job, then it can't afford to promote him or train him for a future promotion. So, not training a replacement can limit someone's career. Nevertheless, scarcity thinking by higher-level managers does tend to limit the developmental opportunities offered younger people.

To fit the values of baby boomers, it is important to have managers who will be honest about the company and their position in it. Dealing with people in a frank and open manner is the ideal of the performance-appraisal systems which exist in most companies but which are rarely well implemented by managers. Developing the ability to deal with people honestly is something that companies can foster in their management-training activities.

"Older managers are simply too authoritarian," said another man. "They view their job to be decision-makers who give clear direction to subordinates. But young people want to express their views or discuss alternatives."

Do baby boomers want to have a role in making their bosses' decisions? Do they want to have decisions made by vote or something similar?

Apparently baby boomers differ considerably in this regard. Some older managers insist that their younger subordinates really want to take part in making decisions. A vote by a committee of involved employees is what is desired, these managers believe.

Others say that boomers do not go that far in their desire for participation. Instead, most young people want an opportunity to put their ideas forward before the boss makes a decision. After that, however, it's the boss's responsibility to make it.

This latter attitude is probbly the most common among baby boomers. By and large, Americans are suspicious of decisions that emerge from a committee vote or a consensus process. We even joke about it. "A camel is an animal put together by a committee," goes an old one-liner.

Still, it is necessary to recognize individual differences. Some young people insist: "I want to have a role in the decision—not just an opportunity to have some input." Other baby boomers are undoubtedly looking for a consensus type of decision-making. One young manager of a large communications-services company explained his views in the following way:

"My generation," he began, "means something different by the term 'consensus' than do older executives. What they mean by a consensus is when they twist a guy's arm to go along so he agrees. But he doesn't want to agree, so they all know it isn't really a consensus and they don't act as if it is.

"But what we mean by 'consensus' is a real agreement among people so that everyone supports the decision completely. We expect it and we have a lot more tools to achieve it."

Regardless of his or her role in decision-making, if a boomer doesn't get consulted at all, he or she does not feel bound by a manager's decision. If any obligation is felt, it is only of a formal sort and there is no feeling of real loyalty or commitment to the decision. Baby boomers who have not been consulted do not put themselves out much to make the decision work out well.

Another thing business can do to improve its working relationship with baby boomers is to modify the usual standards of selection for promotion. Business ought to seek people who are influential in their peer group, not simply those who are able to present themselves as sympathetic to top management. Usually senior executives try to promote younger persons who are like themselves, sharing the values dear to the previous generation. But boomers who are like the previous generation make poor leaders of the rest of their age group.

I once talked to a group of executives about which of two candidates would make the best CEO for their company. The older managers picked a fellow who was described as dedicated to the company and decisive in his actions. What they seemed to mean was "We'd be happy to take orders from him." The younger managers picked a fellow who had traveled a lot, spoke several languages, and was an accomplished musician, in addition to being a good businessman. What they seemed to be saying was "We'd be happy to be influenced or led by him."

Baby boomers think a person ought to be honest with a company about what he or she is really like. One young man told us that when he had a job interview once, he thought, "I'd like to be hired," but still decided to go to the interview dressed casually. He said to himself, "After all, you're a casual person, and if you're going to be happy there, you'll have to be casual."

Some respondents in the survey told us that they had a good relationship with their supervisors. What they pointed to as the attractive aspects of the relationship is significant.

"My boss at the textile mill is forty-one," said one man. "I can talk to him and he listens. We sit down and discuss things all the time. It's a small business and I'm like his right-hand man. He's real good to work for."

Most married baby boomers have working spouses. Of those in our survey who were married, 79 percent had working spouses, three quarters of whom worked full time. Since many also have children, the conflicts between caring for children and work obligations can be frequent and dramatic. These conflicts occasioned a number of comments about employers.

"Companies need to be more yielding to employees, especially females," said a twenty-five-year-old woman who is now self-employed because of her disappointment with working for larger companies. "Female employees have more going on at home than men. Men don't have as many things to worry about. Women have family, husband, home, kids. Male supervisors need to be more sympathetic to the different needs of women. They need to be more encouraging to women."

Another woman told us, "I'd be back to work by now if it weren't for the lack of child care." She added, "I'm a very business-motivated person, even though I'm not working now because of the baby. I'm a competitor when I'm working."

"I'll tell you how I manage the young tigers who report to me in our company," an older manager told us. "I can't get them to trust me if they think I'm going to be in on their next promotion review. So I tell them, 'I won't be the decision-maker in your next promotion; it'll be done two or three levels up in the company.' That's true, too," he added. "And I tell them, 'I'll help you get that promotion,' Then they think I'm on their side, and I get them on my side."

Baby boomers are generally upset at the manipulativeness and dishonesty that this approach entails. Yet it is a very common procedure.

Large companies have long recognized that the baby boomers are different. In the initial research for this book, 250 large companies were surveyed. Some of the comments made by top personnel executives at those companies about the new generation of employees were as follows:

"Employees are more demanding . . . curious. They want to become involved. This means a lot of changing of attitudes is necessary."

"There has been a generation change. Workers today are a better-educated group. Their attitudes are different."

"Folks are more interested in getting time off rather than having better benefits. The work force is changing. . . .Companies are not dealing rapidly enough with the changing needs of the work force. We're not maximizing the productivity of the work force. We're not in tune with the under-thirty-five set. We're a generation apart. We're out of sync with them. The turnover is much too high. We don't have any program for technical brilliance. The needs of the current generation of workers are very different from the managers currently running our company."

"There has been a substantial increase in the assertion of individual rights by employees."

"There has been a shift from dealing with unions as representatives to direct dealing with employees."

"People are more willing to question. A job is a valuable asset of the individual. They have become more assertive."

PROPOSALS FROM BABY BOOM MANAGERS

Recently a major corporation assembled one hundred of its best baby boom managers from all over the United States. They were middle managers who had been selected for their high potential.

The young managers were first treated to a morning's presentation by the six top officers of the corporation, beginning with the chief executive officer. The top men were all over fifty years of age.

The company was in a difficult position. Its markets were declining, and it was facing intense competition from both domestic and foreign firms. As a result, the young managers were working long hours and were under great pressure from top management, other employees, and their own families, all of whom were demanding time and attention.

Concern about the morale of this critical group of young executives had caused the company to convene the session.

In the afternoon the young managers were divided into teams to evaluate the company's potential for the future. The following morning they made presentations while the top officers of the company listened.

What did the baby boomers say about the company as a human organization? They said what any reader of this book would expect them to say. They voiced the values of their generation and called for changes that would conform to those values.

The following are suggestions they made for revitalizing the organization:

First, they proposed that the company recognize each individual for his or her own contribution, and do it, in many instances, by recognizing their families. "We work long hours," they said in one report, "and we leave a tension-filled environment at work for one full of resentment at home. Our spouses and our children are angry that we are so rarely with them. Find a way," they said to the company's top executives, "to help us with this tradeoff, for it is adversely affecting us at work and in our lives generally."

"How can the company recognize your contribution by paying attention to your families?" one top officer of the company asked one speaker. "Give us some specific ideas."

Various of the younger managers then made suggestions, including employee lunches, flowers sent to spouses, parties for children, tours of facilities, and others. "Each of these things is small in itself, but each helps," one man said. "Why?" he asked. "Because the company is doing something for people who are very important to its managers— their families. Doing something for my children is more important than doing something for me."

Second, the group proposed that the company provide education and training so that each person could grow as an individual and do more in the company. This was very important to the group, since because of financial pressures the company had been cutting back on its human-development activities.

Third, top executives were urged to tell each subordinate exactly where he or she stood with the company. "If we have a high potential for promotion, tell us," they said, "and let us tell our high-potential people. Be direct and honest with us and let us be direct and honest with our subordinates."

Fourth, the suggestion was made to have the company spend far greater effort to making the work environment enjoyable. Tension and pressure are not a performance-producing climate at work, they insisted.

Fifth, the baby boomers proposed that the company strive for a "family type" organization. "Even if this sounds hokey," a spokesperson said, "we want to feel like we belong to a supportive organization."

Sixth, they said, "We want to be able to follow a leader's example. We want to continue to build trust; to be listened to, and to be actually heard; to have open and honest communications made to us, and for the actions of the company to match its words."

Seventh, the young people suggested, the company should give its people substantial assignments across different functions. "Often," a boomer said on behalf of the group, "people are kept in the same narrow function because the company is reluctant to lose their experience or fears that they will not perform well outside their specialties. But," the reporter insisted, "the company is being inconsistent. Periodically, it takes the far greater risk—in fact the ultimate risk for the company—of making a one-function, one-dimensional person the chief executive officer of the corporation."

WHAT COMPANIES CAN DO

The opportunity for a close match between the needs of companies today and the younger generation is very dramatic. Corporations are under intense competitive pressures and are often trying to cut costs. Baby boomers are aggressive, and ambitious; they want to work and are anxious to take responsibility to do things. This is especially true of the competitors.

It would appear that these are exactly the kinds of employees American companies need for today's difficult economic situation. The companies ought to be delighted to find the boomers, and the young people ought to be finding the opportunities they seek in those companies.

Unfortunately, this is too often not the case. Instead, there appears to be as much mismatch as fit between the baby boomers and established companies. Why is this opportunity being lost?

Asked about the friction between the companies and the baby boomers, each side gives a different interpretation. The companies say the young people expect too much, are too impatient, and in general do not fit into the corporate way of doing things. When boomers object to aspects of American business culture that they do not like, companies often reject their complaints out of hand. "They are too demanding, too impatient, too abrasive," older managers say. "They don't fit in. We can't accommodate them."

The boomers say the companies are too stodgy and bureaucratic.

The essence of the conflict concerns who is going to be forced to adapt to whom.

The struggle is a stand-off in many situations. Some companies have the power to enforce their standards on anyone who works for them, but talented young people simply stay away from the companies they consider least desirable.

In today's very competitive world, to be deprived of top talent is a very great price to pay for maintaining the traditional practices of a company. In the long term, adhering to policies that starve a company for top talent is almost certain to be self-destructive. For companies in this position, the core of the problem appears to be an unwillingness to adapt to the aspirations and needs of the new generation.

Corporate systems of compensation are generally rigid. They stress carefully defined job duties and so encourage employees to do only what they are formally required to do. Compensation systems reward people slowly over time, when baby boomers are impatient and want big rewards, if they have big successes, now.

Corporate assignment patterns are traditional, providing an opportunity for employees to gain experience by spending time in a particular position. But baby boomers are bored rapidly; they want variety and challenge and have a horror of being told to wait in line. Why must corporate assignments be so unimaginative? The usual answer from executives is, "That's the way it was for me. Why should they be better treated than I was?"

Promotion procedures often, but not always, stress time in grade. Baby boomers who are competitors fear that if they wait patiently for promotion, the many people in their age group will overtake and pass them in the race to top positions.

American business spends great sums on training employees. Because of the desire of baby boomers to learn and experience new things, training ought to be an area of mutual interest. Often it is. But in many companies, the opportunity is squandered by providing narrow and uninspiring training programs which do not really provide much information about the business or challenge employees to do more.

Many of the most creative baby boomers are casual in manner and have developed to an especially high degree their generation's distrust of authority. In the corporations they encounter formality in how people dress and behave and a status-conscious hierarchy. So many turn away.

Ironically, the companies sometimes foster in management-education programs for boomers the very attitudes and behavior they try to suppress on the job. "My company," a thirty-year-old manager at a large automobile company told us, "sends managers like me to university programs and they teach us new management techniques. I think to myself, 'I'm doing that; I must be on the right track.' But when I go back to my company, there is no connection. My boss operates the old autocratic way without any modification. When I challenge him, he says the university is just a place to go and fantasize about how things might be."

A twenty-nine-year-old sales representative at a midwestern natural gas company echoed the complaint in a comment she made to our interviewer. "I would like to see my company have more interpersonal communication. We had some human relations and communications courses in college. They need more seminars on that for top management."

It is not difficult to identify what companies who wish to recruit a productive work force from the new generation ought to do.

First, companies need to professionalize the jobs they offer. This can be done by increasing the scope of responsibility and providing an opportunity for interaction with peers over business problems, and a substantial degree of self-supervision. Organizing work into project teams, varying assignments frequently, and making available training and learning opportunities are significant elements of the new approach.

Second, pay systems need to be more individually directed, with opportunities for earning more provided on an infrequent basis when job requirements are exceeded. Baby boomers respond to short-term objectives with high work effort when there are direct payoffs.

Third, where close supervisory relationships exist, there needs to be more concern by management for the individual. High standards can be applied without confusing performance with the human quality of the individual. Managers need to respect the special pressures raising children places on people who are in two-earner families. Since this category includes more than half of the baby boomer work force, an employer who is sensitive and responsive to this issue is especially important.

Fourth, work ought to be performed increasingly in office or even campuslike settings, which are most attractive to professionals. This includes new factories, which are often highly automated and susceptible to such settings.

Finally, rigid hierarchies tend to strangle initiative and smother creativity in large organizations and are very self-defeating. However, not all hierarchies do this. What is important is how people in the management ranks perceive their responsibilities and how they relate to other people. When status in a hierarchy becomes an occasion for suppressing talent and initiative, as it often does, the more talented young people simply depart, and those who remain perform at a fraction of their capacity.

The popularity among boomers of companies that have adapted to them is evidence of the significance of the above suggestions. To attract talented people, many entrepreneurs consciously follow these precepts.

For example, a twenty-eight-year-old woman recently accepted a job at a rapidly growing new company. The company's founder, who is thirty-two, told her at her hiring interview, "We're hiring you at a better salary than the market. We think you're a smart person; and we're a growing company, so we have lots of opportunity for people like you. Hang around our offices for a while after you start work and figure out what you should do."

(This approach is anathema to most large American companies. I have mentioned it to groups of managers in large firms and watched their discomfort.)

How did it work out in the above situation?

The woman's first week was frustrating. "What am I to do?" she asked herself. Then she began to notice things to do. Her specialty was marketing, so she assisted on some projects. Later she saw an opportunity to open a new location for the company; proposed to her boss that she do so, and progressed well on that effort.

It is hard to escape the conclusion that this informal style makes better use of the human potential in the baby boom generation than does the far more common traditional style of management.

In the past the largest group in the work force were the blue-collar workers in our factories. That is no longer the case. Factory workers were almost one fifth of all employees in the early 1950s. By the end of this century, they will form about one twentieth of the total.

Research and staff professionals in corporations were always a distinct minority. In the future professionals will be the dominant force in the labor market.

Too many American companies still structure their management practices as if they were dealing with masses of blue-collar workers who traditionally expect close direction of their work. Today's work force looks to the now more numerous professional and quasi-professional occupations, and seeks an opportunity to oversee itself.

16

THE GLASS CEILING

WILL WOMEN MAKE IT TO THE TOP?

"My mother worked for years in a bank," said one woman. "She learned all aspects of the business. She had a college education and could have done any job they gave her. But for years she watched men with less education come into the bank and pass her. She used to tell me, 'There's a glass ceiling above me. I can see up to the top jobs through the glass, but the ceiling keeps me from ever getting there. That's how they treat a woman.' "

Among the baby boomers more women are at work than among previous generations in America. In earlier chapters we have seen that many baby boom women are giving a very high priority in their lives to their careers, and are making sacrifices to advance themselves. In large corporations there are now a large number of middle-level executives who are women. How are they doing in the large corporations? Are they making it to the top?

Years ago, there weren't many women in the middle-management ranks with experience and aspirations for top jobs. Today there are a great many. In 1970 among executives, administrators, and managers, only 18 percent were women. By 1985 the percentage had risen to thirty-five. This is the largest change that has occurred in any broad occupational category in the American economy.[1]

It is also the only large change that has occurred in the distribution of people by sex among jobs in our country. A few women have moved into blue-collar occupations, and a few men are now flight attendants and secretaries. But on a percentage basis, these changes, though important as possible indications for the future, are insignificant. In contrast, the stream of women into lower and middle-level management has become a flood.

The pipeline to top-management jobs now contains many women. Colleges feed the pipeline, and today's college enrollment is more than 50 percent women. The MBA programs at the nation's top business schools are more than one quarter women. There is no shortage of trained and capable women entering management.

But the evidence is growing that the glass ceiling, while higher than it was, is still there. Statistics are difficult to obtain, but it appears that top-management ranks in major companies contain very few women. Among 1,362 top executives surveyed in 1985 by a management search firm, only 2 percent were women. Among corporate directors, one frequently cited estimate is that only 4 percent are women.[2] Nor is the situation confined to business. Government, religious organizations, schools, and unions face a similar shortage of women.

The women who now attend graduate schools of business, and who are filling the middle-management ranks are largely baby boomers. They are young, competitive, well educated, and ambitious.[3] But among them is a growing suspicion that they are going to be denied an opportunity to fill top positions in the companies for which they work. Along with this suspicion is a burgeoning resentment that may have considerable consequences for the personal lives of many individuals and for society as a whole.

EXAMPLES OF THE PROBLEM

Two years ago I visited a class at a major business school. The top officer of a big venture-capital firm was there lecturing.

A woman in the class asked him, "When will women run big companies?" He paused, and then answered, "When they create them themselves."

There was silence in the room for what seemed a long while, though it must have been only thirty seconds or so. Usually there is so much give-and-take that there is no silence at all. So the visitor knew that the students were thinking.

Then another woman asked him, "How many applications have you seen at your firm from women to get financing to start up a new company?"

The man hesitated before answering, and the woman continued. "You have a big venture-capital firm, don't you? You see a lot of applications—of business plans for new companies?"

"Thousands a year," he responded.

"How many of them are from women?" she asked again.

"I haven't seen one," he answered.

After the class a woman student told me, "That's just what I expected. It's the kind of runaround men give women about business. First, the guy tells you that if you want to get to the top, you have to do it yourself. Then he tells you he won't support you in getting a business going.

"Why do you think he doesn't see any business plans from women? Because women know he won't support them, so they don't waste the time or money trying. They get started on their own."

Linda Wilson works in the home office of a large corporation. She is twenty-nine years old, has two years of college, but dropped out after that. She says that then she had no motivation. It took her a while to set her sights high. She went to trade school and became a court reporter. She came from a farm in Ohio, but the reporting firm sent her to Los Angeles, where she joined another company as a secretary. Management soon realized that she was a relentlessly driven person. She got her typing up to 180 words per minute, and let management know that she wanted to be the CEO's executive secretary one day.

Her boss told her that she ought to finish her education. She did four years of night school in one and a half years with straight As. Then she took the standard tests for management education aptitude and got a very high score.

After this kind of performance, she lost interest in the executive secretary position and took a managerial job instead. She also applied to two top schools for the MBA program and was accepted.

Her boss told me he sees in her a classic example of the enormous and largely untapped resource of young women as competitors in business. He says he is lucky to have several such women working for him, and he sees them as the competitive edge he has as a manager. He thinks that women these days are just hungrier for top managerial positions than men.

In preparing this book, we talked to one of the first women to become an ordained rabbi. She recounted how, when she was in the seminary during the holidays, a call came from a nearby nursing home asking for a rabbi to hold a Holy Day service. An administrator offered the young woman's name. Hearing this, the person from the nursing home objected. "We don't want a woman," she said. "We've always had men before."

The school official said, "You get her or no one." So they accepted her. "We have to have a service," the nursing-home woman said.

When she arrived at the home, the rabbinical student was introduced in this way: "A woman rabbi—fancy that, a woman rabbi."

There was a stunned silence. The rabbi blushed bright red. Finally, a woman in the audience rose to her feet with great effort. She was old and weak. But she stood proudly. "A woman rabbi," she said. "I think that's wonderful," and she began to clap. Soon the rest of the group joined in, and the young woman was accepted as a rabbi.

We asked her, "Who resists you in your position?"

She responded, "People who have left the religion—yes, left it, because they saw it as old, tradition bound, and generally out-of-date. The people still active have come to accept me. But those who have left are very upset by me. My ordination as a rabbi challenges their view of the religion as an unchanging, stick-in-the-mud institution. I force them to rethink their position. They either have to return or find some other, probably less satisfactory, ground on which to reject it. So they resist me and are antagonistic because I destroy their stereotype of Judaism."

Perhaps if big business put women in top-management positions it would have the same impact. It would force those who think big business is carved in stone to reexamine their lives.

Women told us in interviews, "Big corporations won't do it." One woman told this story. "I went to school in accounting twenty years ago. More than half the people in accounting schools are women. My company can't ignore them all," she said. "Who would do the work? Who'll manage them?"

She described the big accounting firms one by one. "This one has one woman partner," she said. "That one has none."

She has been with her company, one of the Big Eight, for seven years. She is not yet a partner.

"The company used to hire women who wore men's pants to work— literally," she told us. "They were weird people. That was the idea then—hire the weird ones. None of them made partner. 'No qualified candidates,' the company said. Now the company is hiring women who look like women."

We asked her if she was going to make partner. She said she hoped so. It generally takes ten years. Now she is a senior associate who manages an office with twenty-one junior associates. There are also three male senior associates, none of whom, she said, have any management skills. So when she took over the twenty-one juniors, they were all getting ready to quit. She was sent in to get those people into the company's system of learning and development.

She also mentioned her husband. "We've been married a number of years," she said.

We asked her why she didn't wear a wedding ring.

"Should I wear a ring in my nose, too?" she asked in response.

"No," we answered.

"After you've been married several years, who needs a wedding ring?" she said. "I've got a stable marriage, now I can build a career."

Another woman described a major incident in her career. "I was working for an investment banking house for six months, doing financial analysis. When my six months were up, I went to my boss.

" 'Where is my merit increase?' I asked.

" 'You're in the secretarial ranks,' he told me.

" 'I'm not doing secretarial work,' I told him. 'If I don't get my increase, I'm leaving the bank.'

"Soon a vice-president came to see me. He asked me to stay. 'In five years,' he told me, 'you'll be able to enter the managerial ranks.'

"I said, 'No way,' and I went to business school. When I got my MBA, the same vice-president of that company was at my school recruiting. I told him, 'Now I'll come back, at twice what you would have had to pay me at the entry level to management from secretarial.' But I never went back. I got out at the right time.

"Still, as much as I want to be successful in business, I also have a desire to be happy in life. There's this big conflict in me, and I don't know which I want."

Two years ago, two hundred women who run companies went to a business school for a two-day program with some of its faculty, all of whom were men. The participants wanted the women on the faculty to be in their program, too, but there was only one high-level woman in the place at that time.

The women came in flashy clothes. They didn't wear the business-woman's uniform, the type about which consultants say, "It isn't settled what women executives should wear to work, so be conservative." They didn't bother to be conservative; they wore what they looked good in. After all, they were running the companies in which they worked.

One participant commented, "The program was a disaster. The women found the male faculty condescending. The women got angry. The men couldn't handle them.

"The men said the women didn't deserve to be at the high levels which they had attained. 'They aren't bright enough,' the men said. 'They fell into their jobs. They don't have the credentials to be here in the first place, so why are they complaining? We're doing them a favor.' "

A GENERATION GAP IN HOW MEN TREAT WOMEN EXECUTIVES

In 1883, Henry James explained how he had chosen the subject for his now classic novel, *The Bostonians*. "I wished to write a very American tale," he said, "a tale very characteristic of our social conditions and I asked myself what was the most salient and peculiar point in our social life. The answer was: the situation of women . . . and the agitation on their behalf."[4]

Slightly more than a century later, the issue of women's role in our society is as intense as ever, but it has also changed. What was in Henry James's time to a large degree a political issue—should women be allowed to own property in their own behalf, to vote, to hold office—is today a much more intensely personal matter. With many legal rights attained, women now struggle with what freedom means in their own lives, with what choices to make. They struggle also with vestiges of prejudice against them, especially in terms of their potential roles in the high ranks of business and other institutions.

In a previous chapter I mentioned that men in the baby boom generation by a large majority say that they think a woman should do whatever she wants in her life, including having a career. However, it's one thing for a man to say a woman ought to be free to be in the workplace if she wishes to. It's another for a man to help a woman along her career track, especially if she has aspirations that might bring her into competition with him. And this competition is aggravated by a generational aspect.

Many older men are not sure of the capability and potential of women as managers. They stereotype women as belonging at home or in clerical jobs. But ordinarily the worst a woman can expect is to be discounted by them.

The younger businessmen are very different. They don't doubt the talents of women. Rather than condescend to them, they take them very seriously. Because men under forty generally seem more accepting of women in business, and seem to have greater respect for their compe-tence, women often hope that when these men achieve top corporate office, they'll open the doors for women to move up, too.[5]

This may occur, but there is also the possibility that a different sort of problem will arise. Younger men appreciate the intelligence and business capacity of women, and so see a professional woman in the company not as out of place, but as a potentially tough competitor. They try to elbow women aside; it's no holds barred in the struggle for success. Some women today say they don't know which is worse: to be stereotyped, discounted, and discriminated against by the older men, or to be pushed aside, run over, and bad-mouthed by the younger ones.

"I first got an inkling of what it would be like from my male peers when I was at business school," one young businesswoman told me. "One day one of my women classmates made a proposal that we discuss women's issues in a class. Immediately a man in the class said, 'Why should we discuss women's issues in management? We don't discuss Jewish issues, or Indian issues.'

"The worst time of all, though, I've never even told my husband about," she continued. "It happened during my first year in business school. One of the instructors divided the class into teams for an exercise in which we were to negotiate the purchase of a company—an acquisition game, they called it. I was on a team with three men and one other woman. We were to negotiate with another team of five students in a classroom which we had all to ourselves. Most of the students, myself included, saw this as an important opportunity because we wanted to do investment banking after we got our degrees, and this was a chance to get some practice.

"Anyway, no sooner did we start the meetings than the men on my team shoved the women, including me, aside. I wasn't allowed to sit in the middle of our team, where I could take a key role in the negotiations. The other woman and I were put at one side of the table. Nor were we allowed to speak. The men just conducted the negotiations themselves.

"I got furious. The other woman seemed to accept being relegated to second place. I didn't. Finally, while we were caucusing, and again I wasn't being listened to, I just blasted the men. I told them they were being petty and unfair, that I could do as good a job as they could and I wanted the chance. I was really angry and I said so.

"The men just looked at me. Then one of them turned to the others and said, so that I could hear very clearly and so could the other woman, 'Oh, don't mind her, she's just uptight. All she needs is a good orgasm to calm her down.'

"That was it. They never let us into the game. After the exercise was over, all the women in the class met with the professor about what had happened. Other women had been pushed aside, too. I was furious about the whole thing. That's when I learned about how rough it was going to be in business when the men of your own age saw you as a competitor.

"There are more men in most businesses than women, and when they gang up to exclude you, there's not a lot you can do.

"This is one of the reasons lots of women are dropping out of the big companies now. They're saying, 'I don't need this hassle,' and are either quitting work or starting their own companies."[6]

The number of self-employed women is growing faster than men, and women now own one quarter of small businesses in the United States.[7]

Myra Strober of Stanford University has commented, "The problem of the seventies was to bring women into the corporation. The problem of the eighties is to keep them there."[8]

A NEW FACTOR

An older man told us about his daughter, who is a petroleum engineer. She is twenty-eight and works for a big oil company. The company sent her to various out-of-the-way places where it has drilling rigs or pumping stations. He told me how the men had embarrassed her. They would put *Playboy* centerfolds around where she worked just to see her reaction. Once they painted her truck pink.

Another woman told us, "There's usually stuff like that; we've seen that all our lives," she said. "When I was a girl, I was a candy striper. I wanted to be a doctor. Then in high school I took tests and counseling for a career. The counselors told me I should be a teacher. Later I found out that the list of occupations for women didn't include doctor or lawyer. Those were on the men's list."

"That must have changed," we suggested. "The law schools and medical schools have many women students today."

"I don't think it has changed that much," she said. "The women are just fighting the counselors' advice more."

One new development is that men are trying to get their daughters into the professions and business. This has happened just in the last few years, and it has had a powerful influence. Fathers can push aside the advice of guidance counselors. They can make the companies they work for treat women better, because that's how they want their daughters treated. They can help prepare their daughters early for business and professional careers. They can help pay for school.

In the words of one woman, "I think the kind of relationship a woman has with her parents is crucial for how she approaches business. Some women have supportive fathers; they think it's natural for them to go into management or the professions. Usually, they underestimate the struggle ahead. Some women have mothers who were professionals. They think it's natural, too, but don't underestimate the obstacles. Others see only the traditional roles at home, and for them it's a lifelong struggle to adapt."

Recent statistics indicate that among the probable choices of careers by college freshmen, at the top of the list for women was the position of business executive. For men the top career was engineering, then business. Teaching was fourth on the women's list, but much farther down on the men's list. So there is some change, but the traditional occupational choices still remain.[9]

Getting into a profession or a business is one thing, getting ahead once you're in is another. In a big company there's a testing level for jobs. It's the level at which a person has to prove him or herself in order to advance into higher management.

"In my company," a male executive told us, "the testing job is that of the product manager. It's a killer position. You have to work all the time and really perform well. If a person can't make it, then he or she won't go any higher in the company. If you perform successfully, then you can move up the ladder. Women tell me that they think many other women are reluctant to make the sacrifices necessary to do the testing job. But if they don't, they don't move up."

Women have always been tested during their progress up a management ladder, our women respondents told us, and other in more difficult ways than men are. Nonetheless, most of the female managers we talked to agreed that to have the assistance of a parent or spouse in identifying the key testing jobs and being told what to expect is of potentially great value to a woman on her way up.

ARE THERE MALE AND FEMALE STYLES OF MANAGEMENT?

We have talked to many young women managers about their styles and approaches to leadership positions. The question whether or not there are styles of management that are particularly male or female occasions great controversy among them.

At one extreme there are women who insist that, as one did, "Women ought to move up. They're the best managers."

In the center are those who say, "I think that depends on the definition. I think women are best at developing people. But I don't think we're best at pushing an organization."

The other extreme belongs to women who say they have no style of their own. "In my job I just try to ape the male style," said a third woman. "I stay away from fashion magazines and *Cosmo*, even at home. They make me seem too typically female."

The essence of the disagreement is whether or not there is a management style that is especially female because it is based on characteristics that are perceived as female. A managing style that is less aggressive and stresses developing and encouraging individuals rather than pushing them and the organization is said to be female. A woman is considered to nurture and care for people, while a man challenges and demands.

"I try to care for people as individuals," one woman said. "I try to get them to perform. Men are careerists; they're not as interested in developing other people.

"All this careerism the men bring to the job is very destructive in companies," she added. "I had a thought once that the reason so many companies decline is that managers worrying about their own careers and wanting to be sure they get ahead causes men to hire and promote people somewhat less capable than themselves. Then, as lots of people do this every time, the company's average quality declines, and the company isn't as able to keep up in the marketplace.

"Years later when the company is in bad trouble, people look back and say, 'What geniuses started this company? We don't have people like them anymore.' And they're right. The company doesn't have great people anymore. Not because they don't exist—they're out building the competition—but because the people already in this company didn't hire top talent in order to make themselves irreplaceable. I think men are much more likely to do that than women," she said.

Whatever the reality of women's underlying psychology, our society is growing more tolerant of them as managers, and of what is called "the female style." Taking the view that a nurturing and developing style is female, and a challenging, pushing style is male, some are now calling the best managers those who combine the best of both styles.[10]

It may be that the best managers combine both styles, but not because they are male or female. Instead, the combination is powerful because both management styles are different and have something to contribute.

On another plane of thought, the dispute over female and male management styles may seem irrelevent. The important issue is whether women at lower levels are managing with a style that prevents them from going higher. Is their management style self-effacing and passive and do they take little credit for what they do so that higher managers don't recognize their effectiveness?

In some companies these two approaches are referred to as "macho" and "submissive." The women don't want to be submissive, but social pressures deny them the opportunity to be macho, so they get confused about what to do.

In service companies today, female managers more often come up from the ranks than men. This is the opposite of the experience in industrial companies, where men more often come off the plant floor into management positions; and it will be of increasing importance as the economy becomes more service-dominated.

Often people who come up from the ranks into management positions have an advantage; and in service companies today, female managers often seem to understand clerical, advertising, and other processes from the bottom up. Men come in from graduate schools to high positions in the organization, but often don't know as much about the business. Despite this, the advancement of women to top-management positions is very slow or nonexistent.

Many female baby boom managers are very concerned about their identity in management positions. How should they behave? Who are they really? But they are often given contradictory instructions by those who are seeking to advise them.

The issue is reminiscent of what writers in the sixties said about the baby boom generation: that it was counterculture, antimaterialist, and noncompetitive—so it would reform the world and overthrow capitalism, which was the social and economic expression of materialism and competition. But it didn't happen.

Today writers seem to say similar things about women: "Here's the new utopia, provided courtesy of women rather than courtesy of baby boomers." It was a wrong perception before and it's probably wrong now.

The women's movement started with the conviction that men and women are the same and so ought to be treated alike. The initial idea was that men and women would share the load. Men would take their share of women's work. This would be utopia: equal responsibility.

It didn't happen. Women kept their jobs at home *and* men's jobs in business. It was, and is, too much.

So now the movement says women are different; they are socialized differently and get different responsibilities. Companies ought to recognize that women can have their own effective management styles.

It is ironic that just as women are making their way through graduate schools and going into managerial jobs in large numbers, they are facing a crisis of self-confidence. Many are saying, "Maybe I'm different from the men. Maybe I can't do all the things required to be a top executive and still be myself. Maybe I should drop out."

"More and more women realize they can't conquer the entrenched good old boy system and are . . . leaving their achievements in corporate life behind," wrote a woman journalist about this phenomenon.[12]

A successful woman executive, now approaching forty, commented: "It's too bad because women are not really different. They can make it and they can do it by being themselves. Instead, they're getting sucked into another of these 'Let's reform the world' scenarios. 'Let's be loving, nurturing, compassionate in the office just like at home with the children.' It isn't true, because women aren't like that underneath, and it won't work in business. So it's self-defeating.

"In big companies women are in an environment characterized by stereotypes and where they are often held back and discriminated against. No wonder lots of them get out. Only the toughest ones will advance."

REMOVING BARRIERS

What is surprising is that our society and companies continue to put barriers in the way of women at work. The nation needs women at work. Without them, living standards will drop. Also, with so many people getting older, we need all the workers we can to support people who aren't working. Having women in the work force helps the nation's economy at a time when it needs help.

But the economy needs people to be real contributors, not just low-wage fodder for the economic machine. Hence, the general social importance of having women in management positions. Yet with all this need, it's surprising that companies are doing so little to help women employees, especially the managerial ones.

There is an enormously talented pool of women workers, intelligent and experienced, in whom a great deal of education has been invested. They are ambitious, capable, and looking for advancement to the top. On the other hand, there are corporations that desperately need new ideas and approaches. So it's strange to see companies keeping women out of key jobs, turning them off, and driving them away.

How can a company best utilize and advance its women managers?

First, it can give them the same assignments as it does the men. Without such opportunities, women cannot show what they can accomplish.

Second, the company can adjust for the social pressures that make it more difficult for women managers to do their jobs. Two surveys of corporate officers, one of males and the other of females, show how great have been the personal sacrifices women have made to climb corporate ladders. Twenty percent of the women had never wed, contrasted to less than 1 percent of the men; and more than 50 percent of the women were childless, versus 5 percent of the men.[13] It's unreasonable for companies to expect or accept this degree of personal sacrifice from women who want to get ahead in management. Increasingly, those who are working their way up will want to marry and have children. Generally, our social system is such that they will have to bear a disproportionate responsibility for the care of their children. Managers have often mentioned to us how they lost, or came near to losing, a very good woman subordinate because she couldn't find child care. To keep people like this, managers often assist them in locating child care when the company itself is not helpful. Corporations can aid women enormously either by providing child care or helping them to locate it.

Third, companies should make a special effort when evaluating female managers to look at results, not style. Too often is a female manager passed over for promotion not because of poor performance, but because of a conviction by top executives that she lacks the aggressiveness and toughness required in a higher position. This standard, which is in reality one of personality, may be effective when applied to men, but it is likely to be very misleading when applied to women.

Fourth, male executives should encourage more openness with women managers about the special problems women face in the workplace. Many companies have informal organizations of women managers. They meet to discuss common experiences, opportunities, and problems. Such a group is potentially an excellent vehicle for top management to learn about the problems and aspirations of women managers. But many male executives are fearful of dealing with such groups, or even of discussing career matters with women executives individually. Recognizing that companies are social systems that share many of the prejudices and stereotypes of the larger society is simply being realistic. That problems exist is not necessarily such a reflection on any particular company that its top officers must become defensive about it. Instead, there needs to be much more communication about women managers' problems, and much more effort by women managers to grasp opportunities that enhance their ability to do a productive job.

There are extremely effective communication networks among female executives. A company that builds a reputation as a good place for women to be managers will find that it will attract top talent. In today's very competitive business climate, this is an advantage firms should very much desire to have.

17

THE END OF SOCIAL CLASS

THE ONENESS OF THE GENERATION

The conventional wisdom is that there are significant differences in values, attitudes, and aspirations among people, based on their occupations and income levels. These differences are supposed to be reflected in economic behavior and political affiliations. According to most observers, the differences between poor, middle income, and well-to-do people are just as substantial among baby boomers as among other groups in the population. But there is evidence from our interviews that people in the baby boom generation—over a wide range of income and education levels—share the same values, attitudes, and aspirations, regardless of occupation and income levels.

When baby boomers meet in a bar or at the beach, it's harder to tell who is rich or poor than it used to be. Most people in the generation wear similar clothes; they read the same magazines; they watch the same

TV shows; they listen to the same music, regardless of how much money they have. The easy identification of people by social class is passing.

These basic similarities are often disguised even from baby boomers themselves because human beings tend to want to find differences among people. The reason for this is a desire to stand out, to be individualistic, to be better educated and more successful than the others. So distinctions are sought and found. But to a person who doesn't have his or her own personal reasons for wanting to find distinctions, there aren't so many of them.

People in this generation are alike—whatever income level, schooling, or occupation—in the things that they value. They want honesty in personal relationships, the opportunity to be individuals and be respected for this, a chance to have fun at work, and to make a lot of money. They want respect, to be listened to and responded to. They want to be treated as adults—not bossed around. They want to learn. They desire an opportunity to do well in their work; and they want to be let alone to do their own thing. They also want an opportunity for self-expression, learning, and growth. They want to be recognized for their individual contributions, and to have the opportunity to go beyond the scope of their jobs.

Though differences can be identified, they are not the sort that suggest a major division of our society into social classes. America today has a fringe group of the poor, an underclass; and it has a fringe group of the very rich. In between, there is an enormous center in which generational and stage-of-life differences dominate all economic or social-class distinctions.

The American melting pot continues to boil. But immigration has slowed in this century, so that the pot is no longer composed primarily of people of different nationalities who are being fused together into a dominant culture. Instead, today's melting pot is composed of people of different social origins being fused by increased education and the mass media. Melded so as to be very much alike in terms of values, they are also encouraged to seek uniqueness in personal experiences and relationships.

It is in this crucial sense that baby boomers, whatever their income level, are most alike.

AMERICA'S BABY BOOM
WORKERS

In the course of the interviews conducted for this book, we talked with many nonmanagerial working people, drawn from different occupations and geographic areas. None are extremely poor, but in no case is the annual family income above the national median. They are either working class or middle income, according to the customary definitions.

The basic values set forth above resonate in these people. So we were not surprised to find them pervasively suspicious of authority. They look for enjoyment in their work. None speak of duties or obligations as much as of the values of honesty and openness in personal relationships. These people are more conscious of opportunity than of risk to survival.

Little loyalty to institutions or causes was revealed in these interviews. People are concerned with themselves and their own families or friends. There is a continual stress on the individuality and uniqueness of each person. There is no interest in being viewed or perceived as part of a group. Even religion, which is mentioned as of great significance in many lives, is treated as a somewhat private spiritual matter, not as an affiliation to a doctrine or institution.

Experiences dominate possessions in the thinking and desires of these people. Most see these values as different from their parents' values. Feeling good about themselves dominates career advancement or aspirations to improved social standing.

In each of these many dimensions, these people are not significantly different from professionals or managers in their generation. Too often, however, they tell of triumphs in their working lives under the old system and values.

Instead of being treated like professionals, many say they are viewed as children and bossed around by supervisors. So they don't commit themselves to their work. Then the boss says, "These are lazy people. I've got to push harder." He pushes harder, and they resent it more and do as little as possible. So the whole process is a self-fulfilling prophecy and a downward spiral.

Despite their respect for themselves and the interesting things they are doing, both on and off the job, only a few give any indication that their employers care about them as people. This realization seems to be very bitter.

A TEXAS BUS DRIVER FROM WISCONSIN

Now forty-one years old, this man is one of the first of the baby boomers. Recently he moved to Texas from Wisconsin, where he had grown up, attended college for one year, and then worked for a few years. Today he describes himself as "a professional driver" who works for a nationwide bus company driving long-distance routes.

"I used to be a police officer," he said. "How did my change to a bus driver come about? Well, I liked the road and I wanted to try it out. I had never thought about being a driver, but the money was double what a police officer made and I decided to go where the money was."

He has made new friends since being in Texas, mostly among his co-workers, but he has also met people in his community. He finds the Texans are "for lack of a better word, more rowdy—more the party types. Texas attitudes have rubbed off on me and I'm more like my new friends now.

"What's special about me? I'm a unique human being. I'm good at what I do. I've got a lot of good qualities. I'm warm and friendly.

"Over the years my outlook on life has changed. What really worries me is that there'll be no future with this nuclear thing hanging over our heads. The environment is number two; the pollution on this earth, the raping of the earth by man. Crime is number three.

"The most important thing in my life is my own happiness—to be happy with myself, with my own personality. It's being able to look myself in the mirror in the morning and saying, 'I like that guy.'

"I think women should do whatever in society they are capable of handling. They're people first. They should be able to do anything they want. Men should have no more reaction than someone would have to me as a man. If I met a male or female driver, I'd simply say, 'Hi, how're you doing?'

"But the thing that does bother me is that sometimes when the weather gets bad, women bus drivers don't want to be out there on the road. If she gets the same wage as me, then she should be out there when I'm out there. They shouldn't get any special favors.

"I think corporate heads are so wrapped up with the almighty dollar that they could care less if someone gets laid off. They don't care enough about the individual. All they're concerned about is keeping their country club memberships and their big homes. They just don't care about the people who work for them as long as they're making money.

"I keep up with politics. I have a tendency to vote Republican, but I'm really registered as an independent.

"I know two or three pleasure-seekers. They spend the winters skiing. But this area is pretty conservative, so you don't find many people like that around here.

"My ex-wife's a competitor. I don't want to say much about her.

"Most of my friends are kind of doubtful. They're happy more or less, but they ask themselves questions quite a bit.

"I don't have many friends that are contented, but I suppose some people are. And I know one person who is deeply into drugs.

"As for me, I'm happy with what I'm doing. I'm at peace with myself and my job, but I'm not content with what I have materially. I'm not the type of person who gets wasted on drugs. The only thing I really want to know for sure is that my kids can go to college.

"I'm single now; divorced as I told you, twice. I support six children. That's my hobby—sex, not children. Or maybe I have that backwards.

"I've had some pretty interesting experiences as a bus driver. I have to say that my company doesn't carry the jet set. Actually, if you want to learn about America, the bus is the way to go. Sit in the last fourteen rows and you'll get a real education."

A COCKTAIL WAITRESS IN NEW JERSEY

This young woman is twenty-seven years old. She has three children and lives with her husband in Atlantic City, New Jersey.

She has found her life changing considerably as the children have arrived. "I used to party a lot," she said. "Now I don't anymore. Now I go to soccer games with my kids, who are into sports.

"A few years ago I never thought I'd have three children. These days I work as a cocktail waitress and take care of the properties we own.

"Most of my friends are people I went to school with or who live in our neighborhood. I'm crazier than the bunch. They're more calm.

"I'm lucky for what I have. My husband has a good job as a dealer at a casino. A lot of people our age don't have as much as we do.

"Aside from my family, the most important thing in my life is God. I turn to God a lot, because I believe in God. I've never believed in born-again Christians. I don't care about having money in my pocket anymore. I just ask God for what I want and you wouldn't believe it but it usually comes true.

"What worries me is health and growing old. I worry about growing old a lot. I try to be as young as I can.

"In five years I'll be doing something different. I want to get my real estate license. And I'd like to join my husband as a dealer at the casino.

"But I think companies should pay more attention to the people they employ. They don't care about people. They just want them to work. My husband has to work whether he's sick or not. He always has to be there.

"I was just a baby when the Vietnam War occurred. I don't think it should have happened. I don't think any kind of war should happen. People should just make peace.

"The war turned some people into doing drugs—people I know, anyway. People became harder because of having to deal with the war.

"I don't belong to a political party, or get much into it. But I probably will eventually. I would like to get into politics eventually. They're all crooks. I worked at a city hall once. The guy I worked for, he never even came in to work.

"What's important to be in a relationship is caring, showing feelings. I like for my husband to give me a lot of attention.

"I think women my age ought to be boss over the men! We should be making more than the men. But it would be O.K. to treat the men equal.

"Men should treat us as equal. My husband doesn't allow me to go to a bar, but he does. If he goes, I think I should be able to go. We should be treated equal. I have to do all the housework. They should help out at home."

A MASON IN TEXAS

This man is thirty-four and works as a mason in Texas. He said that in the past five years his life has definitely changed.

"I found the Lord Jesus," he told us. "Before that, it was just fun and games—just work and play. My belief in God has really changed my life.

"Originally I thought I'd probably be a schoolteacher. But somehow I got interested in construction. I developed a liking for working outside. I really enjoy what I'm doing. I can see what I accomplish, and it gives me a real sense of enjoyment. I never wanted to work in some office, just pushing papers around.

"For ten years I ran with a group of people who just played a lot. But in the last three years I've made a lot of new friends at church. My friends from church are in more professional positions, so there are some big differences between us.

"I have a wife and two children. I'm very family-oriented. So what's happening to the younger generation really concerns me. The moral values of this country are going downhill fast. I'm concerned for my children—what will happen to them in the future with all these drugs and the lack of values in society.

"In five years what I'd really like to be doing is helping other people with the problems that really bother me—like doing something about the drug abuse and alcoholism.

"The problem with large companies is that most of the employees are union . . . the employees are the problem, not the company. The employees want and expect too much. When you work for a small company, you try to do the best job you can because it's more competitive for small companies. But small companies can't give you the benefits a larger company can. Small companies can't take care of their employees in terms of benefits because they are trying to be competitive. In large companies morale is terrible . . . employees take too much for granted. That's because the unions have gotten them too much.

"During the Vietnam War, I was a draft dodger. I didn't run away, but I avoided it. I stayed in college.

"I think it was a money-oriented war. It was a big political move to bolster the economy. That war was fought purely for economic gain by the U.S.

"I don't belong to a political party. I vote for the person, not the party. I think the one works against the other. When I vote, I want to know how the person feels on certain issues I believe in. Motives are more important than getting anything done. Like it's not Reagan's fault if Congress won't agree with him.

"In a relationship I think honesty and sincerity are most important. Honesty is number one. If someone is honest with me, then I can love and understand them. If someone is sincere in what they believe in, even if it's different from what I believe in, then I respect them. If they live their lives with their own morals and they are sincere, then I can live with that.

"I think a woman ought to be home with the family . . . that's the way I was brought up. My mother didn't work. It's real easy to look at my own children and see what a difference it makes. When I look at other people's children, their behavior and values are much different if the mother works. Parents who work try to make up for lost time by buying their kids material things. I think God created women to have children, so they should do that.

"But I recognize that most women would probably say that their careers are more important. I guess men need to learn women's values more. I know if you're trying to raise a family, men would probably desire to have their wives at home.

"When I was twenty-four to twenty-eight, I was a pleasure-seeker. I ran with a group who was very close. Some were just coming out of divorces. That life-style seemed pretty good at the time. A person is at an experimental time in life between ages twenty-four and thirty-one. Everyone I know in that age group is a pleasure-seeker.

"I guess I'm contented. I don't fit the other groups. I'm just trying to make a better life for myself and my family and to make life better for other people as well.

"I think people's morals make a lot of difference. They have a lot to do with how a person is. There's too much pornography everywhere.

"I experienced everything in the nineteen-sixties. I was in Haight-Ashbury. I was a flower child. We're just beginning to find what's important in life. We always avoided church as children. Now we're coming back to religion.

"I think that I'm very different from my parents. In my life money isn't the all-important thing like in my parents' lives. Money rules their lives. You might say that my parents follow what society dictates. Society accepts women working now, so my parents say to me, 'Why doesn't your wife work, if you're getting into financial trouble?' Of course, my mother never worked. I say to them that I want to have a different relationship with my children. My dad was assigned to a submarine fleet. I never saw him much. I want to spend time with my children. I'm more family-oriented than my parents were. We're more worried about our children than ourselves, I think.

"Too many children are being abused and not being taken care of. More and more people are worrying less about jobs and position in life. More are making their children a priority in life. We're thinking of our children first."

A FACTORY HELPER IN KANSAS

At thirty-two years old, this man says that his most important goal is to find someone to be happy with. He is not married, but enjoys taking trips with his friends. "The experience is what I enjoy," he said.

He did not attend college, and now works as a helper in the receiving department of a factory. When asked if his outlook has changed over the past fifteen years, he answered that it hadn't.

"I thought then that today I'd be being my own boss . . . and that's what I am doing." He described himself as much like his friends. "I get along with everybody. I care a lot about my friends."

What is the most important thing in his life? "Being myself."

This is also what's important to his friends, he told us. "They do what they want to do. They don't let others boss them around that much."

What is striking about this man's responses is that he is not in any formal way his own boss. He has a direct supervisor to whom he is supposed to report. Yet he thinks of himself as very independent. No one bosses him around, he says. He has no sense of inferiority or resentment.

Asked what he sees himself doing five years from now, he responded, "The same thing I'm doing now. Just sitting back and enjoying how life is going along."

ARE UNIONS FOR BABY BOOMERS?

The generational changes in values and attitudes, and the emergence of middle- and low- (but not lowest) income people into the mainstream of values, popular culture, and attitudes, have been particularly challenging to the nation's labor unions. Several of the people in the profiles above are members of unions. However, none chose to mention that fact until specifically asked late in our interviews. In contrast, several nonunion people stressed being nonunion. This is a small indication of the current estrangement between many baby boomers and the labor movement.

People did talk to me about the unions when I asked, which I did occasionally. A selection of comments about unions follows:

"Unions are the advocates of seniority in the workplace. They're for the older generation, not the new," I was told.

"Unions are what I and my friends wanted to escape from," another baby boomer added. "They are things our parents were involved in. When younger people wanted to escape our parents' control, we also wanted to escape from unions."

"Isn't it ironic," I asked, "that the young people who in the nineteen-sixties worked for the poor and supported antiwar efforts didn't make an alliance with the unions?"

"The unions didn't protest the war," one boomer said with some heat. "They supported it."

"Well, I guess you're right," I said, "for most of them. But some unions opposed the war."

They shrugged.

"My friends never saw unions as helping the powerless or disadvantaged," a woman said. "The unions kept the minorities out.

"I know several people," she continued, "who haven't entirely lost the nineteen-sixties priority on helping the disadvantaged. They still volunteer to work against hunger or to help poor people in their communities. But the direct protest kind of activity is gone.

"None of them see any role for unions, however. They will volunteer time to work for the hungry and the homeless, but none would volunteer to work for the unions."

As a result of these generational changes, the unions now seem confused. Unions often represent the middle-class worker, but they talk as if they are working for the poor. This combination was effective for thirty years because it brought the unions votes and financial resources from their middle-class members, and public legitimacy for supporting the poor. There was always tension between the two roles, and accusations of hypocrisy were made, but there was also a careful balance.

However, that strategy is in difficulties today. The big numbers of blue-collar workers are disappearing. So unions won't have enough of them to provide votes and financial support. The poor, for their part, are always hard to represent, politically inactive, and provide few or no resources. Yet unions continue to identify with the poor in public. They seem to forget the need to represent the middle class. So the balance of yesterday is off somehow today.

It's obvious that unions want more members among baby boomers, but they seem to represent the old values and attitudes. Unions often fight attempts to give workers more responsibility. They apparently wish to preserve an old antagonism between workers and management. They say they are for the workers, but sometimes, to support broader objectives, they don't hesitate to let the workers' jobs go abroad or put their companies out of business.

"When I was in the union and they had membership meetings," said a man of twenty-eight, "only a few people came. I'll bet the leadership didn't have direct contact with more than a few percent of the members. When I'd go to a meeting, the old members would not listen to me if I said anything. They ran the union. The meetings were disorderly. There was no agenda. The young people couldn't be heard. So we dropped out."

The unions offer a form of participation, a form of democracy. Isn't that important?

"The vote a person has in a union," a baby boomer, who had been a union member, told me, "is so diluted by all the other members that it's meaningless. A person just gets submerged in the group. Young people don't want that.

"Unions give people contracts and rights. But these are less important today to many young people, who want to belong to an organization, not just to be an employee with rights.

"At my company they started a program of what is called 'positive discipline.' When management thinks a person isn't performing or is out of line, they send him or her home with pay."

"With pay?" I asked.

"Yes, with pay," he repeated. "They say, 'Take the day off and think about it. You know whether you're off base. Go home and think about your job—whether you want to risk losing it.'

"Most of the young people respond real well to it. They say, 'It embarrasses me to be singled out,' and 'I guess the company does treat me okay; I ought to be fair to them.'[1]

"It's much more positive than a suspension without pay. There you're trying to coerce the individual."

"What did your union say about it?" I asked.

"What do you think they said?" he asked me.

"I don't think they are opposed to it," I said. "How could they oppose something that so clearly benefits the worker. He gets paid for the day off?"

"Well, they can oppose it," he replied, "and they do. They say it lulls the worker into thinking the company isn't the enemy.

"People don't want to work for a company that's their enemy, even if they have a union to protect them. They want to work for a company that lets them belong, that cares about them. But the unions oppose this. So people go look for the kind of employer they want, and they leave the unions behind."

Still, many companies don't care about people or let them belong. Our survey shows that clearly. Because baby boomers generally recognize this, they acknowledge that there is a role for the old-style union. Yet most seem to credit many companies with trying to improve human relations. But much of this effort is fairly shallow.

In the fall of 1986, a group of managers at a large corporation met to discuss how to have better relations with people in the company's plants and offices. They had just issued a corporate-level guideline in support of that objective.

But some of the managers asked, "Did the top executives approve this?"

The corporate-level staff member, who was making the presentation of the new company policy, stopped, hesitated, and then said, "Well, they approved it in the sense that they didn't stop us from putting it out."

"So they just let some middle-level younger people put it out?" one person asked the man from corporate headquarters. "Do they treat people here at corporate headquarters like the policy says to treat them?"

"I'm being very honest," the presenter said. "I hope this talk isn't being taped. No, they don't act the way this memo says to act at all," he said.

Some baby boomers there were asked whether the employees in that company need a union.

"Some of them do," answered one of them. "But outside corporate headquarters, people are being treated decently in lots of situations in that company."

Many of the baby boomers' complaints are about the age of the union leadership, whom they view as not only older but also not in sympathy with their concerns. "Union leadership is mainly old people," one young man said. "They worry about other old people who are their friends. They give up anything to protect pensions. They care more about retirees than about the young workers. They don't even trust young people. Our values are different, and they look down on us because of that.

"I remember the people my age with whom I worked when I was in the union," he continued. "We worked hard, and were proud of what we did. But we felt we were being constantly mistreated on the job by our supervisors and by the union's stewards. Both were unresponsive to the young workers. We, the young people, were very ambitious—but we also were willing to help the older workers. If they were slowing down, the younger people would pick up for them. Still, the union didn't seem to be concerned about us at all."

"When I was in a union," another one said, "I heard two union officials talking. One was in his early sixties; the other in his late twenties. Actually the older man was a national vice-president; the younger a local union president. The old fellow said to the young guy, 'There are all these young workers in the big companies. They are ignored, mistreated, unheard. They can't get any attention in those big organizations. Why don't they come to us?'

" 'You don't understand,' the young guy told him. 'We're a big organization also.' "

LET THE INDIVIDUAL SHOW THROUGH

From the point of view of many baby boomers, the unions are muddled up. They stand for participation and involvement and fairness, which the baby boomers want. But the unions couple these objectives with organization and group discipline, of which baby boomers are very suspicious. As one baby boomer put it, "People our age want to be involved, but they want to do it as individuals, not as people whose individuality is lost in a crowd."

The problem is one both unions and management face: How can individualism be preserved in a group?

It's possible. One of the strengths we have in America is the ability to combine individualism with team effort. As one Japanese executive commented, Oriental companies have the advantage of group effort, while American companies have the advantage of individual initiative. But he also said that he had seen American companies where people competed with each other as individuals, yet also worked together as a team. He found it difficult to comprehend how people could do both, but when they did, it was a really powerful combination, one that companies abroad had trouble matching.

The same analogy can be applied to a sports team. The really good teams have players who are outstanding as individuals, but nonetheless work with each other as a team. The Boston Celtics are an excellent example. The team has superstars, like Larry Bird, who get the most public attention and who compete with other players on the team for attention and rewards. But these stars also work together with the team when they play.

That's the real American strength: not to be totally individualistic, and not to submerge people in the group, but instead to mix the two.

The problem with unions today, according to the baby boom generation, is that they won't let the individual shine.

A CONTEST FOR THE ALLEGIANCE OF THE NEW GENERATION

In the past unions, like trade associations, did polling only to drum up support for some lobbying campaign. It was rarely done to learn what members really thought.

Today a union leader or a corporate executive cannot really understand the new generation unless they make extraordinary efforts. The techniques used are not just simple polling, but include in-depth telephone interviews, focus groups, and personal interviewing.

It's not easy to get information. One pollster spoke about calling a union member once and his wife answered. "I said I was calling for the union," she told us, "that her husband belonged to and wanted to speak to him.

" 'How do I know who you are?' the wife said. 'Why should he talk to you?'

"She was so abrasive, I got mad. 'Look lady,' I said to her, 'your husband pays twenty dollars a month dues to this organization. They want to find out what he wants them to do with his money. If you don't want him to talk to us, fine. But don't complain that no one ever listens to you.' "

"And?" I asked her.

"She put him right on the phone."

More than ten surveys have been taken by the bricklayers' union over a four-year period.[2] More than a thousand members have been interviewed, as well as several hundred former members and a hundred or more people who were never members but who work in the same industry. These surveys, each taken by an independent company utilizing up-to-date sampling and analytic techniques, provide an unequaled in-depth look at a segment of the skilled blue-collar work force in America.

One of the most striking findings provided by these data concerns the social confidence of blue-collar workers. Several questions about self-confidence were asked of the bricklayers' union members and also of middle managers from a variety of companies. Respondents were asked to agree or disagree with a group of statements according to a five-point scale. The statements included: "I like to be considered a leader"; "I have a great deal of confidence in myself to get anything done

I set my mind to do"; "I would like to be responsible for checking the quality of my own work." And there was one negative statement: "I have never really been outstanding at anything."

The responses of the two groups were extremely close on these questions. Both registered very high agreement with the positive statements, and very high disagreement with the negative statement.

Baby boomers in both groups scored more strongly in agreement with the positive statements, and in disagreement with the negative statement.

There is no evidence in these remarkable data of a downtrodden social class of workers. Probably the managers enjoyed far more income, but the workers felt no less good about themselves.

On two other questions asked, there was a difference in response. The workers felt themselves to be less a source of information for others about their company or union, and said they were less likely to give advice about company or union issues to others. In our society some people are supposed to have answers, so others consult them. Other people have just as much confidence and willingness to be helpful, but are less sought after.

The reader may recall that in our surveys working people continually repeated that their managers and supervisors did not respect them as individuals. But the evidence is clear that, by and large, they respect and feel good about themselves.

There is a lesson for all leaders of large organizations in the bricklayers' experience with in-depth polling of its members. Ours is an increasingly populous society. For a business executive or a union leader to rely on personal contacts as a reliable source of information about people in general is a mistake. A leader has to have a systematic way of learning how and what his constituents (whether members, employees, customers, or voters) think.

There ought to be a parade of top officials of labor and business organizations to top-quality opinion-research companies like the one which did the surveys for the bricklayers.

There is certainly some truth in the observation that the relationships between managers and employees are changing in many workplaces. But though this observation applies in some places, it does not apply in others. Many women get little respect in the workplace. Male supervisors still joke about them. And in businesses where the competition is intense, people are still exploited.

It is possible to overestimate the enlightenment of managers in many companies. When unions were stronger, managers treated people well to avoid unionization. Today managers have told me, "We treat the people well." And they often add, "And if the workers don't think they're well treated, and if they bring a union around, then we'll get a lawyer and use the law to keep the union out."

In America there is a very mixed picture. Much of the blue-collar and clerical work force is well educated and aspires to being treated by management as professional. But only rarely does it get such treatment.

Unions, on their part, have been slow to accept the different values and aspirations of the younger generation. In part, that has contributed to the decline of unions. But as unions decline, managers in many instances seem to be less concerned about the people they employ than when unionization presented a more significant threat.

So a contest between management and labor continues for the loyalty of baby boomers. Management has held the stronger hand, but may now be seeing its advantage decline. Opportunities may be opening for the unions, but only if the unions can identify themselves more effectively with the values and aspirations of the new generation.

18

THE POLITICS OF VALUES

"That fellow who ran for governor last year," Bif said to Gary. "Susan told me he was a friend of yours. Was he?"

"Yes," Gary replied.

"I thought he was going to win," Bif said.

"So did he," Gary answered, smiling.

"The reason I asked," Bif explained, "is that I remember that he complained that it was our generation who beat him."

"Yes," Gary said, "he did say that."

"So I thought," Bif continued, "that maybe we should talk about the impact of our generation on politics."

"Well, he was an interesting case," Gary began. "I was with him the night the primary returns came in. He had already served as lieutenant governor, and his family was prominent in politics. His father had been a very influential congressman. So he expected to win. But the votes came in against him, and I remember that after he'd made his concession speech, he sat there over a drink and said, over and over again, 'They've forgotten where they came from.' "

"What did he mean?" Susan asked.

"I think he meant that the people who had moved up in life and left the city for the suburbs had forgotten the politicians who helped them get there."

"His was the same old message though, wasn't it?" Susan asked.

"I think the main thing was," Gary said, not seeming to hear her question, "that the organization he'd depended on to deliver the vote to him hadn't done it.

"No one can deliver votes anymore," Gary continued. "When I was younger, political parties and unions could deliver votes and so could some political bosses in the big cities. They'd tell their members, or the people who lived in their district, how to vote, and the people would listen to them. Not everyone, of course, but the majority.

"Just look how the political party has changed. Thirty years ago when I started to vote, the political party was a provider of patronage, a communicator to the masses, and a selector of candidates. Today none of that remains in any significant way. Today the political party is a service and finance organization for the candidates, who identify themselves and are chosen by the voters in campaigns in which values dominate.

"Voters don't pay attention to parties anymore. They're better educated, so they want to make up their minds for themselves. They watch TV, and they see the news, and they say, 'See, I heard the news. I know enough to make up my own mind about this matter or that one.' And they say, 'I've seen this candidate on TV, or that one, and I know I don't like him'; or 'I know I like him.' No one needs to get their information from a party or a union or a boss anymore. They rely on TV instead, or on friends who rely on TV. They think they don't need a political party to tell them about a politician, to say, 'He's a great person, so likable, so like the people, not at all aloof or like the rich.' That's what the parties used to say. They'd tell you all about him because you wouldn't have a chance to know him yourself.

"Not today, though, not today," Gary concluded. "Today everybody looks at the candidates on TV and says, 'I know each of those people, and this one is a regular guy and that one is stuck up'; or 'This one is tough,' and 'That one is too weak.'

"Nobody looks to the parties or unions or business for information or direction about how to vote anymore. So no organization can deliver the votes."

"That makes the unions just like business," Bif commented.

"What do you mean?" Gary asked.

"The people who manage my business haven't been able to influence how I vote. Our executives endorse candidates and give them money, but they can't tell anyone how to vote. The unions used to be able to turn out the vote. Now they just endorse and give money. So union leaders are now like business executives in how they influence politics."

"I think that's one of the things that beat my friend," Gary said. "He was relying, like his father did, on the party regulars and the union leaders to get out the vote for him."

"So union leaders and business executives don't have any power in politics anymore," Bif said.

"I think a person ought to vote for the most qualified candidate and then rely on him or her to use judgment."

"That's an old attitude," Gary said.

"No, that's a new attitude," Bif corrected him. "It's the old generation who vote on the basis of their own interests, i.e., who vote for politicians who tell them what they want to hear. My friends pick the person they think is most like them, and then let him make up his or her own mind about questions that come up."

GROUP INTERESTS VERSUS PERSONAL VALUES

When baby boomers vote for candidates on the basis of who is most like them, they are, at a fundamental level, choosing values. By and large, the generation is not concerned about public issues. It is concerned about people. Baby boomers' values have to do with how individuals should deal with other individuals. When these attitudes are applied to political matters, it results in a personalization of politics.

There is a tendency among those who view politics primarily as a struggle of different interests to see a focus on the candidates as shallow. In their view people should know about issues and vote their own interests. But to many baby boomers, this view is simply the old politics: the politics of interest groups.

Instead, today's politics is about individuals. It is as if election choices are made by voters by comparing the candidates as if they knew them personally. But in our large society, there is no realistic opportunity for voters to know the candidates personally.

In place of personal acquaintance, stands the television set. Through television, each voter feels that he or she can make a personal evaluation of the candidates; it seems to provide one-on-one communication between candidate and voter.

Even though this communication and knowledge through television is essentially an illusion, it is the illusion that makes personalized politics possible. In this sense politics is like entertainment on TV. It gives one the illusion of face-to-face interaction. In consequence, people confuse entertainment and politics.

Baby boomers follow people they admire, not necessarily someone who says what he or she wants to hear, but someone who is liked, someone with whose values the young persons are comfortable. They identify with values that neither political party owns. Candidates of either party can embody and express their values.

It's also the politics of feeling good. "Vote for me; I'm a strong leader," says a candidate. "You should feel good about yourself. You should feel good about America. I'll bring back pride."

In itself, there would not appear to be anything wrong with this approach to electoral choices. But the criticism is often made that the issues that really matter to people get lost. Not every baby boomer is a professional and makes good money. What's wrong with the politics of feeling good is that people will vote against their own interests, their own pocketbooks. Many will vote for a seemingly reassuring candidate like Mr. Reagan who later will sometimes work against their interests while in office.[1]

Many baby boomers seem to have a different assessment of what matters to them. They give less priority to economic interests and more to attitudes and values of a candidate. An excellent example was provided by the 1984 senatorial primary elections in a northeastern state. The odds-on favorite to win the primary (which in this state was tantamount to election) had not served in the Vietnam War because of a draft deferment. His opponent had fought in the war. So the favorite tried to play up the unpopularity of the war by attacking the morality of the war and insisting that his opponent shouldn't have fought in

Vietnam. This strategy backfired. The Vietnam vets went to his opponent as volunteers, and in the last five days of the primary, put together a telephone campaign that turned the elections around.

The candidate who lost had not understood the attitude of the majority of baby boomers about the war. He said that his opponent shouldn't have fought in Vietnam, implying that he, and the other vets, had had a choice. That was very naïve. People voted against him because he was naïve—and they felt insulted.

The concrete facts aren't very important politically anymore. What matters most is the mood, the emotion, or the belief that results from how the media present an event. The political reality is what people think. If the information received is a distortion of the event, then the truth about it never catches up. A story is old once it's been reported, and no one cares about an old story. So reality is not events, but perception.

When the image and the events don't merge, it's the events which give way, which get lost. An event is only a fact—subordinate, anterior, of less importance than the imagery. The Texas oil boom is *Dallas*. The Miami drug scene is *Miami Vice*. The Vietnam War is *Platoon*. The entertainment event defines the reality. The medium isn't just the message, it's the event itself. Fictional dramas and fictional news both become realities to the voters, and so they affect politics and help to determine the future.

Because this is how information is presented to the public, in a context created by a script or copywriter, what matters is not what people think but what they feel. Politics ends up not being about what to do, but about people's emotional responses; it's not about policy, but about therapy.[2]

The baby boomers accept this sort of politics as natural. Their parents did not and do not.

Like a minister at a small church once said, "There is a difference between the old and the new generations. The new generation can't sing the old hymns because they don't know them, and the old generation doesn't like the new hymns."

What is happening in politics has its counterparts elsewhere as the baby boomers bring their own particular brand of values and attitudes and ways of doing things to our society. The evangelical churches are growing, not because of their moral teachings—which is the reason the press gives for their growth—but because of their emotionalism, because they let people feel good.

What a successful politician needs today is a sure touch for the values and expressions of the baby boomers; not a program or a policy, but the ability to react to an event or a news story the way the voters react. Then people know that the politician shares their values.

A successful politician is less a leader than a participator. He or she leads only in expressing or exemplifying certain values. The politician is a facilitator—to help people express how they feel about things.

But politics is not only candidates and elections, which have been the focus to this point. Politics is about legislation as well as elections.

Although baby boomers are well on their way to remaking elections so that they are concerned with values and personalities, and not with interests—on the legislative level, interest-group politics remains.

As a result of generational change, American politics is now split in two. On the one hand is the politics of issues, interest groups, and ideologies, which determines the way candidates vote on legislation. On the other hand, there is the politics of values and personality by which candidates obtain elected office.

The politics of issues is the old politics, and it is also today the politics of money, because the World War II generation remains in control of the nation's wealth. The politics of values is the new politics, which is the politics of elections, because the baby boomers are more numerous and more energetic in election campaigning.

During the coming decade, baby boomers will increasingly grasp control of the nation's wealth. As this occurs, the politics of values will also become the politics of money, and the current split in the political system will disappear. Only one system will remain—the new politics.

Today the inconsistency between the politics of interest groups and those of values is flagrant, and as a result, attempts at reform are beginning.

Both baby boomers and their parents have well-defined generational personalities. American politics represents a conflict between the two. The result is that the old labels are now useless. People who grew up talking about liberals and conservatives nowadays don't know what labels fit political realities.

When Pierre Trudeau was prime minister of Canada, a reporter[3] asked him where he fit into the political spectrum.

"I am in the radical center," Trudeau replied. "I am an extreme moderate."

Initially the answer appears to be double-talk. But he was using an apparent contradiction to express the approach of a politician who tried to straddle the gap between the old politics of issues and the new politics of values. He was saying that the conventional labels don't apply.

Perhaps this is why politics is so often about symbols—there are so few new ideas. For two centuries politics has been thought of in terms of the workers. The blue-collar worker in manufacturing was both poor and the individual most representative of industrial society. He was so numerous that the political parties contested for his vote. The social commentators worried about his living standards, education level, life expectancy, and political role. Communist, socialist, radical, liberal, conservative—the labels are all defined in terms of the role they see for the blue-collar worker.

Now that worker is disappearing. The political categories of workers and the poor remain, but America doesn't have as many of either anymore.

Voting for Reagan and against Carter made baby boomers seem conservative. But the liberal and conservative labels don't fit well. Boomers generally don't fit the traditional political categories. If the liberal and conservative labels are used, then the boomers require both labels. A traditional conservative believes in a free market for goods and services, but in government regulation of life-styles and personal expression. The traditional liberal, on the other hand, believes in a free market for ideas and self-expression, but not for goods and services, which he wants to have regulated. Baby boomers believe in a free market for both goods and self-expression, particularly as the latter applies to life-style.

Since it's hard to label baby boomers as conservative or liberal, it's hard to predict how they will vote. As a result, some political consultants are saying that a politician who proposes a free market in both goods and self-expression would get the new generation's vote. This is not certain. Voters among the baby boomers do not seem to have a positive program for government.[4] They just want to be left alone. From many of them, a politician gets votes by being antigovernment.

The representative boomer is socially liberal and economically conservative, and when the two conflict, he or she makes a choice or a compromise on the spot. Boomers are individuals and personal relationships connect them to each other. Their politics is made up of loosely defined networks, just as is their social activity.

Many see politics in terms of individuals versus the special interests. "What people want is a chance," a twenty-nine-year-old man told our interviewer. "They want more opportunity. They don't want to be cut out of good professions or businesses. We've had one hundred years in this country of letting big companies and professions use government regulation to limit competition, because people thought that was the way to improve service and enhance living standards. So there were regulated monopolies and self-regulated professions.

"Now there's been a revolution in our thinking. We are using competition to open the door to new people in industry and in the professions in order to lower prices to consumers and to give more people an opportunity to get ahead."

The old way of thinking emphasizes scarcity, a key element of nineteenth-century economic theory that is deeply embedded in traditional economic thought. We learn in college economics courses that there is always a scarcity of resources, and everyone always tries to protect what he has. So people got government regulation to keep others out of their businesses, and they controlled the number of people to be trained in their professions. But there's another way to think: A person can think about opportunity and growth, so that over time, scarcities can be overcome.

Reagan was a puzzle to many experienced commentators because he claimed to be a conservative, but wouldn't raise taxes to eliminate big budget deficits. But this position is very consistent with the baby boomer's values. Reagan opposed tax increases because they limit individualism and initiative. He kept spending up because this helps people have a better life in a stronger economy. And he doesn't connect the two, as most baby boomers don't.

"RAMBOOZLED" BY THE POLITICANS

"What do you think about the new tax bill?" a thirty-year-old professional in Maryland asked our interviewer.

Without waiting for her reply, he answered his own question. "Taxes are eating me alive," he said.

"I work for a medium-sized company," he explained. "Small and medium-sized companies are really going to take a beating with this new law. The working couple has been shafted. I have a wife who works full time and has four children. I've been ramboozled by this whole thing."

Despite being "ramboozled" by the politicians from time to time, baby boomers by and large stay out of the political fray. They are too involved in their own lives to get deeply into politics.

"I voted one time," a thirty-three-year-old Texan told us. "Then I got called to jury duty. I was really bored doing jury duty for two weeks. So I decided not to register to vote again so I wouldn't have to do jury duty ever again."

"Do you concern yourself with politics?" our interviewers asked baby boomers. "No," responded 45 percent. "Yes," answered 31 percent. "A little," replied the remainder.

"Do you associate yourself with a political party?" we asked. "Yes," said 54 percent. "No," answered 46 percent.

"Which party?" we asked those who did have a party affiliation.

"Republican," answered 56 percent (30 percent of the entire group). "Democrat," responded 37 percent (about 20 percent of the entire group). "Independent," replied 7 percent (4 percent of the entire group). Independents are not strictly speaking a political party, but many baby boomers think of them as such.

Why is almost half the baby boom generation not associated with political parties?

"I stay apart from them," said a thirty-eight-year-old Virginian. "I believe in a little of both parties."

"I don't believe in one party all the way," said another person. "Some people vote strictly upon the Republican or Democratic guidelines. I go with who I feel is the best candidate—not upon a political guideline."

"I don't feel it's important to associate with a party," said a thirty-year-old New Yorker. "When it comes down to it, we're all Americans. Whoever I like, I vote for. Parties are silly. There's no reason to commit yourself to one party or the other."

"What about the primary elections?" we asked sometimes. "Don't you need to have a party affiliation to vote in the primaries?"

Many baby boomers told us that they don't vote in the primaries, and so a party affiliation isn't necessary. Others answered that they reside in states where they are able to vote in primaries without a party affiliation; and they do so when they are interested enough in the candidates.

"To associate with a party stifles your choices," said another man. "I'm never sure who I'm going to vote for. It's always a toss-up. I don't feel very secure with any politician in a high position. I rely on the news media. They usually bring out the best and worst in each candidate. I weigh the odds and vote."

"No one party is better," said a woman. "As I get older, I see more differences; but I pick and choose ideas from each one, and neither one has enough for me."

It's hard to avoid the judgment that such political views are somewhat naïve. People who stay so much on the political sidelines are not likely to have much influence on politics or understand how much of importance is actually accomplished through the political process. Nonetheless, a great number of baby boomers stay aloof from politics much of the time, and when they do participate, they do so primarily on the basis of the personality and values of the candidate.

An insight into the reluctance of some baby boomers to affiliate with a party was offered by a twenty-seven-year-old southwesterner who said, "Neither party takes the time to explain what each stands for and who's for who. I don't know who to believe in when it comes time to vote. I usually just ask my friends. I vote for whoever a majority of my friends are voting for."

Other baby boomers who seemed confident that they understood the basic orientation of each party were not made more comfortable thereby with either party.

"I don't agree with the mainstream," said one. "I don't agree with either party. They're either for big business or for welfare people. Neither one represents most American people today."

"I have trouble aligning myself with one party," said a man. "I agree with Republican financial policies, but their social policies bother me. And it's reversed with the Democrats."

It is very significant that most of the baby boomers who expressed an affiliation with a particular party indicated that it was not a very firm attachment.

"I'm registered as a Democrat," said a forty-one-year-old woman in Maryland, "but I don't always vote that way. It's not in concrete as for whom I will vote. I guess you could say I'm associated to a party since I'm registered that way, but I don't consider myself as being associated to a specific party."

This response may seem a bit self-contradictory, but it articulates quite clearly the ambivalence which many, and probably most, baby boomers feel about being part of a political party. "I'm associated," they say, "and I'm not."

There might be some indication in this situation of a realignment in favor of the Republicans. Certainly the younger generation is less heavily Democratic than its parents; but it is less Republican than nonaligned. This is a new phenomenon in American politics, if not in kind then certainly in degree, for the baby boomers stand on the political sidelines. It almost seems as if they were waiting for some nonparty alignment possibility, perhaps an American version of West Germany's Green party.

While America waits for a more coherent version of the politics of values, the politics of personality prevails. Lacking a political home, most baby boomers look for candidates who express their values rather than for those who support their interests. They look for politicians with whom they are personally comfortable and who provide, if such a choice is presented, excitement and diversion.

19

TURNING THE TABLES ON THE MEDIA

"You," Gary said to Susan, but glanced at Bif as well, "still like to shock people, don't you? Years ago you wore beads and used drugs and demonstrated, and you loved to upset your parents and outrage college administrators. Now it's almost twenty years later, and you still delight in flouting convention. Why? Shouldn't you have outgrown that by now?"

Bif and Susan exchanged glances. Then they looked at Gary.

"No," Bif answered. "I don't think we should outgrow that. People have always been telling us what we should do. When we were younger, they said we should be quiet and go along with the war, or stay away from drugs and rock music, and when we didn't, they condemned us. I was going to college and making good grades and helping people but because I wore a gold ring in my ear, older people, who didn't do any of the things I did, would sneer at me.

"It was fun to see how upset people would get. There'd be this man in his business suit and his wife in her neat dress, and they'd have the kids with them, all decked out in their best, and I'd come by with my ring and my long hair and cutoffs and sandals, and they'd look at me like I was a slave trader or something, destined to corrupt their kids."

"I remember how funny it was to see the expression on people's faces," Susan added. "They'd get so upset. They'd take it all so seriously that we began to take it seriously ourselves. After all, we were only their children, but they treated us as if we'd come from Mars."

"I can understand it then," Gary persisted, "but why haven't you outgrown that kind of stuff by now?"

"I guess we got to like it," Bif answered.

"The greeting card industry is cleaning up on it," he continued. "They do cards that are outrageous and satirical, and people our age buy them by the millions."[1]

"When you think about it," Gary said, "it isn't so strange that people in your generation should be attracted to satire. If you are suspicious of authority, then you would naturally like to see things that represent authority or conventional behavior made fun of."

"But it's more than that," Susan said, sending Gary a sharp glance. "When you say that, it's so simple and it makes us seem so simpleminded. It's more than that."

"Well," Gary responded, "what more is it?"

Susan hesitated and thought for a while. "It has to do with showing that you're an individual," she said finally. "It's a way of saying, 'I'm more than what other people are prepared to let me be.' I don't fit into the mold that they want me to fit into. I'm more than what they have decided I should be. Whether it's my parents or the society at large who want to tell me what I can be. It's a way of saying, 'I'm my own person.' "

"Susan's right," said Bif. "When you take a delight in confounding the expectations of others about what you do and what you say, then it's a way of saying that you are an individual."

"But the trouble," said Susan, staring directly at Bif, "is that people who used to be willing to be individuals and shock other people, now want to make money, and so end up looking just like the people they ought to be trying to shock."

Bif frowned at her. "I try to agree with you and help you out," he said, "and you dump on me."

Susan looked a bit ashamed of herself. But she recovered quickly. "It's that I still care about you, and I hate to see you giving up being yourself," she said to Bif.

"You're saying," Gary asked, "that it's your insistence on the uniqueness of the individual that causes you to act uncivilized and embarrass other people?"

"To a degree, yes," Susan responded. "I don't think we're uncivilized, but we do like to shock people. It may seem strange to you, but that's a way of showing a deep conviction that each combination of traits in a person has value, not just the combination of traits that society endorses for the moment."

"So it isn't political?" Gary asked. "When you set out to shock people, it isn't because you reject their society, but because you want the freedom to do your own thing?"

"Yes," Susan answered, "that's right."

"It isn't because you think America is too materialistic and there ought to be more equality for everybody—a different distribution of income?" Gary said, continuing his questioning.

"Maybe that's true," Susan responded. "Maybe some people think that, but that's not what's involved here."

"When the media say we're all yuppies," Bif said, "they're telling people we don't care about anything but shopping—about what kinds of clothes we wear and what kinds of cars we drive. Other generations got into that, and all they said was 'See how their living standards are improving, isn't it great?'

"I thought it was good the way there were those rock concerts to benefit the people in Africa," Bif added. "Those things helped other people to see us as more than just yuppies. It showed what we can do. Those were the first really big charity fund-raising efforts on an international scale. Other generations did a lot of talking about how generous they were, but they never did anything like that on so big a scale."

"Other generations sometimes had to make sacrifices to give aid to people in need," Gary chided Bif. "Your generation may be generous, sometimes, but it's not self-sacrificing."

"I don't see why it should be," Bif responded. "Our generation wants to combine work and fun. I think it also wants to combine generosity and enjoyment. To my mind, that's great. It serves as an example to people in other nations. It says we in America don't just have so much money that we can give it away, which it seems is often the message of charity, but it says we get involved emotionally in the process of helping other people, and we want people like us who are in other countries, and can also afford to give money to help others, to get involved as well."

"You're right," Susan said emphatically when Bif had finished. "Big business and the media are constantly trying to exploit us. I saw one big company do a commercial that said that our generation knew there was more to life than a VCR, a food processor, and the latest pair of running shoes. It said we did volunteer work and helped our communities. I thought it was great.

"Then I read in a newspaper that the company which had sponsored the TV messages had done so only to try to exploit us. The company even called it a 'hook.' There was a hook in the message, they said. The idea was to get people like us to see the TV spots and say to ourselves, 'There's a company that really understands us and our life-styles.' Then they thought we would all buy from their company.[2] It made me mad that the only time a company would say anything good about us, it was only to try to get our business."

"I think we've always been subjected to unfair criticism," Bif said. "I once made a list of the adjectives that people applied to us in books and articles they made us read in college. They said we were selfish, irresponsible, and narcissistic—I didn't even know what that meant until my teacher made me look it up."

"I read the same stuff," Susan said. "What always got me was that the same people who said we were so full of self-love also said that we had so much self-hatred that our personal relationships with others were ruined. I was young and trying to understand myself, and I was being told that I loved myself too much and that I hated myself too much. I decided they didn't know what they were talking about."

NOT A YUPPIE

It is surprising to their parents how conscious baby boomers are of themselves as a generation. There was no generational consciousness on a similar scale previously. But to a baby boomer, his or her generation is very special. They are very conscious of it and very protective. They listen to what people say about them and take it very personally.

Such an attachment cannot have grown in a vacuum. Baby boomers have responded to what has been written and said about them, in the process becoming conscious of themselves. The Vietnam War also taught them to think of themselves as a special group. They were supposed to fight the war, and were concerned that they were being turned into cannon fodder for their parents' generation.

The media are a major source of the labels attached to baby boomers, so that there is a love-hate relationship between the generation and the media. The media are continually rediscovering the baby boom generation and attaching new labels to it. Many baby boomers resent the labels.

"The media don't really portray anyone right," a thirty-three-year-old woman told our interviewer. "They just try to get sensation and novelty. It's all entertainment for the masses, and we're the freaks.

"They invent the caricature, and then they demolish it. They went through this business about 'having it all.' We were supposed to be the generation that was going to have it all. They said to people, 'You can have it all' and they invented the term 'Superwoman' to be the person who did all they said she could do. Then after a year or two that got old, so they came up with 'the end of the juggler.' They said that people were giving up trying to have it all, and were picking just certain things to do. But the fact is that some people in our generation have always been trying to have it all, and others have chosen only certain things from the start.

"Several years ago the media invented the yuppie who was supposed to be our generation. He was rich and spent all his time trying to get the latest in fashion. But after a while this got tiring to the public, and the media so overdid the caricature that everyone loathed the yuppie and no one would be one—so they rediscovered the people in our generation who don't make a lot of money and they wrote about them for a while."

An aspect of media attention which offends many baby boomers is that broad generalizations seem continually to be made about the entire generation. In the sixties they were said to be the counterculture, and were labeled "hippies." When they got out of college and into jobs, the media labeled them "materialists."

The interplay between the media's portrayals and the generation's reactions to them is both constant and intensely personal. "The media are always trying to put us in a neat package," a man told us. "Every few years they rediscover our generation and attach a new label to it."

A woman in her mid-thirties, who lives in Florida and is a quality-circle facilitator in a factory, was interviewed for this book. She had spent two years in college, when the Vietnam War intervened. "I dropped out of college to become a candle carrier at the moratoriums," she told the interviewer. "I still feel bad about those who lost their lives. I'm still very bitter about it all."

After the war she was married, then a divorce sent her looking for work in a distant city, and she took a job in a factory. She had been there several years, but did not like it. "The factory I work in has an employee involvement program," she said. "But it's just a hollow promise. I wasn't allowed to do the work they said they wanted me to do. People aren't satisfied with just money and benefits anymore," she continued. "They need more satisfying work.

"I think I've mellowed over the years," she said. "I care more about myself now than I used to. I run, take aerobics and exercise. I used to party a lot, but now I don't do much of that anymore.

"This is the most satisfying time for me," she continued. "I'm going through a career change. I'm taking a chance and becoming a real estate agent. Some people say it's just my midlife crisis. I don't agree. I'm feeling better about myself and my life.

"I wonder what kind of person I am? I have a picture of a yuppie posted on my wall at home. I don't think I am one. I don't care as much about material things. I'm more happiness-oriented. I read about a man who said that the media are preoccupied with hype and don't really care about the people they cover. I think it's true."[3]

This is far too harsh an indictment. Many reporters are very honest people who don't dream up stories or categories, and who care about those they report on. Increasingly, they are themselves baby boomers.

Baby boomers are unable to trust the labels the media attaches to them—"hippies" or "yuppies" or whatever—because the motivation of those creating the categories is suspect.

"I think we can tolerate some manipulation by Madison Avenue and the media," a woman told us, "but it has to be rejected when it goes too far. I think there ought to be a declaration of independence for this generation from the media and Madison Avenue."

The media haven't really helped people to comprehend baby boomers, and if professionals or business people or politicians don't understand them, then they are out of touch with America today.

Most of the baby boomers themselves are not much better in their self-assessment. They know who they are as individuals, but they don't know America. They are only dimly aware of our nation's history; they are rarely reflective; and though they know themselves as a group, they are not good at articulating what makes them special.

Sometimes the media's presentation of the baby boomers is like looking into a mirror in a fun house: They can recognize themselves in it, but only as a very distorted image. Still, because they are recognizable, the media perform a kind of service. They let boomers see aspects of themselves in extreme exaggeration. There is usually some truth in the picture, enough for a person to think about himself or herself more deeply.

Much of the time boomers don't like what they see in the media mirror. Years ago, when they were called the "counterculture," most knew they didn't want to end up in a commune, so they rushed into business. More recently, when they were presented as yuppies, those who didn't want to be shallow and silly tried to put more depth into their lives. The media say now that boomers are too materialistic, and a revival of interest in the spiritual side of life is emerging among them.

There is a constant dialogue with the media who try to pin labels on the generation which boomers don't like. So the boomers do unexpected things to turn the tables on the media. There are still a lot of surprises to come from this generation.

20

"WE'RE ONLY SPIRIT"

Several weeks later, Bif and Susan agreed to a final meeting. She suggested that since the weather was good, they should meet at the beach near her house. She had planned to spend the afternoon sunning, and he agreed to join her there after work.

When he caught sight of her reclining in the sun he was surprised that she was alone. She had not mentioned Gary in their conversation, but Bif had assumed he would be present.

So surprised was he that he neglected to greet her. "Where's Gary?" he asked as he came up to her.

Susan languidly opened one eye. She was lying on a brightly colored beach towel and wearing a small bikini.

"Is it Gary you wanted?" she asked.

Bif said nothing. He slipped off his shirt and shorts, under which he wore a bathing suit, spread a towel, and sat down beside her.

"Gary couldn't come," Susan said, not looking at him. "I'll tell you why later." She hesitated, then continued. "He and I talked, and I'm supposed to tell you what he said."

"I'm just as glad that he isn't here," Bif said. "But what did he say?"

"He likes our classifications," Susan replied. "He thinks they work well."

"Where does Gary fit into the classification scheme?" Bif asked, now lying back and idly gazing at the sky.

Bif and Susan were silent for a while. They lay side by side as the first chill of oceanside evening crept up the beach from the water.

"I wonder," Susan said, "whether we really should be classifying people. It's something I don't entirely approve of. It's kind of a persistence of the old ways of thinking—trying to put people in groups rather than accept them as individuals."

"You know, you're right," Bif responded. "I was interviewing a young man for a job at our firm the other day. He was part Japanese, part Cape Verdean, and part English. Quite a mixture. So people are continually asking him what his ethnic background is. He said people always want to identify with some group so they can stereotype him. I think he told me that, hoping I would not try to classify him but would look at him as a separate, unique person."[1]

"Are you going to hire him?" Susan asked.

"I recommended we do," Bif answered. "I think he's a competitor, and we need them."

Susan laughed. "So you avoided one classification—based on ethnic background—to use another?"

Bif grinned. "Of course. But I think it's better to classify people by their priorities and behavior than by their ethnic background. If you're going to stereotype or be stereotyped, I think our classifications are better than racial or ethnic ones."

"I do too," said Susan.

"You know," Bif continued, "the top brass in my company have given up on our generation. This guy I was interviewing was very young, just a junior in college. They want to hire him after he graduates next summer. They've decided to hire younger people and train them to be like the company wants. They think the next generation is going to be more like they were. It's a cycle, they think—or it was Vietnam that made us like we are—independent. But they don't want us. They want people like themselves. I keep hearing via the grapevine that more and more companies are doing that. They're all hoping that the next generation is going to be more accepting of authority, more docile, more like the older people were when they were young."

"Will they be successful?" Susan asked.

"I don't know. What do you think?"

"I don't know either. I don't have any children."

"But we have some allies. I met a guy in his fifties at the bar last night. He told me it's not only people in our generation who have our values and want the things we want. Many of the older people want those things, too, he said. 'Many of us have tried for years to get changes along the lines you want.'

"So maybe it's an even contest. Someday a study by a survey company will tell us whether we passed our values on to the next generation—or whether our influence just died out."

Another long pause ensued. Purples, oranges, and deep blues appeared in the sky. The underside of the few clouds glimmered with the reflection of the water until they acquired a rosy, silvery mother-of-pearl cast.

"Well," Bif finally asked, "what have you and Gary concluded about me?"

"What do you mean?" Susan asked.

"You know what I mean," Bif said. "This whole thing started with you telling me that my values had changed. Then you brought Gary in to check me out. Well, where did you come out of the question? Have I changed?"

"Gary says you haven't," Susan responded. "He says your values haven't really changed, but your priorities have. You're involved in the conflict all of us have about what our priorities are. You're asking yourself, 'Am I too much a competitor? Should I be more of a pleasure-seeker? Should I become a better-balanced person?' Gary says I've been complaining because I think you've become less balanced and too competitive. It's a matter of priorities."

"That's what Gary says," Bif responded. "What do you think?"

"I think," Susan responded, "that when you get to be too much of a competitor, you adopt so many of the characteristics of the older generation that I have trouble distinguishing you from them. I think our values stress independence, but you are becoming too conformist. I think our values stress individualism, to be a bit bizarre and to shock older people; but in trying to compete successfully, you're adopting all the conventions and hang-ups of the old system."

"But you're not saying that's how I am now?" Bif inquired.

"No," Susan admitted. "I'm saying that you're heading that way."

"Then maybe you're not saying much at all." Bif defended himself. "Sure, I'm more pro-business than I was years ago; almost all of us are, even you. As we've grown older, we've learned the importance of business.

"But I'm no less anti-big business than I ever was, and I'm still pretty entrepreneurial."

Hearing this, Susan rose on one elbow, turned her face toward Bif, and shading her eyes from the brilliant red of the sun, asked in amazement, "Are you serious?"

Bif was taken aback. "Well, I'm not as entrepreneurial as you, I admit," he said abashedly. "But it's natural for people to evolve in their interests," he insisted, defending himself once more. "It's natural for a young person to be a pleasure-seeker and to evolve into a competitor as he gets older and takes on more responsibility."

"Does that mean I'm unnatural?" Susan asked.

Bif looked startled by the question.

"You implied that it was unnatural to stay a pleasure-seeker and I'm more a pleasure-seeker than you are." Susan insisted.

"I didn't mean to imply that it was unnatural," Bif said.

"Good, because I don't think it is," Susan said. "Maybe you should think about being more of a pleasure-seeker again," she suggested.

"When we first talked about my life last spring," said Bif, "I got mad at what you said. Then later I began to think about it. You really challenged me. 'What is my life about?' I asked myself. 'What is important to me?' Then as we met and talked, I began to say to myself, 'What is happening to the spiritual aspects of my life? Am I one thing or another? Am I all materialistic today, or is there anything spiritual left?'

"I think I'm a combination of both. There's a materialistic side of me; but there's also a spiritual side. I think maybe I was losing sight of the spiritual side.

"So I've been thinking about this. I used to have a vision of what was spiritual. But I've lost that in recent years, just as you said I have.

"Back then, I wandered around without income, without a job, like the Indian mystics do. Then I rejected materialism. I thought it was incompatible with my spirituality.

"But I couldn't wander around poor forever. Now I'm less sure that materialism and spirituality are so different. I see them as supporting each other. Earning money makes it possible to do things that add to my spiritual development. If I want to travel, to add to my understanding of the world, then I have to have money. If I want to have experiences, I need money to pay for them.

"Back in the sixties I thought of spirituality as revelation or self-insight. I thought it would come intuitively if I were just to free my mind of everything material.

"Now I think spirituality is an awareness you develop about life from living it—not from running away from it. Spirituality develops out of challenge and overcoming self-limitations.

"So material and spiritual aren't opposed; they complement each other. You can go too much to the material, like you say I've been doing, and probably you're correct. But I can also go back a little and emphasize more of the spiritual side of my life."

"What I want," said Susan, "is satisfaction in life, even though not all my wants are met. I know I can't have everything. It's as if there's at least one thing that a person doesn't get. Everyone doesn't get something or another. One of my friends doesn't have a child; another doesn't have a husband. Another doesn't have a house and won't start off with a condo. So it just eats at her that she doesn't have a house.

"There's always something you think you ought to have, but don't get. I recognize that. But I want the kind of satisfaction that comes from having freedom and opportunity and using it, not just from acquiring goods.

"I saw an interview with Bob Dylan on the tube a few months ago, but I didn't make much of it then. Now it means something to me. He is into religion now. 'We're only spirit,' he said. 'That's all we are.'[2]

"What I wondered," Susan continued, "was how each of the groups in our generation feel about material things. The way I figured it out was that the competitors always want more, so they can get ahead of others. Most of the pleasure-seekers can get enough for their life-styles, so generally they're satisfied with the material goods they have. The trapped need something else than material things; they need freedom. The balanced have scaled back their desires to what they can afford. And the self-destroyers don't care what they have or don't have anyway, they're so deeply into their own problems."

"That makes sense," Bif said. "I was a pleasure-seeker first, then a competitor, and now I think I'm in between. Thinking about all this—

which you've made me do—has made me more comfortable with myself. I feel better about myself."

Susan smiled wanly but said nothing. She understood that Bif was talking to himself more than to her.

Bif fell into silence and Susan still said nothing.

"Don't you ever turn over?" Bif finally asked her at one point, as he rolled onto his stomach.

"I like to tan my front first," Susan replied, speaking absently, as if her attention had been recalled from a great distance.

Now the sun was dipping into the ocean. The first tremors of a shiver passed through Bif. He sat up and opened his eyes, surprised to see Susan already sitting up, hugging her bent legs with her arms, her chin resting on her knees. She was wearing her sunglasses and staring fixedly into the setting sun.

Suddenly Bif realized that she had been somewhat withdrawn and less playful than usual. A sadness in her manner, which had been only dimly apparent to him earlier, was now unavoidably evident. Obeying an impulse, he put his arm over her shoulder and pulled her near. She shuddered and leaned toward him.

"Susan," Bif asked, "what's wrong?"

She didn't respond.

Then he understood. "It's about Gary."

She threw her head up defiantly, not facing him, as if to deny his suggestion. But when she spoke, it was to say instead, "Yes."

"What happened?"

"He told me he's going to get remarried."

"Is that why he isn't here?"

"Yes."

"Didn't you try to hold on to him?"

"It's hard to hold on to a person when he confronts you with another woman.

"He told me he was going to get remarried and he had me meet the woman. I know not to try to hang on."

"So it's all over?" Bif asked.

"No," she insisted. "None of my relationships end. I'll stay in touch, and so will he. That's why he brought his fiancée to meet me. But it will be very different. We won't see each other like we did.

"I get scared," she said. "I know it's my life-style, but its frightening.

I have to look for a new person again. I worry, will I be able to find someone stimulating and enjoyable.

"People who are single have to realize they have to start over again. I have to meet new people, do new things.

"This is why some people get married. They marry to make life easier. They are looking for security. They want to get out of the struggle to change and grow. They don't want to have to be interesting and attractive. They want to hide, to find security. Even if it's only an illusion—even if marriage doesn't last. At least, it's the illusion of security.

"Maybe I should get married. Maybe my life-style is disappearing. Maybe people are giving up sex because of AIDS, and settling down and having families."

"What you said about having options and marriage as a trap," Bif asked, "was that all a pretense?" He tried to make the question challenging but gentle, since he knew that she was very vulnerable at this instant. Also he wanted her to understand that he was asking because he really cared about her. "Did you really mean what you said, or do you wish you and Gary had gotten married?"

"I don't think it's all a pretense," she answered. "Once I could have married Gary. We talked about it. I didn't want to. But still sometimes I have doubts. Even if you're independent, you care about people. So sometimes when you lose somebody, it hurts."

"Maybe," Bif said cautiously, "it's because you're not supportive enough. Maybe you're so busy thinking about what's next in your life that people think you judge them too harshly."

"Do you think that?" Susan asked.

"Sometimes, yes," Bif answered.

"Maybe," Susan acknowledged, "but I think I'm often supportive. Gary had a tough time when his first marriage broke up. I met him a year or so after the divorce. He'd had a real trauma. I helped him out of it; gave him lots of support. Then in the end he fell in love with another woman.

"Once I asked him, 'Would you marry again if you had it all to do over?' He said, 'No, I wouldn't marry. But children? Yes. Children are wonderful—my whole life. Marriage is up and down.'

"He must have found a woman he was comfortable with and thought it would be good for the children if he remarried. I know I should be glad that he's found someone he can be happy with, and I *am* glad. But still it's hard for me to be left behind because I really cared about him."

Bif saw in her eyes a defiance of her own pain. But he had never seen her so upset and depressed.

"Come on, let me buy you a drink," he suggested.

Susan nodded in agreement. They rose, gathered their belongings, and headed away from the beach.

Three days later Susan sat in the Boston airport. She was indifferently dressed; her hair, usually so carefully brushed, was tousled and unkempt. She was still upset.

"Why am I here?" she asked herself.

After a moment's thought she answered her question, "I've got to break my ties here; I've got to do something unusual."

From the corner of her eye she noticed a tall, slender man in jeans and a blue shirt enter the waiting area. He wore a moustache and had wavy brown hair.

"Maybe that's what I need," she thought to herself. "Someone who is more relaxed, out of the pressures of the East. Nothing like Gary."

Her flight to San Francisco was scheduled to stop in Denver. "Perhaps," she thought, "he's going to Wyoming or Montana." Years ago she had driven her van through the upper mountain states, and in the back of her mind had nestled the intention to return. Now it was time to find a new challenge; to start a new relationship; to do something different. It was time to close one chapter of her life and open a new and different one.

"He is really good-looking," she told herself, examining the man carefully as he sat down opposite her, still out of the corner of her eye.

She ran her hand through her hair to straighten it and tucked in her blouse for a neater appearance. Her eyes brightened and her chin lifted in anticipation as she saw the man rise from his seat and cross the aisle to where she sat.

"Are you going to Denver?" he asked.

21

THE REVOLUTION OF THE NEW GENERATION

WHAT BABY BOOMERS HAVE DONE FOR AMERICA

In 1969, Charles Reich predicted confidently that the college students of the time would make a revolution in the United States and around the world. "This is the revolution of the new generation," he wrote. "Their protest and rebellion, their culture, clothes, music, drugs, ways of thought and liberated life-style . . . We can see that the present transformation goes beyond anything in modern history. Beside it a mere revolution, such as the French or Russian, seems inconsequential."[1]

In the years since 1969, generational and technological transformations have in fact given us substantial social change. American society is different, but not in many of the ways Reich had expected.

The baby boom generation, through its multiplicity of interests and endeavors, encourages multiple dimensions in each life. The single-minded commitment of previous generations to a job once gave us many colorless and uninteresting personalities. Also, people were exhorted and sometimes compelled to fit the one-dimensional molds their leaders designed. People were forced into jobs without variety and into lives without balance. There were exceptions, of course. And it is the exceptions who became models for the baby boom generation.

Often criticized as selfish and as wanting it all for themselves, this generation has, by its activities, made it possible for both older and younger people to enrich their lives as well. To have it all is to have a fulfilling job at decent pay, an interesting avocation, time for family and friends, and enough variety and adventure to permit growth in mind and spirit.

In the old system, a person played during childhood, worked during adulthood, and, in old age, was free to pursue his or her own interests. Unfortunately, childhood in those days did not provide a good base for adult activities, nor did work provide a base for the leisure which was to follow. Each segment of life was specialized and encapsulated from the others. It was thought that people's mental capacities deteriorated as they aged, leaving retirement essentially for simple pleasures, for which no preparation was needed during their working lives.

The baby boomers have enriched each of the periods of life. To childhood they have brought a renewed emphasis on education as preparation for an adult career. Since they are often criticized for pushing their own children too hard in school, they should not be denied the kudos they have earned by recognizing the importance of learning. In other words, they ought to be recognized for the good as well as the bad in what they do. As adults, they have refused to be wholly consumed by a job. The interests and capabilities they develop instead will serve later as the basis for a far richer old age.

Modern research into the functioning of the brain is demonstrating that with a stimulating environment, mental capacity (measured in neurological terms) continues to grow even in old age.[2] A likely result of the myriad interests that baby boomers developed early in life is environmental stimulation.

This generation is enhancing human freedom. From adolescence, the baby boomers have insisted on the uniqueness of each individual. They have enshrined the legitimacy of each person's expression of his or her own particular consciousness. "Do your own thing" is a clear statement of the freedom accorded each person. It has often been said that free expression has been given too loose rein by this generation, but it cannot be denied that the generation has also insisted on and acquired greater freedom in thought and behavior than did its predecessors.

The baby boomers are attempting to promote a peaceful world. In the place of jingoism is a more sophisticated comprehension of the confines of national ambition and the limitations of military power, a concept in large part born of the Vietnam War.

Simultaneously, this generation has an extensive experience and understanding of the international economic and political scene. It seeks international involvement via media, travel, and trade. But it eschews foreign conquests. It is uncomfortable with the pursuit of narrow national interests because it aspires to multinational leadership in the world.

To the great issue of the risk of nuclear war, this generation brings little romanticism regarding Soviet repression, but it also has an abhorrence of risking war by seeking to alter the Soviet system.

The great foreign-policy movements in American history—expansionism, isolationism, crusading against totalitarianism—any of which if applied in today's world would create significant risks of nuclear annihilation, are each rejected by boomers. Whether or not peace can be preserved remains to be seen, but the baby boom generation is more determined in its pursuit of peace than any previous American generation.

This generation is creating an explosion of entrepreneurial effort and technological innovation. Committed to individualism, desiring material rewards, and fascinated by the potentials of new technology, the baby boomers are pushing at business and technical frontiers in all directions.

Entrepreneurship, for this generation, is an avenue of escape from the red tape of large firms. For women and blacks it is a means of escape from the frustrations of racial and sexual discrimination. Always independent in their personal lives, many of the most capable people among the baby boomers now look to their own companies as expressions of their uniqueness and as vehicles by which to create their futures.

Entrepreneurship and technological advances are two of the most important engines of economic advancement. Two others, often used in the past, are rapid population growth and large-scale military conflict. But these two are denied the United States today—population growth is slow and military adventures are by and large rejected for good and sufficient reasons. So only entrepreneurship and technological change are left to fuel America's growth. Thus it is of crucial economic significance that the baby boom generation is deeply committed to both.

Virtually all of the free world's industrial nations are in a situation very similar to America's. Each has slow population growth; and each is endeavoring to avoid military conflict. Only Japan now matches the United States in entrepreneurial drive and technological effort. Western Europe, in particular, has lagged behind in both; these countries have lacked a home-grown impetus for expansion, and to achieve it, have depended to a large degree (with Japan, to be sure) on America as an overseas market. In this circumstance, Europe is finding the American example of innovation—in business and in technology—a valuable model. By exercising initiative in America, the baby boom generation is providing leadership to the world.

This generation has turned the focus of American domestic politics away from the divergent interests of groups and regions to values and personality.

Baby boomers are pushing aside the political categories of the eighteenth and nineteenth centuries, with which we are still burdened, and are creating new categories. "Liberal" and "conservative" are terms that have lost their meaning, though still retaining symbolic value to many. "Where have all the liberals gone?" ask pollsters, who find there are very few voters who will identify themselves with the label. And while the number of self-described conservatives has risen, this may be misleading because many are opposed to restraint on what traditional conservatives believe are morally offensive publications, films, and broadcasts? We have a dominant generation that is liberal about personal expression and conservative about economic issues. Of what value then are the labels, since they characterize virtually no one in the generation accurately?

With the decline of the old politics has come notoriety for interest groups. Already influential at the presidential level in American politics, noninterest politics are now making their way into the congressional and local levels.

In place of economic and social-class interest questions about the candidates' understanding of and expression of the values and aspirations of the baby boomers are appearing.

The struggle against the depersonalization of large institutions, which the young people of the nineteen-sixties initiated, continues. No longer does the resistance take the form of street protests and mass movements, but instead finds its expression in individual acts—less of protest than an affirmation of values and attitudes often ignored by conventional institutions and large organizations.

Each person now struggles with the claims and pressures exerted by the conventions of society. Individuals are trying to preserve the liberty and promise of youth from the demands of employers, spouses, offspring, and peers. There now occurs a continuing contest in the life of each individual between liberty and bondedness.

Partly as a result of depression and war, the World War II generation developed qualities and concerns that made it seem to its children regimented, captive to the bureaucracies of large organizations, and possessed of a mentality which stressed economic advance over other concerns. In reaction, younger people grasped at independence; they embraced honesty in personal relationships and the preservation of the natural and human environment. Today, entering middle age, most still hold to those goals.

As they enter middle age, people who were free spirits are striving to preserve their independence against the claims of traditional society. This has emerged as a key human drama of today. It is a question of values—remaining true to certain values or betraying them. Some are unable to retain their freedom. They have become bound to one or another aspect of the traditional society. They have become captives. Others have resisted.

Commentators in the 1960s saw the young generation as advocates of freedom and of a different ethos, as leaders, carrying a torch of change for the minority in the older generation that sympathized with them, but was ineffectual among its peers. In this important sense, the struggle which young people engaged in for greater freedom was extended to all. It still is.

DO CHANGING PRIORITIES MAKE BABY BOOMERS LIKE THEIR PARENTS?

In our survey we asked each person whether or not his or her outlook on life had changed during the past five years. Seventy-eight percent told us that it had.

"How has it changed?" we asked.

"I am more conservative," was the answer from 38 percent. "I am more realistic," said another 19 percent. "More pessimistic." "More independent," said others (31 percent). A few (4 percent) added, "More religious."

Why do so many say that they are now more conservative? The explanation that most give is that they have acquired families and, with them, responsibilities that have altered their outlook on life. They have new concerns and additional worries.

In consequence, new priorities are emerging for many baby boomers. Now that many are entering middle age, they are concerned about excesses in drug and alcohol use, primarily, it seems, because of the implications to their own children of extensive substance abuse. They are concerned about the mistreatment and abandonment of children, for similar reasons. And they have developed a growing interest in religion and the spiritual aspect of life.[3] The emergence of these considerations as significant elements in their lives is what baby boomers mean when they say they have become more conservative over the years.

Today many members of the post-World War II generation are making some of the same choices their parents did about marriage, children, careers, and life-styles. Does this mean that the generational differences have been obliterated? Do concerns such as these mean that the baby boom generation is really no different from its parents' generation?

The answer is no. The basic values that underlie the new concerns, and that largely determine how they will attempt to deal with these concerns, are shared by baby boomers, but are quite different from those of the older generation. Because these values are dispersed so broadly, there are really almost no traditionalists in the generation.

Traditionalists do not harbor the deep reservations about the institution of marriage that many baby boomers have. Traditionalists do not nurse the profound suspicion of big business and big government that baby boomers continually express. Nor do traditionalists accept the legitimacy of pleasure as a priority in the life of many people the way the new generation does.

The new generation remains different. Its basic values are distinctive, even though the individual priorities within the generation change over time. The generation has changed the way Americans view work; it has introduced a new style to human relationships; and it has turned the American philosophy about the meaning of life upside down—from duty to self-expression. The generation's attitudes, behavior, and commitments are very different, even though as most of the baby boomers progress through life, they may appear to become more like their parents.

To some, today's convergence of priorities between the old and the new generations suggests the failure of Reich's predicted revolution. They believe that the old society was not swept away. But this narrow view focuses unduly on political developments. In part, the power of institutions has been replaced by skepticism about the purposes and value of such institutions. Meanwhile, baby boomers have pushed ahead with major social changes. Women are in the work force in large numbers, with their aspiration to the top jobs recognized if not wholly endorsed. The concept of the "organization" man, wedded to his job and nothing else, has given way to the "modern" man who increasingly makes time available for other pursuits. The hard-boiled professional or executive has given way to a more sensitive and concerned person.

From today's vantage point, it is clear that Reich and other commentators of the sixties failed to understand the full range of values of this generation and, therefore, emphasized some out of context. Rather than sweeping away the old society and establishing a new, unfamiliar structure in its place, the sixties revolution produced changes in existing social institutions that were in concert with the generation's values. That the resulting structures also incorporated much of the collective experience of previous generations should not be surprising.

Probably the most important area of change has been in human relationships. The younger generation coined a new vocabulary about people's feelings; it sparked the sexual revolution; it brought a new openness and honesty to personal relationships. Through its efforts, a rigid and moralistic society has softened and been made more tolerant.

So there has been a revolution. Not the political upheaval and surge to the left that was predicted, but a revolution nonetheless. A revolution in social mores, in technology, in interpersonal relations, yes—but not a revolution in the economic and political system. Despite the prophets of leftist revolution, the sixties generation never really desired one. It found the system flexible enough to meet its requirements, though some are still reluctant to admit this.

After these adjustments of the past two decades, there is now a slowing of the push for change. People of the post-Vietnam War generation are looking back and asking themselves what did they really accomplish by storming the barricades of society years ago?

BABY BOOMERS: BETTER OR WORSE THAN THEIR PARENTS?

Baby boomers have brought to our business organizations a new inventiveness and intolerance of bureaucracy, at a time when international competition requires our companies to be more innovative and cost-effective. The baby boomers are bringing the right qualities to business. That large organizations are often so unwilling to adapt to them seems unfortunate. A great opportunity is being lost.

To our politics the baby boomers have brought a suspicion of authority which is, on balance, healthy. They have also brought tolerance, which causes American politics to have less rancor and bitterness than ever before in our history. But the majority are unwilling to devote much effort to public issues, and the nation suffers as a result. Also, the lack of a feeling of duty or obligation to others that characterizes most boomers leaves our society with few who are willing to address the great unmet needs of the poor and helpless.

AN EXPLOITED GENERATION

The media and social commentators have generally portrayed the baby boomers as an affluent and self-indulgent group. The new generation is made to appear the largely undeserving beneficiary of the hard work and sacrifice of previous generations of Americans.

This judgment is inaccurate or at least should be subjected to qualification. The baby boom generation has not been particularly well treated by the America of its parents. Tens of thousands were killed or wounded in an ill-conceived, poorly directed war in which young people were the primary victims and for which they received in return mostly resentment.

Acquiring considerable education, most were nonetheless directed into jobs in large organizations where they have been given very little opportunity to apply their talents.

Encouraged continually by marketeers to expect considerable leisure for sports, adventure, and exciting experiences, many have instead been required by a weak economy to spend a great part of their lives at work. In fact, a larger proportion of this generation is compelled to work to make ends meet than was the case with its parents.

Baby boomers have had less in the way of economic gain than previous generations, although admittedly they started from a higher base. They began work in a period of rampant inflation and high interest rates, and then found themselves in a series of recessions, followed by a period of very slow growth. Living standards for baby boomers have risen at a much slower rate than for most previous American generations. The overhang of government debt and of foreign debt, is the legacy of recent years, makes it unlikely that economic growth will be any more rapid in the foreseeable future. Furthermore, responding to the nation's economic challenge from competitors abroad is likely to result in falling living standards in the near future.[4]

Unless the economy improves dramatically, many baby boomers may not be able to afford the living standards of their parents.[5] All the publicity given to young professionals who are affluent has suggested that all young people are doing well, but that isn't the case.[6] Many young professionals are even having trouble making ends meet. Most of them are loaded with debt.[7]

It also seems likely that baby boomers are already paying considerable taxes, and will pay more to support an increasingly large population of retired people. By the time baby boomers reach what is now the normal retirement age of sixty-five, there will be almost one person retired and drawing Social Security and/or some other pension for every two people working. The result is that young people must expect to pay up to 30 percent or more of their earnings, through taxes or by their income being diverted into private-pension contributions, for the support of the elderly.[8] It is not surprising that many young people are concerned that there will be few resources left to support them in *their* retirement.[9]

Many baby boomers hope to retire early so that they may avoid working until they are so close to death that they do not have any golden years. But the financial security necessary for early retirement is going to be more difficult to achieve. Our government is already attempting to make early retirement more difficult by reducing the benefits early retirees can receive from their own pension plans.[10] Even if baby boomers set aside savings for early retirement, the government will attempt to keep them from retiring by imposing ruinously high taxes if they do so.

Finally, baby boomers who are competitors are very ambitious as well as very talented. They aspire to climb corporate ladders and to attain top jobs. This is as true of the women as the men. But there are few top jobs, despite the large number of young people with the capability to perform them well. The result will be that the full potential of many baby boomers will never be achieved.

It is not common for the young people to complain or to be pessimistic. By and large, they are an optimistic generation. But more and more of them are perceiving that they have not been well treated by American society. To be blunt, they have been made to work more than previous generations with less to show for it, and they are being taxed more heavily while being denied top jobs in recompense. The redistributions of income which take place in our society through government taxation and spending policies are generally made at the expense of the baby boomers.

Despite the situation in which American society has placed baby boomers, insult is added to injury by the continual barrage of media and political criticism. Some commentators deny that baby boomers are benefiting less from the economy than have previous generations.[11] Americans are told repeatedly that baby boomers are selfish and overprivileged. "I guess you have to have been born after World War II to be a real skunk," says a character in a recent novel.[12]

Neither history, nor economic data, nor our interviews support this indictment of the baby boomers. On the contrary, baby boomers would appear to have a legitimate concern that they will turn out to be the first generation in American history to have been exploited by its parents.

22

WHAT LIES AHEAD

LIFE IS A PROCESS OF CHANGE

Baby boomers accept that they are living in a time of rapid change. They recognize that as the years have passed, their outlook on life has altered. Most recognize that their lives will continue to change.

A twenty-eight-year-old artist, who described her national heritage as "American-Russian-German," told our interviewer about the changes in her life.

"I had great expectations about life several years ago," she said, "about what life should be like. But now I'm letting go of my expectations. I'm relaxing a lot more.

"I thought I'd become an artist, and I did. Nothing took me away from that. I knew I'd always be doing something creative, but I didn't know what. The media I was interested in changed. I was going to go into theater, but there are too many things out of your control in the theater business. So I went into the visual arts because that's something I can do myself.

"People I'm friends with," she continued, "are going through similar changes in their lives. My friends have been drawn together. We have gotten to a point where it's necessary for us to be in each other's lives.

"Crazy things happen to people; things you don't expect at all. Some are very good and some are very bad. But these are the growth-producing events in life, and people come into a person's life at these times.

"What is really important to me?" she asked rhetorically. "A long time ago I worked in a company. My needs certainly weren't being met there, so I left. I couldn't do what I wanted and work for a company. I wanted to express myself by being creative. Once I knew I could support myself on my own, I left.

"I'm more and more contented. I'm learning to accept the traumas life brings. I think I'm where I'm supposed to be.

"I like people who grow, who aren't afraid to take risks or to change. That's what life is about. I've learned that it's okay to live like that. Life is a process of change."

What are baby boomers today concerned about? When asked, people gave a variety of responses, among which certain themes stood out.

People with children expressed concern about the economy and having financial security, though only one quarter of the respondents mentioned that it was a serious concern. Another quarter of the group were concerned about their children on a more personal basis, involving such questions as the quality of their education. Fully 15 percent were most concerned about nuclear war or the possible destruction of our environment and ourselves.

Almost everyone seems worried about the possibility of nuclear war. Some have it up front in their minds. Others repress the worry. But the fear of nuclear destruction crouches in almost everyone's consciousness.

In the words of one young woman, "I concentrate on my own individual life, because things could go so quickly. Nuclear weaponry has been a predominant part of this generation's lives. It makes me not want to pay attention to what goes on in the world because I realize that it's not in my control."

We also asked people what they expected to be doing in the next several years. Only one third answered they expected to be doing the same thing as currently. One person in seven expected to make a career change. Another one in seven expected a significant advance in career.

Six percent of the group hoped to go into business for themselves. Finally, one person in seven hoped to achieve a dream—to break into the entertainment world in a big way; or to make enough money to quit work before age forty; or to found a great business that will dominate its field.

Several people who are trapped recognized their situations and said they were going to get out. They told us they would refuse to persist in such unhappy circumstances. One said she would break up her marriage. Others said they would not stick it out in companies they didn't like. They would change jobs.

We encountered several people who said they wanted to retire early. "Our parents got stuck," they said, "in the same company for years. They finally retired, only to die soon afterwards." Baby boomers don't want this to happen to them.

"The thing I keep coming up against," a thirty-six-year-old real estate salesman told our interviewer, "is that I want to play music as a professional, but I have to sell real estate in order to make money. I'm striving to become more into my music. I feel trapped and I'm struggling to do what I want to do. I'm just not there yet."

Like this man, many baby boomers are just not there yet. Some want to change careers, others to raise families successfully, still others to deepen their spiritual lives. Others are unsure what they want.

Because they are so talented and adaptable, baby boomers have emerged from the womb of traditional social roles without having established secure nontraditional roles into which to go. The result in many of their lives is a considerable tension that does not seem to be alleviated as they get older. Choices made do not foreclose other opportunities the way they used to for previous generations.

The need for choices is at the core of each baby boomer's life. There is first the difficulty of making choices, and then the greater difficulty of living with the consequences. Each individual is confronted with the need for dealing with the restraints on personal freedom which traditional institutions wish to place on him or her. Families, employers, and peers each reach out to claim one's adherence. Rarely does any claimant reduce the pressure to make room for the others. Nor is any claimant very respectful of a person's desire for room for himself or herself. It is not possible simply to put aside all traditional claims. Hence each person is involved in a daily balancing act among those claims.

Tension is both a concern to be dealt with and a source of energy and creativity. The openness, impatience, and broad tolerance that baby boomers express have their roots in the confusion of opportunities they face. These tensions, and their associated attitudes and behaviors, will be as significant in the future as they are today.

WHERE THE BABY BOOMERS ARE TAKING AMERICA

Today, and for the next few years, we are entering a period of consolidation. Previous generations have also gone through this phase of life as they became parents and householders, but because the baby boom generation is so large, the effect of this shift will echo loudly in American society.

As millions of baby boomers age and tire of a fast-paced life-style, the desire for stability that comes with middle age will tend to slow the process of social change and make it more predictable. Visible signs of this in the social sphere can be seen in the decision of people to have children and in sexual-behavior changes in the face of threats like AIDS.

New technology is no less profuse, but what once seemed an unendurable pace of change has been accepted. Alvin Toffler's "adaptive breakdown" (which he labeled "future shock" and attributed to the fast pace of change) has been avoided by most people. [1]

This is not due to a lack of technical discoveries; rather it is the result of people becoming surfeited with technical novelties. Swamped by already announced discoveries, they fail to be astounded by even greater novelties.

Negative reactions to technology can be seen in the movement to limit the use of nuclear power; the constant media attention to the adverse effects of modern chemicals in the food chain; the fight over acid rain and other forms of industrial pollution; and the early commercial plateauing of the latest mass invention (the home computer). Such shifts away from technology as a sign of progress to technology as a sign of uncertainty are signaling a slowdown in the twentieth century's fascination with new technologies.

A slowing of the pace of personal and technological experimentation does not mean that life in the future is going to be as it was in the past. The changes that the baby boomers have brought to America have provided a foundation for a future that will be different in important ways.

Nor is the current period of consolidation and slower change likely to exist for very long. The pressures for adaptation to a rapidly changing world are too great, and the interests, enthusiasm, and ambition of baby boomers are too strong. Renewed bursts of technological progress, economic advance, and social redefinition are certain to occur.

The future will be characterized by a different order of social relations in which economic factors will be less significant than they were before.

What will occur is not just a change in the economy, but a qualitative shift in what human beings are concerned with and how they relate to one another.

The future will be even more than now an age of individual expression. Though the new era emerges from the past, it is in conflict with the many centuries of conformity that preceded it. The new era is one of increased human freedom, of enhanced liberty. It carries the long struggle of the beginning of human freedom forward in a gigantic step.

The emphasis which baby boomers have placed on the uniqueness of the individual is especially significant in a generation most commonly noted for its large numbers. It is logical to think that our most populous generation might be the most likely to submerge the individual in the group and to subordinate the singular to the collective. That this has not happened is a major indication of what the generation values and the direction it will take in the future.

The stress on the significance of each human personality is a very important message in this rapidly crowding world. Four billion people inhabited our planet in 1970. By the end of the century, there will be 8 billion. In 1980 some 1.5 billion people struggled to make a living in the nonagricultural work forces of all the nations. By the year 2000, about 2.25 billion people will be seeking to support themselves and their families via nonagricultural jobs.[2]

In the years ahead, when the population explosion makes its influence felt, the danger is that human beings will be more and more regimented in the search for survival.

Hence it is of the utmost significance that the generation now coming to power in America, large though it is in a national context, insists upon the value of the individual. This message of confidence in individual freedom will resound very strongly at home and abroad for years to come.

The period we are now entering in the United States will be less characterized by great factories, social classes, human regimentation, and interpersonal relations based on group identification. Instead, at its core will be networks of individuals, sometimes connected by hierarchies but not always. Professionalism will emerge at all levels of work, bringing with it considerable freedom for the individual and interpersonal relations based on the individual's values and interests. In dramatic contrast to industrial society, the economic system will have the potential to be harnessed to the human being, not vice versa.

Some fear that the new electronic and biochemical-based technology will put people out of work and cause lives to be lost in wars that it makes more likely. But technology is not driving our society. Instead, the values and attitudes of human beings are taking us wherever we are going. Today's technology is permissive—it is flexible and will allow change to occur as people desire it.[3]

The new electronic and biochemical-based technology is likely to be liberating in its impact—not just of humans as a group but of individuals. It will give individuals freedom to move about, to communicate widely, to design customized products and individual expressions. It will expand human knowledge, advance mental concepts, and extend and refine personal reach. It will be useful to the scientist and artist alike.

Though we will be its masters, it is necessary to ask the right things of the new technology. Otherwise, we risk becoming enslaved to it—not as a result of its essence but by our own limited imagination.

THE YEAR 2000

Baby boomers are now making choices that will take them and America in new directions. By the year 2000, where will we find ourselves? This look ahead will be limited to the consequences of the generational change that has occurred in values and attitudes, and will deal with possible economic, social, and technological developments only as they interrelate with personal values.

America will be a more open society than it is today. Public discussion of human relationships, including sexual relations, will be more open. In part, this will happen because public-health concerns like AIDS will require more explicit discussion than in the past. Sexual morality will probably not change much from what it is today, but general public awareness of choices and discussion of their consequences will be more open.

Business and investment morality is likely to increase. The secrecy which provides a cloak for dishonesty in the economy will have given way to stringent investor- and consumer-protection legislation the essence of which is fuller disclosure.

Politics will have been altered by the same forces. The cozy relationships between interest groups and legislators that now determine the enactment of laws will have given way to greater disclosure. In their place will be a greater reliance on polling and other methods of determining voter sentiments about particular issues so as to affect the direction of legislation.

There will be a new political organization, which will appeal to those who are concerned about environmental issues—including the risk of large-scale war, which will increasingly be seen as an environmental rather than a geopolitical issue. Probably this organization will be an autonomous element within the Democratic party rather than a separate political party itself. The new organization is not likely to have the support of a majority of baby boomers, but may be the creation of an activist and influential group among them. Its influence on the direction of American policy is likely to be disproportionately large, compared with numbers of members.

Probably the greatest significance of the new political organization and the thinking it embodies will be to cause America to reach a *modus vivendi* with the Soviet Union in order to avoid a nuclear war. Such an accommodation between the United States and the Soviet Union will remove Europe's protection from Soviet conventional power and cause Western Europe to slip out of the western alliance and into a more neutral posture with respect to the Soviet bloc. This will occur because the baby boomers are not prepared to risk nuclear war to preserve Europe's close alliance with America, and they are also unwilling to match the Soviet Union's conventional arms buildup. Europe will be increasingly on its own in international politics, and will seek an accommodation with the Soviets. The great geopolitical lesson of World

War II to the generation that fought the war was that we must involve ourselves in European disputes early if we wish to avoid involvement later at much great cost. This lesson was not experienced by the baby boomers and so is lost on them. As a result, American policy with respect to Europe, which has been essentially unchanged since World War II, will be drastically altered by baby boomers. Our alliances in the year 2000 will look more to Asia and to Latin America than to Europe.

Elections will be, to an even greater extent than today, personality contests in which the media are used to create images. Charisma will increasingly dominate American politics. The identification of the voters with the values and attitudes of candidates will be the most crucial factor.

None of this suggests that as a result of these developments America will be a better-governed society in 2000 than it is today. On balance, the legislative process will have been improved by the reduction of the dominance of interest groups, while the executive process will have been damaged by the divorce of elections from issues and by the increased openness in which policy will have to be determined and conducted. The country is simply too large, and the issues the executive faces are too complex to be handled effectively by a process that increasingly resembles a giant town meeting conducted electronically. But that is what politics in 2000 will be like.

America's population will be much older at the end of this century on average than it is today, but we will have made revolutionary adjustments to cope with the change. We will have reversed today's efforts to restrict immigration in order to reserve jobs for our own citizens. Instead, we will accept substantial immigration from Latin America and Asia as a work force to support a large population of retirees and to bolster a renewed emphasis on economic growth.

On balance, living standards will have improved somewhat, primarily as a result of technological advances embodied in new consumer products. The volume of what is consumed, measured in terms of miles driven, products purchased, travel undertaken, etc., will decline. Economic statistics will show these developments as a small reduction in average living standards.

Baby boomers today are searching for organizations to which they can comfortably belong. As they do so they will redefine companies to fit their emphasis on the individual. They will create organizations that allow people freedom in determining how work is accomplished, that provide status, recognition, and rewards other than promotions, that deemphasize authority and hierarchy, and that are more supportive of the individual.

Manufacturing, transportation, retail, and financial companies, in which hierarchical structures are dominant today, will have modeled themselves somewhat after professional firms in the fields of law, medicine, investment banking, consulting, accounting, and education. The new organizational structures will stress semiautonomous work groups, flat hierarchies, and communication via networks rather than chains of reporting. The computer will make this possible; the baby boomers' demands for professional treatment at work will make it necessary.

Large companies will adjust to the new organizational style by altering today's balance of centralization and decentralization. The large company will become increasingly an investment manager, centralizing allocation of capital and strategic direction (and thereby major acquisitions or divestments). Top-management personnel will also be centrally allocated, as it is in many companies today. Other activities will be decentralized, and controlled via electronic data systems.

In the operating units of companies, there will be far fewer specific jobs. A manufacturing plant which today has ninety distinct jobs will have only two or three broad classifications. Despecialization is necessary for efficient use of a labor force. It also corresponds to the baby boomers' desire for variety and opportunity for personal growth in their careers. This process is already under way in manufacturing and will be far advanced by 2000, and the service industries will follow.

Women will have broken through into top-management ranks by 2000, but not in significant numbers. From today's 3 or 4 percent, women will form 5 or 10 percent of the officers and directors in large corporations. Middle-management ranks will contain some 40 or 45 percent women. The nation will have legislation providing day-care facilities and requiring leaves for parents at the birth of children.

To retain and enlarge membership, unions will be very differently organized and administered. There will be fewer national unions, most of which will be administered on a more decentralized basis. Union presidents will keep in touch with members by extensive polling and interviewing efforts. The values and attitudes of baby boom members will cause the unions to redefine their roles. Unions will support and encourage individual growth in companies. Wages and benefits will be no less significant to members and to unions, but improvements will be sought not only through demands put on management, but by union cooperation in the development of economically viable enterprises. The effort to build businesses that can afford to pay good wages and benefits will replace today's concession bargaining with companies that are no longer competitive.

In summary, America in 2000 will be a more open society with a more complex and quickly responsive political system. There will be more decentralized organizations, and a professional work style will be applied in old-line businesses and in occupations not now considered professional. Unions will be growing and have altered their roles somewhat. The population will be increasing more rapidly as a result of increased immigration; economic growth will be at higher rates than at present; but living standards on the whole will be stagnant. The nation will have redefined its international political goals and shifted its alliances away from Europe to Asia and Latin America.

These are the likely results of the control in 2000 by baby boomers of America's business and politics.

Two hundred years after the Enlightenment, another opportunity to concentrate not on class and groups in human society but on the individual, and on a firmer foundation and a far larger scale, will be presented to us. This is the broad significance of what the baby boomers will bring to America.

APPENDIX A. SURVEYS USED IN PREPARING THIS BOOK

This book was based on a series of survey-based studies. Each deals with a somewhat different topic, but each tells something about the baby boom generation and how American management and unions view the younger generation. One survey involves the opinion of baby boomers about themselves; another, the opinions of corporate personnel executives about them; yet another, how participants in a top-management education program differ by age in their attitudes; still others concern how blue-collar workers see themselves and their employers and unions.

This appendix briefly describes the surveys used. It describes in more detail the key survey utilized in the book, which took a random sample of baby boomers in the population as a whole. Two surveys were made specifically for the book. Others were done for other purposes, but provide relevant materials.

None of these surveys has been published before. All except one were conducted by LDG Associates of Gardner, Massachusetts. Most were done by telephone; one was conducted by personal interview and another by printed questionnaire. In the case of the latter, all 136 respondents assembled to take the questionnaire simultaneously. The questions were read to respondents, and any necessary clarification was provided so that all understood the inquiries. This procedure provided far greater confidence in the quality of the questionnaire responses than can ordinarily be obtained with a printed and mailed questionnaire.

In general, the surveys relied strongly on "open-ended" questions rather than on the more common system of choosing answers from a group of alternatives. This procedure was used primarily to understand the attitudes and values of baby boomers, and only secondarily to gather quantitative data.

One survey (of attendees at the Harvard Business School's Advanced Management Program described below) was analyzed by discriminant techniques, allowing the data to drive the categories into which the population was eventually divided. This is a common technique and has been utilized in other major values-oriented surveys. It seems to have the virtue of putting the researcher's own judgment as far from the analytic results as possible. Some researchers believe that this method-ology is the most objective possible. It allows statistical analysis of the data to drive the researcher's results. That is, the researcher's role is merely to attach labels to categories in the population which are identified by statistical means only.

I do not agree that this is the best method. Instead, for this book I coupled discriminant analysis of survey data with in-depth interviews, in which certain broad ideas, supported by discriminant analysis, were tested directly with a random sample of the target population, i.e., baby boomers. In effect, I asked the sample respondents to comment on my tentative conclusions and modified the conclusions to fit their responses.

Rather than permitting the data to drive the analysis exclusively, I relied to a great extent on the opinions of survey respondents and on my increasingly informed judgment. I do not consider this a subjective procedure. My purpose was to understand the phenomena under investigation to a far greater degree than permitted by attempting to interpret and label the always perplexing categories resulting from a factor analysis.

Of the two surveys that are of special importance, one was taken in 1985 of 136 members of the Advanced Management Program at the Harvard Business School. This survey demonstrated that there existed among these managers a significant difference in attitudes and values based on age.

The survey is summarized below.

STUDY OF ADVANCED MANAGEMENT PROGRAM
ATTENDEES VALUES RESEARCH QUESTION

The study of managerial values started with the basic question: Do managers of different generations demonstrate statistically different values?

METHODOLOGY

In order to answer this question, a survey instrument, consisting of sixty-nine statements covering a number of life situations, was developed from a variety of sources. Several demographic items—age, sex, and citizenship—were added.

The study was designed to tap similar values more than once to provide stability in the analysis. To ensure that respondents could not go back to previous answers for guidance, the items were read to the respondents in a predefined sequence. Subjects were requested to respond to each item by writing a number from 1 to 5 indicating the strength of their feelings toward that item. (The number 1 represented "strongly disagree"; 2 was "somewhat disagree"; 3 was "neither agree nor disagree"; 4 was "somewhat agree"; and 5 was "strongly agree.")

To control the impact of as many exogenous variables as possible, it was necessary to obtain a sample of managers, some of whom were in their thirties and others who were forty-one or older, who were reasonably diverse in background. Such a sample was found by using an Advanced Management Program (AMP) class at the Harvard Business School; 136 members of the AMP participated in the study.

ANALYTIC TECHNIQUES

In order to determine if there were significant differences between the values of younger and older managers, a discriminant-analysis technique was used. The sample of 136 managers was reclassified into two populations, based on reported age. One subsample (group 1) included subjects forty-one years or younger, and the other (group 2) included subjects forty-two years and older.

A computer-generated random sample of ninety subjects from both groups was selected and subjected to an iterative discriminant-analysis procedure. Each questionnaire item was, in turn, considered by the computer program. Two different mean scores, based upon the responses given by each group, were calculated, and the difference between the means was used as the basis of a variance test to determine if the difference was statistically significant. Those items showing statistical significance were then collected and subjected to a combined-variance test and used as the base for a discrimant function of the form:

$$ax + by + cz = \text{discriminant score}$$

where a, b, and c are statistical weights and x, y, and z are numerically coded values expressed by subjects in the study.

This function, in turn, was tested for stability by utilizing the values expressed by the remaining forty-three subjects on the significant items. Each of these subjects' numerically coded values was substituted into the formula, and a discriminant score was calculated. Using this score as a base, the computer assigned each person to group 1 or group 2, and then compared the assignment with the actual group membership based on reported age. The computer then reported the numbers of people correctly classified and misclassified as to age based on their value scores.

THE RESULTS

The analysis did turn up a significant difference in values based on age: 74.4 percent of the smaller population sample that was used to test the discriminant function were correctly classified into age group based on their discriminant scores.

This suggests that there are significant differences in the managerial population's values based on age, and that the new generation of managers has different attitudes from those of its predecessors.

STUDY OF A RANDOM SAMPLE OF THE
BABY BOOM GENERATION

The second survey, which was of special importance, was taken in 1986 of 153 persons aged twenty-one to forty-one, the baby boom population. The sample used was randomly chosen from the population as a whole. The purpose of the survey was to identify their attitudes, values, concerns, and priorities.

The characteristics of the respondents are listed below. Of those in the sample who were actually contacted (all interviews were done by phone), 80 percent participated in the study. A significant number of people in the sample could not be located.

Among our survey respondents, some two thirds were married.*

TABLE 1

MARITAL STATUS	PERCENT
Married	67.3
Single	30.1
Refused	2.6

Twenty-three percent of the sample had been divorced at least once.

TABLE 2

EVER DIVORCED	PERCENT
Yes	22.9
No	75.1
Refused	2.0

We obtained some data regarding ethnic background. The topic, however, is fraught with confusion. People described themselves as Americans who are a mixture of nationalities, or were simply born here and have lost any ethnic identification.

* Here and in tables to follow, percentages are accurate to within ±1%.

Our interviewers asked people about ethnic backgrounds and recorded the answers. We did not offer a list of choices and ask respondents to choose one. What people told us is summarized in Table 3.

TABLE 3

ETHNIC BACKGROUND	PERCENT
Other	64.7
Spanish	3.3
Black	4.6
Italian	7.2
Irish	7.2
Polish	1.3
German	8.5
French	0.7
Jewish	2.0
Not Sure/Refused	0.7

We separated our sample at the annual family income level of $35,000. This is a moderate income level for an average family of two adults and one and a half children. That the generation is not unduly affluent is indicated by almost 60 percent having family incomes of less than $35,000 per year.

TABLE 4

FAMILY GROSS INCOME '85	PERCENT
Less than $35,000	58.6
Greater than $35,000	39.5
Refused	2.0

Our respondents were predominantly male. The poulation as a whole has a slight preponderance of females. The composition of the sample reflects less population distribution by sex than it does work-force composition by sex. The sample is skewed toward men because of an underrepresentation of housewives, as indicated by a comparison with census data.

TABLE 5

SEX OF RESPONDENTS	PERCENT
Male	64.5
Female	35.5

The distribution of survey respondents among occupational categories is also somewhat skewed. More people described themselves as professionals and fewer as sales, clerical, and service workers than census data suggest are appropriate. This is consistent with the baby boomer's general aspiration to have professional or professional-type occupations.

TABLE 6

TYPE OF WORK	PERCENT
Does Not Work	2.0
Housewife	6.5
Managerial	10.5
Professional	39.2
Clerical	4.6
Blue Collar	18.3
Sales Clerk	0.7
Service	7.2
Student	4.6
Military	3.3
Creative (Arts)	2.6
Refused	0.7

Because of the biases in the data—toward men and toward professional occupations, the text of the book does not rely on quantitative analysis of the categories of sex or occupation. Qualitative data and insights obtained from our interviews with respondents are utilized, of course.

Also, significant quantitative estimates, especially of the distribution of the baby boom population among the five categories described earlier, were adjusted for the biases in the data, as recounted in the text.

The regional and age distribution of survey respondents is reasonably consistent with national distribution, as indicated by the census data.

TABLE 7

GEOGRAPHIC REGION	PERCENT
South Central	8.5
Southwest	11.1
Pacific	6.5
Mountain	2.6
South Atlantic	13.7
Midwest	5.9
Upper Midwest	22.9
Northeast Mid-Atlantic	24.8
Pacific Northwest	3.9
	99.9

TABLE 8

AGE GROUP	PERCENT
21–25	11.8
26–30	32.7
31–35	27.5
36–40	21.6
41–45	6.5

The questionnaire used for the survey is at the end of this appendix.

OTHER SURVEYS USED AS SOURCES

Other surveys from which insights were drawn include:

1. Surveys of the membership of the International Union of Bricklayers and Allied Craftsmen, taken five times over the past four years (1982–1986), and of the spouses of members of the union. Two additional ones were done of baby boom members of the union, and of nonmembers who also work at the mason's trades. In total, some 1,200 people responded to these surveys.
2. Surveys of the local officers of the International Union of Bricklayers and Allied Craftsmen
3. A survey taken in 1983 of personnel vice-presidents of 224 of the nation's largest corporations
4. A survey taken in 1985 of the line and staff executives of 119 large, diversified companies, stratified by strategic orientation to inquire into labor relations and personnel practices
5. A survey taken in 1982 of middle-level managers in different companies
6. A survey taken in 1985 of 400 employees of a large automobile corporation regarding their willingness to relocate to new locations within the United States.

   Information from only three of the surveys is directly reported in this book:

1. The 1986 survey of baby boomers;
2. The 1985 survey of Advanced Management Program participants; and
3. The 1983 survey of personnel vice-presidents of large corporations.

RANDOM SAMPLE—BABY BOOMERS
SURVEY INSTRUMENT*

HI, MR. ___. THIS IS ___. I'M CALLING IN BEHALF OF PROFESSOR QUINN MILLS OF HARVARD UNIVERSITY IN BOSTON, MASSACHU-

* LDG Associates, Gardner, Massachusetts.

SETTS, WHO IS CONDUCTING A STUDY OF PEOPLE BETWEEN THE
AGES OF 21–41 TO GET OPINIONS OF WHAT THIS GENERATION
CONSIDERS IMPORTANT IN LIFE. WOULD YOU HAVE A FEW MINUTES
TO HELP US AND SHARE WITH ME SOME OF YOUR VIEWS?

V1   IDENTIFICATION NUMBER

V2   STATE

V3   WHAT IS YOUR AGE?

____(Actual Number)

(Note: Terminate call if respondent is not between the ages of 21–41.)

V4   LOOKING BACK 5 TO 10 YEARS AGO, HAS YOUR OUTLOOK ON LIFE
      CHANGED?
          (1) Yes, changed   (2) No, hasn't changed

V5   (IF YES ABOVE) HOW HAS YOUR OUTLOOK ON LIFE CHANGED?
      (IF NO ABOVE) WHAT IS YOUR OUTLOOK ON LIFE?

      Open-ended:

V6   ARE YOU DOING WHAT YOU THOUGHT YOU WOULD BE DOING?
          (1) Yes   (2) No

V7   IF I MAY ASK, WHAT DID YOU THINK YOU'D BE DOING AND HOW
      DID THAT CHANGE COME ABOUT?

      Open-ended:

V8	WHO ARE YOUR CLOSEST FRIENDS . . . PEOPLE YOU MEET AT WORK, PEOPLE YOU GREW UP WITH, PEOPLE IN YOUR NEIGHBORHOOD, PEOPLE YOU WENT TO SCHOOL WITH, YOUR FAMILY, OR OTHERS? Open-ended:

V9   HAVE YOU BEEN CLOSE TO THE SAME GROUP OF FRIENDS FOR A NUMBER OF YEARS?
    (1) Yes   (2) No

V10 DO YOU TEND TO BE LIKE YOUR FRIENDS IN MANY WAYS?
    (1) Yes   (2) No

V17	AND, WHEN YOU THINK ABOUT PEOPLE YOU KNOW, IN YOUR AGE BRACKET . . . NOT NECESSARILY YOUR FRIENDS, WHAT DO YOU SEE AS SPECIAL ABOUT YOURSELF? Open-ended:

V18	ASIDE FROM YOUR FAMILY AND LOVED ONES, WHAT IS THE MOST IMPORTANT THING IN YOUR LIFE? Open-ended:

V13	AND, WHAT ARE YOU MOST CONCERNED ABOUT?
	Open-ended:

V14	WHAT DO YOU SEE YOURSELF DOING 5 YEARS FROM NOW?
	Open-ended:

V15   PROFESSOR MILLS GIVES A LOT OF SPEECHES TO BUSINESS MANAGERS AROUND THE COUNTRY AND ONE THING THAT HE SAYS IS THAT COMPANIES TODAY AREN'T DOING A GOOD JOB OF MEETING THE NEEDS OF PEOPLE IN YOUR GENERATION. DO YOU AGREE OR DISAGREE WITH HIM AND WHAT DO YOU THINK EMPLOYERS NEED TO DO TO MAKE WORK MORE SATISFYING?
    (1) Agree   (2) Disagree

V16	(WHAT DO EMPLOYERS NEED TO DO?)
	Open-ended:

NOW, I'D LIKE TO CHANGE THE SUBJECT A LITTLE BIT.

V17 | WHAT ARE YOUR OPINIONS ABOUT THE VIETNAM WAR?

Open-ended:

V18 | WHAT WERE YOU DOING AT THE TIME OF THE (VIETNAM) WAR?

Open-ended:

V19 DID YOU GO TO VIETNAM?
   (1) Yes   (2) No

V20 | HOW DID THAT EXPERIENCE INFLUENCE YOUR LIFE OR THE LIVES OF PEOPLE YOU KNOW?

Open-ended:

V21 DO YOU CONCERN YOURSELF WITH POLITICS?
   (1) Yes   (2) No   (3) Sometimes

V22 DO YOU ASSOCIATE YOURSELF WITH A POLITICAL PARTY?
     (1) Yes   (2) No

V23 (IF YES) WHICH ONE?
     (1) Democrat   (2) Republican   (3) Independent

V24 (IF NO) WHY DON'T YOU ASSOCIATE YOURSELF WITH A POLITI-
     CAL PARTY?

     Open-ended:

V25 WE KNOW THAT PEOPLE FALL IN LOVE FOR A LOT OF DIF-
     FERENT REASONS. WHAT DO YOU STRIVE FOR IN A PERSONAL
     RELATIONSHIP?

     Open-ended:

V26 PEOPLE TELL US THAT THE ROLE OF WOMEN IN SOCIETY IS
     CHANGING. WHAT DO YOU THINK WOMEN YOUR AGE OUGHT
     TO BE DOING?

     Open-ended:

V27	WHAT DO YOU THINK THEY WOULD SAY?
	Open-ended:

V28	WHAT OUGHT TO BE THE WAY MEN REACT TO THAT?
	Open-ended:

PROFESSOR MILLS HAS DEVELOPED FIVE DIFFERENT DESCRIPTIONS OF PEOPLE IN YOUR GENERATION. I'D LIKE TO READ THESE DESCRIPTIONS TO YOU AND ASK YOU TO TELL ME IF THESE DESCRIPTIONS FIT PEOPLE YOU KNOW.

V29 1) THE PLEASURE-SEEKERS—THE PLEASURE-SEEKERS WORK PRIMARILY TO EARN ENOUGH MONEY TO PAY FOR THINGS OR EXPERIENCES THEY ENJOY. WORKING IS IMPORTANT BUT LESS SO THAN DOING WHAT THEY ENJOY.

OUT OF TEN PEOPLE YOU KNOW, HOW MANY WOULD YOU SAY FIT THAT DESCRIPTION?

COMMENTS:

V30 2) THE COMPETITORS (BUSINESS-MOTIVATED)—THE COMPETITORS ARE CAREER-ORIENTED AND ARE CONSTANTLY SEEKING OPPOR-TUNITIES TO ADVANCE THEMSELVES IN THEIR CAREERS. SOMETIMES THEY GET SO WRAPPED UP IN THEIR WORK, THEY CAN'T FIND THE TIME TO ENJOY LIFE. MANY PEOPLE SAY THEY ARE OVERACHIEVERS.

OUT OF TEN PEOPLE YOU KNOW, HOW MANY WOULD YOU SAY FIT THAT DESCRIPTION?

COMMENTS:

V31 3) THE TRAPPED—THE TRAPPED ARE IN SITUATIONS THAT ARE UN-
     COMFORTABLE. THEY WOULD LIKE TO DO THINGS DIFFERENTLY,
     BUT HAVE NOT. SOMETIMES THEY ARE CONCERNED THAT THEY
     ARE BECOMING TOO MUCH LIKE THEIR PARENTS.

     OUT OF TEN PEOPLE YOU KNOW, HOW MANY WOULD YOU SAY FIT
     THAT DESCRIPTION?

     COMMENTS:

V32 4) THE CONTENTED—THE CONTENTED HAVE ACHIEVED ACCEPTANCE
     IN THEIR COMMUNITIES AND ENJOY THEIR WORK. AT SOME POINT
     IN THEIR LIVES THEY MAY HAVE FELT TRAPPED IN SOME KIND OF
     SITUATION, BUT THEY HAVE ALWAYS MADE AN EFFORT TO DO
     SOMETHING DIFFERENTLY TO GET THEMSELVES OUT OF A BAD
     SITUATION.

     OUT OF TEN PEOPLE YOU KNOW, HOW MANY WOULD YOU SAY FIT
     THAT DESCRIPTION?

     COMMENTS:

V33 5) THE LET'S GET HIGHS—THE LET'S GET HIGHS ARE VERY SENSITIVE
     PEOPLE WHO SOMETIMES FIND IT DIFFICULT TO ACCEPT THE
     CONTRADICTIONS OF EVERYDAY LIFE. TO MAKE THEMSELVES FEEL
     BETTER, THEY GET HIGH ON DRUGS, ALCOHOL, DAREDEVIL AD-
     VENTURES OR, IN SOME CASES, RELIGION.

     OUT OF TEN PEOPLE YOU KNOW, HOW MANY WOULD YOU SAY FIT
     THAT DESCRIPTION?

     COMMENTS:

V34 WHEN YOU THINK ABOUT YOURSELF OR PEOPLE YOU KNOW,
     WHAT DO YOU THINK WE HAVE OVERLOOKED IN THOSE
     DESCRIPTIONS?

     Open-ended:

V35	HOW WOULD YOU CHARACTERIZE YOURSELF IN TERMS OF THOSE DESCRIPTIONS? Open-ended:

I HAVE JUST A FEW MORE QUESTIONS FOR STATISTICAL PURPOSES.

V36 ARE YOU MARRIED OR SINGLE?
    (1) Married   (2) Single

V37 (IF MARRIED) DOES YOUR SPOUSE WORK FULL TIME, PART TIME, OR NOT AT ALL?
    (1) Full time   (2) Part time   (3) Not at all

V38 HOW MANY CHILDREN, IF ANY, DO YOU SUPPORT?
    ____ (Actual Number)

V39 HAVE YOU EVER BEEN DIVORCED?
    (1) Yes   (2) No

V40 WHAT IS YOUR NATIONALITY?
    (1) SPANISH   (6) GERMAN
    (2) BLACK   (7) FRENCH
    (3) ITALIAN   (8) JEWISH
    (4) IRISH   (0) OTHER
    (5) POLISH

V41 WHAT TYPE OF WORK DO YOU DO?
    Open-ended:

V42 DID YOU GO TO COLLEGE?
    (1) Yes   (2) No

V43 WAS YOUR FAMILY'S TOTAL GROSS INCOME IN 1985 LESS THAN $35,000 OR GREATER THAN $35,000?
    (1) Less than $35,000   (2) Greater than $35,000

V44 SEX OF RESPONDENT:
    (1) Male   (2) Female

V45 AND FINALLY, I'D LIKE YOU TO THINK FOR A MOMENT ABOUT SOME
PERIOD OR EVEN IN YOUR IFE, ASIDE FROM ONE CONCERNING YOUR
FAMILY, THAT YOU CONSIDER TO BE THE MOST EXCITING AND/OR
SATISFYING. COULD YOU SPEND A COUPLE OF MINUTES TO TELL ME
ABOUT IT?

Open-ended:

TIME _____

INTERVIEWER _____

DATE _____

APPENDIX B. HUMAN PSYCHOLOGY AND GENERATIONAL DIFFERENCES

HOW HISTORY CREATES A GENERATION

History impacts on human psychology by creating generations. The members of a generation reflect in their attitudes and behavior the events through which they have lived, or just as important, have not lived. The older generation in America experienced both the Great Depression and World War II. The older generation was very much influenced by the experiences of those two great events. The attitudes and values of people, and their conditioning, were affected importantly, as was their behavior. A theory of personality that omits these influences is seriously deficient.

The baby boom generation did not experience the Depression or the Second World War. But it was profoundly affected by prolonged economic prosperity and by the Vietnam conflict. Already there is another generation growing up which did not experience Vietnam and which is encountering a slower economy. These are the kinds of definitive historical events that cause substantial differences between generations. It follows that the upcoming generation will be different in important ways from the baby boomers. But we will have to wait a while to be able to identify just how different they will be, and in what ways.

It is true, of course, that the older generation also lived through Vietnam and the long economic prosperity of the 1950s and 1960s. But it was not as profoundly shaped by these events because of the previous influence of the Depression and Second World War. The order in which events occur matters, since although generations reflect to a degree all the influences to which they have been subjected, those that occur in childhood and adolescence are of especial importance.

Individuals in each generation are affected by great historical events in different ways. During World War II, some persons served in the armed forces, others did not. Of those who served abroad, some saw combat, others did not. Of the ones who served in combat, some were horrified by it, others exhilarated. Some fought an especially brutal war with Japan in the Pacific; others a relatively more civilized military conflict with Germany in Europe. These are important differences that have had significant impact on each individual's emotional and behavioral characteristics.

However, despite these differences, World War II profoundly influenced all who experienced it, and in certain basically similar ways. Fundamental conclusions about conflicts among nations, about good and evil, about the purity of one's own nation's motives and the corruption of those of one's adversaries, about the importance of submission to authority in gaining success, all flowed into the convictions of today's older generation as a consequence of the war. Individuals who had very different personal experiences in the war generally shared these conclusions. The postwar generation, which did not go through World War II but had instead its own very different experience in Vietnam, does not share the convictions of its predecessors.

The Great Depression similarly marked those who lived through it. Despite the fact that not all were unemployed and destitute, enough were so as to profoundly affect the attitudes of all. For the postwar generation, who experienced not depression but affluence, the impact of the Great Depression is nil.

Also, each generation is in its own way a reaction to its predecessors. The older generation was largely satisfied with the contributions to the general good which its efforts in World War II had made. Anxious for material security, a residue of the Depression, it devoted itself in the 1950s and 1960s to personal economic advancement with a singleness of purpose that provoked an intense reaction in its offspring. As these baby boomers entered adolescence and young adulthood in the late 1960s and early 1970s, with the idealism which ordinarily accompanies that stage of life, they were given a particular intensity and direction by reaction to the apparent Philistinism of their elders.

In the past many people lived in such isolation and ignorance that some events of history passed unnoticed. Significant attitudes and values were transmitted from generation to generation in families living in small villages and towns. Outside influences were less significant.

This is no longer the case. At a very young age, most people have entered into the communication network of their own generation, and have begun to be affected by it more than by their parents or other adults. Today an adult has only a few years in which to shape a child's values and attitudes before the peer group, affected strongly by the national media, assumes a dominant role.

Some psychologists argue that all the important influences on a child occur before age two. This may be true in shaping the individual psyche, but it errs in denying the later influence on personality that the sequential stages of life and generational-specific influences have.

The importance of considering the generation in human psychology is increasing because the impact of historical events on generations is becoming more pronounced. As media penetration becomes greater, each generation is subjected to a similar set of influences and interpretations of significant events.

The significance of popular music should not be underrated. In this century in America each generation has been characterized by an attachment to a particular style of music that was popular in its adolescence. Music embodies not only style but a set of values. Furthermore, for today's young people, the written material on record album covers provides a message network that is theirs alone and little known or paid attention to by adults.

A generation has its own culture. Although there are classics that are read and are influential from generation to generation, there is also much that is new in popular culture. Each generation has its own motion pictures and sports heroes, and to a large degree, music, literature, films, and sports are specific to each new generation. The national media transmit a broad message and an interpretation of events. But even the TV news, from which each generation appears to receive the same content, is given interpretations that are specific to each generational group. Television is especially influential in shaping opinion, and the often distant events it covers assume a greater immediacy in many instances to viewers than events that occur nearby but are not reported. As a result, the geographic differences among people are minimized, and generations are bound together by common experiences, often obtained via television.

History catches each generation at a different stage in its life cycle, and therefore influences them differently. Interpretations, conclusions, and attitudes drawn from the media are transmitted by word of mouth and become part of the folklore. In the African famine of the mid-1980s, the older generation saw the persistence of poverty and tragedy across time; the baby boomers saw the indifference of the rich nations to the plight of different nationalities and races; and the youngest generation saw the risks inherent in each individual human life. Very different interpretations were drawn from the past and current experience peculiar to each generation, but each was drawn from the same media coverage.

HOW THE MEDIA NOW SHAPES
GENERATIONS WORLDWIDE

The shaping influences of the media are now increasingly felt world-wide. The media reach across the globe; events are shared by all. To a remarkable degree, the generations are beginning to be shaped globally, not just nationally.

As a visitor to the Soviet Union, I experienced a striking example of this. A young Soviet official was accompanying me on a trip within Russia. We became so well acquainted that he permitted me to listen with him to the English-language broadcasts of the Voice of America and the BBC. It is the Russian-language broadcasts that are jammed. The Soviet intelligentsia, which is reasonably fluent in English, acquires its general news from the Western international media, just as do Americans and Western Europeans. Although tuning into the

English-language broadcasts is illegal, the Soviet apparatchik is rarely apprehended for this "crime." Having gotten the facts from the Western world, the Soviet official then turned to the Soviet media for a political interpretation of the world scene (that is, for the party line). What was most interesting was the degree to which the Soviet official had a knowledge of world events similar to mine because that knowledge was drawn from Western sources, too.

In countries with less stringent censorship, the media are today fashioning a worldwide mass culture very much in the America mode.[1] In the free world there is a full range of media influences—news, entertainment, literature, music, and sports—carrying similar messages and interpretations of events that fashion generations not only on a national but an international scale. In the Communist bloc, American influence is less intense, but real nonetheless.

The increasing influence of the media reinforces the need for a complete theory of the human personality to include generational influences. In such a theory, each person's identity at a particular time is composed of three elements: that which constitutes his or her individual psyche, that which is appropriate to his or her stage of life, and that which is provided by the generation to which he or she belongs.

Each personality is a complex intermixture of these influences. Some are unique to a person: parental relationships, upbringing, intellectual and physical capabilities. Others are shared with other people, including stage-of-life and generational influences.

It is the individual psyche that is influenced by a person's unique experiences. The stage of life of a person is determined by the process of aging, and is shared by others who are of the same age. What we call generational influences are the events of history (developments in music, literature, art, education, international politics, and economics) as they affect in broadly similar ways people of similar age.

Basic human nature, as described by the categories of the individual psyche, does not change very much, if at all, over long periods of time. The stages of life, however, do change slowly, because they are increasing in number as the expected life-span increases. Further, exactly where certain critical stages fall in the age cycle alters as the people's life-styles change. Generational changes occur in the shortest periods of time, since historical events exert their influences in the twenty-year-or-so span between generations.

Personality is shaped by the three influences, each reflecting a different length of time. The psyche reflects what is continuing and long-term in the human situation; the stage of life reflects the slowly evolving and intermediate term; the generational influence reflects momentary events of the short term. Combined, these three influences create the full identity of a person.

People have both unique experiences and common experiences. Their personalities are shaped by both, and their behavior reflects both. Only by understanding the psyche, the stage of life, and the generation can (an individual) be fully understood as a personality. The psyche may seem the most important element of personality because it is the most enduring; conversely, it could be considered to be the least important because in its focus on the individual, it gives the least insight into groups.

As I said before, it would be a mistake to conclude that people are all the same because they are at the same stage of life or because they are of the same generation. But it is also equally mistaken to conclude that people are altogether different simply because they have unique aspects in their individual psyches.

Generational considerations in human psychology have received the least careful attention. They are most controversial as to their significance. Yet generational influences are an important aspect of human personality and their significance is most rapidly being enhanced by developments in the world today. They are the way in which the great events and technological advances (especially in communications) of our time have influence on the individual human personality.

Notes

Chapter 1. What a Difference a
Generation Makes

1. Anthony Esler, *Bombs, Beards and Barricades* (New York: Stein & Day, 1971, pp. 30–31), has given us a useful definition of what he calls a "social generation," a concept very similar to that used in this book and one for which I am grateful. Esler writes, "A social generation is . . . an age group . . . people born within a few years of each other . . . [they] advance together through life . . . psychologically and sociologically conditioned by common institutions and social circumstances . . . [and] history.

". . . [they] have . . . been raised according to the same child-rearing practices . . . conditioned by the same family structures, the same parental and sibling relationships . . . exposed to the same pattern of education, formal and informal. . . . Almost any sort of historical trend or traumatic event may leave its imprint on a social generation." See also Esler's two-volume bibliography, *The Generation Gap in Society and History* (Monticello, Ill.: Vance Bibliographies, 1984).

2. See Frances Fitzgerald, *Cities on a Hill* (New York: Simon & Schuster, 1986).

3. Arnold Mitchell, *The Nine American Lifestyles* (New York: Macmillan Publishing Company, 1983.)

4. C. Brooklyn Derr has independently developed from his study of 150 high-potential naval officers a typology somewhat similar in the labels it uses. See *Managing the New Careerists* (San Francisco: Jossey-Bass, 1986).

Chapter 2. The Pleasure-seekers

1. Joe Kane, "Working Less and Liking It," *The World*, March 10, 1985, pp. 9–12.

2. This point has been made in Barbara Ehrenreich, Elizabeth Hess, and Gloria Jacobs, *Remaking Love* (New York: Anchor Press, 1986).

3. *Time*, May 19, 1986, p. 35.

4. Ann Landers, "Is Affection More Important Than Sex?," *Family Circle*, June 11, 1985. Condensed in *Reader's Digest*, 127, 760 (August 1985), pp. 44–46.

5. See Gerald R. Kelly, "Baby Boomers on the Vineyard," *The Martha's Vineyard Times*, July 10, 1986, p. 21ff.

6. Stephen Hills, *The Harbus News* (Harvard Business School student newspaper), September 22, 1986, p. 19.

Chapter 3. The Competitors

1. Charles Reich, *The Greening of America* (New York: Random House, 1970), pp. 242–243.

2. Ibid.

3. Len Schlesinger, interviewed on *20–20*, "What a Way to Run an Airline," ABC, 1983.

4. Reich, op. cit., pp. 417–418.

Chapter 7. The Legacy of Vietnam

1. Richard B. Morris, ed., *The Encyclopedia of American History* (New York: Harper & Row, 1976), pp. 497–505.

*Chapter 8. The Importance of Values
and Relationships*

1. Richard Halloran, "Veterans Value Personal Growth Over Job Skills," *The New York Times*, March 18, 1986, p. 15.

2. Joseph Berger, "Catholic Dissent on Church Rules Found," *The New York Times*, November 25, 1985, p. A7.

3. Seymour Martin Lipset, "Feeling Better," *Public Opinion*, 8, 2 (April/May 1985), p. 8; also "Growing Pains at Forty," *Time*, May 19, 1986, p. 35.

4. World Congress on Human Resources, sponsored by the American Society for Personnel Administration, September 21–24, 1986, Washington, D.C.

5. Janice C. Simpson, "Baby Boomers Have '60's Heritage, but Charities Say They're Cheap," *The Wall Street Journal*, September 11, 1986, p. 37.

Chapter 10. *The Complete Person*

1. Robert J. Lifton, "Protean Man," in *History and Human Survival* (New York: Random House, 1970), first published in 1961 and revised in 1970.

Chapter 11. *A New Meaning of Success*

1. Survey by Liberman Research Inc. for *Money* magazine, cited by Susan Antilla, "Baby Boomers: Debts, Hopes Higher," *USA Today*, April 26, 1985, p. 1.

2. D'Arcy Masius Benton & Bowles, Inc., "Fears and Fantasies of the American Consumer," report in *The Boston Globe*, May 13, 1986, p. 15.

3. Heidrick and Struggles, *Top Management Profiles—CEO Survey*, Fall 1985.

4. Transcript of Show #527, 20/20, ABC News, July 4, 1985, pp. 10 and 11.

Chapter 12. *Chained by Convention*

1. The following is an expression of the same point of view: "The women's movement has played a key role in undermining the very qualities in men that made them attractive to women in the first place, and accordingly, women find today's men 'wimpy' and uninteresting," Cary McMullen, "Liberated Woman Meets Uncommitted Man," in Letters to the Editor, *The New York Times*, September 4, 1986, p. 18.

2. For a similar story, see Charles Kenney, "Up Against the Clock," *The Boston Globe Magazine*, March 30, 1986, p. 24ff.

3. Joann S. Lublin, "Staying Single," *The Wall Street Journal*, May 28, 1986, p. 1ff. Data are from the U.S. Census Bureau, Washington, D.C.

4. "Ratio of Single Women Breaks 1890's Record High," *The Wall Street Journal*, December 10, 1986, p. 14.

5. Alan L. Otten, "If You See Families Staging a Comeback, It's Probably a Mirage," *The Wall Street Journal*, September 25, 1986, pp. 1 and 22. Data are from the U.S. Census Bureau, Washington, D.C.

6. "Six in Ten Women Will Divorce," *The Boston Globe*, April 5, 1986, p. 15, citing a study by Arthur J. Norton and Jeanne E. Moorman.

Chapter 13. The Consequences of Parenthood

1. Jean Dietz, "Family-Job Stress Found in This Study," *The Boston Globe*, November 14, 1985, pp. 1 and 24.

Chapter 14. The Large Corporation

1. James E. Burke, quoted in Tamar Lewin, "World's a Stage for '49 Class," *The New York Times*, April 3, 1986, p. D3.

2. This is a key message of John Kotter, *Power and Influence* (New York: The Free Press, 1985).

3. See D. Quinn Mills, "Managing the Corporate Generation Gap," *IBM: SPD Management*, September 1985, pp. 16–19.

4. Survey in *The Harbus News*, op. cit., p. 19.

5. Thomas F. O'Boyle, "Loyalty Ebbs . . . ," *The Wall Street Journal*, July 11, 1985, p. 27.

Chapter 16. The Glass Ceiling

1. See N. F. Rytina and S. Bianch, "Occupational Reclassification and Distribution by Gender," *Monthly Labor Review*, 107, 3 (March 1984), pp. 11–17 (especially pp. 13 and 14 for the data cited in the text). Most recent data are courtesy of Ellen Siegel, Data Development, Office of Employment and Unemployment Statistics, United States Bureau of Labor Statistics, Washington, D.C.

2. Liz Roman Gallese, *Women Like Us* (New York: William Morrow, 1985).

3. Korn Ferry International, cited by Cathy Trust in "Corporate Women," *The Wall Street Journal*, January 21, 1986, p. 1; and Research Institute of America, *Recommendations*, 37, 7 (February 14, 1986), p. 3. See also Beth McGlodrick and Gregory Miller, "Wall Street Women: You've Come a Short Way, Baby," *Institutional Investor*, June 1985, pp. 85–96. In its June 3, 1985, issue, *Forbes* magazine listed the 785 chief executive officers of U.S. corporations with the highest pay. The magazine commented editorially, "of the 785 CEO's . . . 2 are women, *Ms.* Magazine, please copy" (p. 132).

4. Josephine Hendin, "Introduction" to Henry James, *The Bostonians*, first published in 1885 (New York: Banton Classic edition, July 1984), p. v.

5. See "Executive Women," *The Wall Street Journal*, September 9, 1986, p. 1.

6. Eric Schmitt, "Women Entrepreneurs Thrive," *The New York Times*, August 18, 1986, pp. D1 and D3.

7. See also Karen Cmar, "Women Grads Discuss Careers," *The Harbus News*, November 12, 1985, pp. 19 and 21.

8. Quoted in Robbi Vander Hyden and John Kao, "Note on Women Entrepreneurs," Harvard Business School, *Boston*, 1985 (0-485-161) p. 1. See also Connell Cowan and Melvyn Kinder, *Smart Women/Foolish Choices* (New York: Potter, 1985); and Srully Blotnick, *Otherwise Engaged: The Private Lives of Successful Career Women* (New York: Facts on File, 1985).

9. Cooperative Institutional Research Program, "Career Choices," quoted in *The Wall Street Journal*, March 7, 1985, p. 35.

10. See Alice G. Sargent, *The Androgynous Manager: Blending Male and Female Management Styles for Today's Organization* (New York: American Management Association, 1983).

11. Joyce Baker Miller, *Toward a New Psychology of Women* (Boston: Beacon Press, 1974).

12. Jane Meredith Adams, "Giving Up the Dream," *The Boston Globe*, March 25, 1986, pp. 43, 52–53.

13. "Male vs. Female," *The Wall Street Journal*, December 9, 1986, p. 1.

Chapter 17. The End of Social Class

1. Laurie Baum, "Punishing Workers with a Day Off," *Business Week*, June 16, 1986, p. 80.

2. Michael A. Pollock, "How Jack Joyce Is Rebuilding the Bricklayer's Morale," *Business Week*, September 9, 1985, pp. 73–74.

Chapter 18. The Politics of Values

1. "The New Collar Class," *U.S. News & World Report*, September 16, 1985, p. 59ff.

2. This is a formulation sometimes attributed to Senator Daniel Patrick Moynihan of New York.

3. The reporter was Victor Riesel, a syndicated columnist.

4. See William S. Maddox and Stuart A. Lilie, *Beyond Liberal and Conservative* (Washington, D.C.: Cato Institute, 1984).

*Chapter 19. Turning the Tables
on the Media*

1. Teresa Carson, "The New Greeting Cards: Slick, Sassy and Strange,"
Business Week, December 16, 1985, pp. 49 and 52.

2. Ronald Alsop, "American Express Ads Focus on the Nicer Side of
Yuppies," *The Wall Street Journal*, May 14, 1985, p. 35.

3. Norman E. Isaacs, *Untended Gates: The Mismanaged Press* (New York:
Columbia University Press, 1985).

Chapter 20. "We're Only Spirit"

1. See Meredith Woodward, "Newcomers at Tufts Get Some Lessons on
Discrimination," *The Boston Globe*, August 31, 1985, pp. 17–18.

2. "He knows which way the wind blows," *USA Today*, October 9, 1985,
p. 21.

*Chapter 21. The Revolution of the
New Generation*

1. Charles Reich, *The Greening of America* (New York: Random House,
1970), pp. 2 and 235.

2. Daniel Goldman, "New Evidence Points to Growth of Brain Even Late in
Life," *The New York Times*, July 30, 1985, p. C1.

3. See Norman Boucher, "A Faith of Our Own," *New Age Journal*, April
1986, p. 27ff; and Robert Lindsey, "Spiritual Concepts Drawing a Different
Breed of Adherent," *The New York Times*, September 29, 1986, pp. 1 and B12.

4. Paul W. McCracken, "Toward World Economic Disintegration," *The
Wall Street Journal*, February 9, 1987, p. 18.

5. Pamela Reynolds, "Downward Mobility," *The Boston Globe*, February 28,
1986, pp. 9–10. See also Gene Koretz, Economic Diary, *Business Week*,
March 31, 1986, p. 20.

6. Gene Koretz, Economic Diary, *Business Week*, October 14, 1985, p. 29.

7. Betsy Morris, "Many Baby Boomers Find They Are Caught in a Financial
Squeeze," *The Wall Street Journal*, December 17, 1985, pp. 1 and 29; and
Arnold Kling, "Yuppies Must Work Harder Just to Keep Even," *The Wall
Street Journal*, February 20, 1986, p. 27.

8. Phillip Longman, "Age Wars," *The Futurist*, January-February 1986,
pp. 8–11.

9. Vicky Cahan, "The Shrinking Nest Egg: Baby Boomers Will Have to Secure Their Own Futures or Keep Working," *Business Week*, December 8, 1986, pp. 114–116. See also Marlys Harris, "Backed into the Future: The Age Warfare on the American Horizon Can Be Sighted in Pinellas County, Florida," *Money* magazine. November 1985, pp. 85–92.

10. Janet Novak, "Work Until You Drop," *Forbes*, November 17, 1986, p. 72.

11. Everett Carl Ladd, "Generation Myths," *Public Opinion* 9, 4 (November-December 1986), p. 10ff.

12. Louis Auchincloss, *Diary of a Yuppie* (Boston: Houghton Mifflin, 1986).

Chapter 22. What Lies Ahead

1. Alvin Toffler, *Future Shock* (New York: Random House, 1970), p. 285.

2. See D. Quinn Mills, *The New Competitors* (New York: John Wiley & Sons, 1985), p. 20. See also D. Quinn Mills and Malcolm R. Lovell, "Competitiveness," in Bruce R. Scott and George C. Lodge, *U.S. Competitiveness in the World Economy* (Boston: Harvard Business School Press, 1985), pp. 437–440.

3. See Shoshana Zuboff, "Automate/Informate," *Organizational Dynamics*, Autumn 1985, p. 17.

Appendix B. Human Psychology and
Generational Differences

1. "Exporting American Culture," *Public Opinion*, 9, 1 (February-March 1986), pp. 1–20.